ON WINGS OF JOY

Lou Turner

ACKNOWLEDGEMENT

My grateful acknowledgement goes to Dr Keith Munro, whose wonderful assistance has made it possible for this book to be published and fulfilled a long cherished dream. (Lou Turner)

First published in February 2008 by
Learmount Publishing
94 Learmount Road
Claudy
BT47 4AL

A copy of the British Library Cataloguing-in-Publication data is available from the British Library.

The author asserts her moral rights in this work in accordance with the Copyright, Designs and Patents Act 1998.

Typesetting: Joe McAllister
Copyright © Lou Turner/Learmount Publishing

ISBN 978-0-9558135-0-4

INTRODUCTION

I have known Lou Turner since the 1960s when I too found answers. I knew and admired the two Johns (her husband and son). I met Lou's sister Pat, as well as Hagar, her beautiful and faithful mother. Having these spiritual links with the family and an abiding respect and deep love for Lou herself, I was delighted to meet her again in 2006 at the Scottish Bahá'í Summer School held in St Andrew's.

During our little chats I found that she had kept notes of her international travels over the years. I suggested she write a book. This I felt would not only be of great interest to those who knew and loved her but also of historical significance to the Bahá'í Faith. With typical humility she explained that age and lack of skills would prevent her from such a project. Seeing her sadness I offered to edit and publish a volume for her, if she would provide all the notes as well as the many photographs she had kept over the years.

So, given the wonders of e-mail and a long weekend sitting with Lou in Scotland, we have together produced this book for posterity.

I cannot fail to mention Zoë Turner, the widow of Lou's son, John, who has been a loving and faithful companion to Lou over all these years since his tragic accident. She has been of enormous physical and spiritual support and continues to be so, especially in recent weeks when Lou had a slight stroke and was in hospital for a period.

Lou is one of those extraordinarily rare souls who brightens the life of everyone she meets. She feels everyone's pain. She empathises with them in their troubles and prays for them night and day. Her love for God is deep, lasting and eternal. Her faith is as firm as a rock. While she will be delighted to see this project brought to fruition she is in fact looking forwards, without fear, to passing on to "the next part of the Great Adventure".

Thank you, Lou, for allowing me to share a small part of your adventure.

Keith Munro
November 2007

Dedicated to my beloved husband and son and to all my loved ones in this world and the next; and to Zoë for her friendship and companionship for over thirty years; and to Anisa, my beloved granddaughter.

CONTENTS

Mother and Father, with Joe (9), Lou (7) in the middle, and Pat (5), circa 1928.

1

A NEW PATH OPENS AND MY JOURNEY BEGINS

February 13th, 1962 was a grey wintry day, and I wasn't expecting anything exciting or unusual to happen. I had no idea that my life was about to change in a rather wonderful way.

I walked into a small meeting-room in Daulby Street Spiritualist Church in Liverpool, just before eight o'clock that evening. There were about thirty people present. My husband John and I had been attending weekly Study Sessions in this room for a period of several months. Often our fourteen year-old son, 'young' John, went with us. Amidst the friendly greetings and chatter we settled into our seats to await the arrival of our speaker. I was wondering why on earth I had agreed to go at all. The Spiritualist Church had planned a series of meetings, in which speakers from different religions were invited to talk about their beliefs. Discussions of this kind were usually of great interest to me. They were part of my search for understanding. But the subject that evening was 'The Bahá'í Faith', and this held no appeal for me whatsoever. I had been wondering, for a long time why there are so many different religions in the world and was feeling somewhat annoyed that someone, somewhere had concocted yet another.

It had been a deeply sorrowful and painful event that awakened my longing to know more about the purpose of life and to understand what it is that God wants us to do. That event had set me on a path of search and although this profoundly traumatic event took place in 1950, in my heart, it felt like yesterday.

I had just finished tucking my two year-old son into bed on a lovely, calm April evening. Suddenly, I heard my mother's desperate cry, as she called to me urgently, "Your dad's very ill, ask John to get the doctor!" We were without the luxury of a `phone at that time, so my husband rushed out to the nearest telephone box, while I dashed into the living room where my father was lying on the settee. He looked so very pale and weak: my lovely Dad, who was always so full of vitality and joy. Now, his voice was little more than a whisper as he struggled to speak my name.

Several weeks before, he had collapsed with acute chest pain that was diagnosed as having angina. That obviously had been a warning, and now he was having a massive heart attack. I managed to stumble out of the living room, unable to contain my anguish. Although desperately weak, he was still able to speak to my mother, telling her that he wasn't afraid to die, but he didn't want to leave her. Minutes later the doctor arrived and immediately went to the front room. I will never forget the overwhelming agony I felt, waiting for his verdict. I stood in our small kitchen, with huge waves of sorrow washing over me, scared even to think of going in to see my father. Part of me knew what was happening but in my soul I could not face it. I have no idea what words the doctor used to my mother. I just knew that my Dad had gone.

How could this be happening? How could we possibly be left without my wonderful Dad? It was unbearable! My heart was breaking, not just for my own loss, awful though that was, but for the devastating loss for my mother. I wondered how she would ever cope without him. Tears were streaming down my cheeks.

I prayed long and urgently for God to help her. I returned to the room, after the doctor left. I remember my thoughts very clearly at that moment. My father wasn't old. Six weeks earlier he had celebrated his fifty-fifth birthday. He was such a warm, loving man, with a kind, gentle nature full of humour and a joyful radiance that everybody loved. He had been a great reader and was especially fond of poetry. His little grandchildren adored playing with him. To their delight, he would kneel on the floor and give them rides on his back. All these thoughts passed through my mind as I stared at his motionless body lying on the settee.

My Dad was dead. I struggled to find meaning in the midst of this ocean of anguish. Surely there must be another world where he had gone, perhaps a more beautiful world? I felt sure that God would never cut off such a wonderful life forever. I remember the questions I struggled with. "Where had he gone? Why are we here? What is the purpose of our life in this world?" I was longing to understand, and in those devastating moments of grief, my search for truth began.

In the twelve years that followed, I went to many different churches and bought books on subjects relating to the spiritual aspect of life. I was always hoping to discover even a glimpse of the truth I so desperately longed for. I clung fervently to those words in the Gospel: "*Ask and ye shall receive, seek and ye shall find.*"

There were lectures held at the Theosophical Society, on Sunday evenings. Here I first learned about belief in reincarnation. This doctrine seemed to answer some of the perplexing questions about suffering and injustice in the world. Then one day, a friend mentioned that there was a Spiritualist Church in Liverpool not far from where we lived. I felt eager to attend, as one of my many questions was, "Is there life after death?" Surely this would be the main theme in a Spiritualist Church? To my relief, this urgent question was answered positively. As the weeks went by, my heart rejoiced in the knowledge that our lives continue after we leave this world, and my dearly loved Dad had not gone from us forever and had not ceased to exist. I accepted these comforting teachings with all my heart, reassured that, when the time comes for me to leave my own physical body, I would meet all my loved ones again, in the spiritual worlds that surround us. Everything I learned gave me a new and happier

Dad in 1938.

outlook on life. My husband and I decided to take our little son, John Charles, to the Sunday-morning classes, known as The Lyceum. These are attended by children of all ages, as well as adults. The songs and recitations were uplifting and joyous. My mother, Hagar, was living with us at that time and she loved going to those meetings and seeing all the little ones.

For several years I felt quite contented. Then the thought came to me that perhaps the Spiritualist Church did not hold the complete answer to my search. I began to wonder whether I was really doing the right thing. Had I found the right pathway for me? I became more and more aware of other major religions in the world. Millions of people follow each of these Faiths, with the belief that they have found the true way. How do we know that one particular religion has the right answers, in preference to another? I felt confused, and kept thinking that if I had been born in China, India or Arabia, or in some other part of the world, I would have been brought up as a Buddhist, a Hindu, or a Muslim. This thought puzzled me. I felt so strongly that there is only <u>one</u> God, so why are there so many different religions?

I began to pray with all the longing of my heart, for guidance. After a while I began to get a strong feeling that, somewhere, there really was a truth just waiting to be discovered. I felt that this something would bring everything together, like the missing piece in a jigsaw puzzle. I began to pray earnestly, "O, God, guide me to the truth." I could visualize those words in huge capital letters, "Guide me to THE TRUTH." This made me eager to attend the weekly Study Sessions that were held at the Church, in the hope that I might discover a hint of what I was looking for. This is the stage I had reached on that February evening.

I had seen the name Bahá'í on a small plaque outside the house next door to where my sister Pat lived in Langdale Road. We had not made any enquiries as it appeared to be for members only and not open to the public. However, two of our very close friends, Jessie and Nick Echevarria, had discovered the Bahá'í Faith in Canada, and had written many times, urging us to investigate it for ourselves. But because of my feelings about the appearance of another new religion, I showed no interest at the time. Now here I was – waiting – on a grey, wintry evening to hear about it.

Our speaker arrived, and was introduced as Mrs Madeline Hellaby. She and her husband lived in Prescot on the outskirts of Liverpool. She began to speak very clearly, and within a few minutes her words had gripped my attention completely. I became fascinated. It was as if my years of wondering and puzzling were being washed away. The missing pieces were falling into place. I felt as though many windows in my soul had been flung open, and light was streaming in from all directions. What I learned in that short space of time was astonishingly simple, but it reached deeply into my heart.

Mrs Hellaby explained that God has created us to know Him and to love Him, and she went on to unfold some very logical and beautiful teachings. She was saying:

> Because the human mind is finite, it is impossible for us to comprehend the Infinite. God makes Himself known to man through a succession of messengers. These are the Great Teachers that He sends to guide us. Messengers such as Moses, Krishna, the Buddha, Jesus and Muhammad are all founders of the great religions of the world. They have appeared throughout the ages, to bring the knowledge that mankind needs for each particular stage of our development.

Then I realised that every great religion is part of a continuous flow of divine guidance, and that all are from God. I was amazed and overjoyed as the significance of these words sank into my heart. Those many different faiths! Those questions that had troubled me! It was all so simple. I wondered why I had not seen this before. While I was marvelling at this great discovery, Mrs Hellaby went on to tell us the most exciting and inspiring thing of all. I found myself leaning forward on the very edge of my chair trying to drink in everything she was saying:

God has sent another revelation to the world in the last century, to bring the teachings that we are in need of, at this present time.

As I listened, I was saying to myself, over and over again, "It's true! It's true!" Mrs Hellaby continued to explain that the dawn of this great new age had started in May 1844 in Persia, when a young man, who was given the title 'The Báb' (The Gate) came to prepare the people for the coming of 'Bahá'u'lláh,' which is an Arabic title meaning 'The Glory of God'. The Báb was like John the Baptist, who prepared the way for the coming of Jesus. Sadly, in 1850, after some years of persecution, the Báb was put to death by a firing squad in the city of Tabriz in northern Iran. That horrific event was witnessed by many thousands of people, and amazing, miraculous things were connected with His martyrdom. Already a number of books have been written about that turbulent period of recent history.

I sat there in absolute wonder. What a glorious and staggering thought! It was like being alive at the time of Jesus, in the very earliest days of Christianity. I felt that I was being lifted into an atmosphere of pure happiness, and I hung on every word with rapt attention. It moved my heart deeply when we were told of Bahá'u'lláh's life of suffering. How he was banished from Persia, which was His homeland, and for forty years endured torture, exile and imprisonment. It became clear that the teachings of God for this day touch every aspect of our lives, and my heart responded eagerly to everything I heard. Madeline explained that the Bahá'í Revelation places special emphasis on the oneness of mankind and the oneness of religion. This is a new cycle of unity and eventual peace for the peoples of the world.

I knew that what I was hearing was true. My long search for answers was over. I thanked God and as Madeline's talk ended I felt that I had entered a new dimension. Tea and biscuits were served amidst a lot of happy chatter, and everyone agreed that the talk had been "very nice", and "very interesting". It seemed strange that people around me had not been more deeply affected. It is now more than forty years since that night, and the assurance and joy I felt then has never diminished.

On the table in front of her, Madeline had set out a fascinating display of booklets on different aspects of the Faith. I wanted to read them all, and asked if I could take one of each. She very happily agreed, and because of my intense interest, invited me to what Bahá'ís call a "fireside", on the following Friday, at the home of a Bahá'í in Southport. In the following days my joy and excitement increased as I studied the Bahá'í teachings. When I began to read the history of the Faith, I became filled with a deep sadness. My tears flowed, as I learned of the terrible suffering and persecution that had been meted out to the early believers in Persia. Then one day, while I was absorbed in my reading, my mother, Hagar, arrived home. I began to tell her about the amazing things I had discovered. I will always remember that moment, as she stood looking at me from across the room. "You've got it, haven't you?" she said. "You've found what we were looking for." She, also, had been searching for answers since my father's death. We had talked so many times about the meaning of life and God's purpose for us. We had often wondered about people who had a strong faith, and what it would feel like to experience this for ourselves. Now she realised that I had found this wonderful gift, and it was filling my life with joy.

The very next week my husband and I went to the fireside meeting in Southport. We were given a very warm welcome by a group of friendly people who were clearly delighted to see us. The name of the speaker on that night was Jeanette Battrick. After her most interesting talk, she recommended three books she thought might be helpful to us in our understanding of the Faith. They were *All Things Made New* by John Ferraby, *Thief in the Night* by William Sears, and *Renewal of Civilisation* by David Hofman. We managed to order them from a bookshop in Liverpool, and when we had collected them, several days later, I remember rushing back to the car where I started reading straight away.

For several years I had accepted the doctrine of reincarnation, and was therefore keen to know what Bahá'ís thought on this subject and hurriedly looked it up. It stated clearly, however, that the soul does <u>not</u> return to this world after death. In fact we continue to live eternally and progress through all the spiritual worlds of God. Looking back, I realise that this was my first test of faith. How firmly did I really believe that Bahá'u'lláh's teachings were from God? That He <u>is</u> indeed His Messenger for this day? Thankfully, I had no hesitation in putting aside the beliefs I had previously held, and turning, with confidence to the guidance of Bahá'u'lláh, whose coming I now believed Jesus Christ had foretold.

In my heart and mind I had declared my belief in Bahá'u'lláh, there and then. My registration as a member of the Bahá'í community was postponed until all my commitments at Daulby Street Spiritualist Church had been fulfilled. From then on John and I went every Monday to Madeline and Bill Hellaby's firesides (open house), while my mother attended some of the Public Meetings held at the Liverpool Bahá'í Centre. She had been warmly welcomed by the Bahá'ís there, who were, naturally, delighted to have such an eager enquirer. On May 23rd, while they were commemorating one of the Bahá'í holy days, my mother told the excited friends that she wanted to become a Bahá'í. I will always remember the lovely expression on her face when she came home that evening, with eyes as bright as stars. She gently chided me, "You don't know what I've done, do you?" But, of course I knew, as her face was alight with happiness. I gave her a big hug, and we were both filled with the greatest excitement and joy. I don't think I could ever forget that special, wonderful night of her declaration of Faith.

Less than three weeks later, on 12 June, 1962, all my commitments for the Children's Lyceum were fulfilled, and I felt as free as a bird. I had been hoping and praying that John and I could take this important step together, but he was not quite ready. It was another sixteen months before that wonderful day arrived. Our son, John, sent a letter expressing his belief in Bahá'u'lláh, just two weeks after his fifteenth birthday, on 11 October, 1962. Gladys Pritchard, then secretary of the local Spiritual

Assembly of Liverpool, wrote that John was the first youth from the city of Liverpool to become a Bahá'í, and that he was making history. It made us realize more than ever, that it was a very special time in his life, and in the lives of us all. It has been a great blessing for me that so many of my loved ones accepted this new Revelation, destined to unite the nations of the world and to bring a lasting peace to all mankind. My sister Pat became a Bahá'í in August 1963, just a little while before my husband. In fact they both just missed, by a few months, the first Bahá'í World Congress held in the Albert Hall in London in April 1963.

2

A UNIVERSAL GATHERING

It was a great and momentous occasion, that first World Congress, celebrating 100 years since Bahá'u'lláh's announcement that He was the Messenger of God, foretold in the scriptures of previous religions. That historic event had taken place in a garden, just outside Baghdad, during the latter days of April 1863, where He had spent ten long years as a prisoner and an exile.

It was an unforgettable experience to be present in that hall, mingling with 6000 Bahá'ís from every part of the world. The atmosphere of unity and harmony was overwhelming. Such love and happiness radiated from every face, and the blaze of brilliant colours from a multitude of national costumes, was like a garden of beautiful flowers. In His writings, Bahá'u'lláh describes humanity as being the flowers of one garden. It was like heaven on earth to be part of that unique gathering, where so many races of the world were represented. I was now witnessing the reality of these new spiritual teachings, and it was like a glimpse of the future for the whole human family.

Many inspiring and moving talks were given, including one from Mr Taráz'u'lláh Samandari who, as a young man of sixteen, had been in the presence of Bahá'u'lláh. It was an incredible experience, like listening to someone who had been with Jesus and heard Him speak.

Outside the Albert Hall, the people of London were engrossed in the daily round of work and business. The buses were running, shops were open, and people were hurrying by, engrossed with their cares and schedules. Inside that Hall we were surrounded in an atmosphere of such love and happiness that is impossible to describe. It seemed that we were in a world apart, where time stood still.

One of the most unforgettable moments came when the nine newly elected members of the Universal House of Justice stood before us on the platform. We arose spontaneously, applauding with joy and thankfulness for this very first election of the world administrative body of the Faith. I had learned that Bahá'u'lláh created this unique institution in His book of laws, (Kitáb-i-Aqdas) revealed in 1873 while He was still a prisoner in 'Akká. Now, exactly one hundred years since His declaration, it had come into being.

It was impossible to keep our tears from falling, with so much emotion in our hearts. There was no other way of expressing what we were feeling. The election of that great Institution had taken place in the Holy Land only a few days earlier. Like all Bahá'í elections, it had been by secret ballot and in a peaceful atmosphere of love and reverence. This was so very different from political elections, when love and reverence is so sadly lacking. Bahá'ís from all corners of the earth, members of fifty-six National Spiritual Assemblies of the world, had taken part in that election. For the next five years those nine members would take up residence on the slopes of Mount Carmel in Haifa. From there, they would give guidance and encouragement to the Bahá'ís of the world.

My husband gave selfless service during those five memorable days, in volunteering to help with the children, who had also come from all parts of the world. He wasn't yet a Bahá'í, but spent every day attending to the important work of keeping the children happy and amused. It wasn't an easy task, with little ones from hundreds of different countries, speaking diverse languages, all needing attention.

Each evening, in our hotel, believers from across the world, including our friends Jess and Nick Echevarria from Canada, would gather together to share exciting stories. Most of these stories told how our lives had changed after we found the Faith. So much happiness! So much harmony and laughter! Never will I forget those radiant faces. Our hearts rejoiced at the sheer wonder of this new revelation for the world. We even astonished the waiters when we ordered soft drinks rather than alcohol. For health reasons, consuming alcohol is not permitted in the Bahá'í Faith. With such spiritual love and happiness we all felt intoxicated anyway. During those days of heavenly delight, I could feel how much my life was changing, renewed with dynamic spiritual energies that I had never felt before. Again and again I asked myself, "Why me? Why have I been so blessed?"

My life had always been one of caution. I felt reluctant about change, none more so than moving house. It was now amazing to find that my feelings of insecurity had completely gone. Gradually, there came the deepest longing in my heart, to go wherever we could serve this new cause, even though it might take us to totally unknown places. My love for the Faith seemed to wash away all my previous fears and doubts. I wanted to give something back, to serve wherever that took me. I was now prepared to go anywhere, to aid the spread of this message for the unity of mankind.

3

NEW DIMENSIONS

Bahá'ís were needed all over the world to share the exciting message of unity and peace with the rest of humanity. This called for dedicated believers, willing to move to another town or even to another country. They were not missionaries in the traditional sense. Those who express their desire to move to a new area are known as pioneers. That town, or country, becomes their home. They try and find employment in order to become self-supporting and make efforts to fully integrate with the local people.

My dream of pioneering was first fulfilled in 1966, when John and I decided to help the Bahá'ís in Southport save their local Assembly by making up the nine members. Bahá'u'lláh had laid down the principle of establishing an annually elected local assembly in every town and city on the planet. There are no clergy in the Faith but we still need organisation to help development in an orderly fashion. We moved joyfully and eagerly, John being able to drive to his work in Liverpool, while our son travelled by train to the Collegiate Grammar School. That first pioneer move seemed a very small effort to make, being only twenty miles down the road from Liverpool. But it took us into a new and wonderful life that brought the greatest happiness. Our home became 33 Park Avenue, Southport. From then on we felt the house belonged to Bahá'u'lláh. We had gone there to serve the Faith, so now it became completely central to our lives. Everyone was welcome, no matter when they called, and every Friday night we held what are called 'firesides' when the Bahá'ís could gather and bring their friends.

Those were special days, when the whole atmosphere seemed charged with a harmony and love that I'd never known before. The magic they brought lifted me above this world as I had previously known it, and replaced it with a radiant assurance that came from deep within.

I used to walk Simon, our Boxer dog, along a quiet little path across the fields near our home. While I walked a sense of utter freedom expanded all my thoughts, and I marvelled at the grace of God's love and goodness. Now to be surrounded by the love of so many friends, was like living in a global village.

A passage from the Bible came to mind. *"I am come that they might have life, and that they might have it more abundantly." (John 10:10)* I now understood that this abundant, beautiful life is given to us through our faith in God, in whatever age we are living. I felt it as an enrichment of my inner being, as pure happiness, not affected by any outward changes or conditions.

John (Jr) on the steps of 33 Park Avenue, South- port with Ruth Gillibrand

Simon, our Boxer dog

Carmel, the Mountain of God

There was immense excitement in 1964, when my mother made her pilgrimage to the Holy Land. A Bahá'í pilgrimage lasts a period of nine days when the pilgrim is invited to visit the holy places in Haifa and 'Akká, where Bahá'u'lláh and 'Abdu'l-Bahá, (His eldest son) spent the latter years of their lives under house arrest. These are now the most peaceful and tranquil spots on earth. On her return, she inspired all the Liverpool Bahá'ís to make their own spiritual journey as soon as possible. Several of us sent our requests to Haifa straight away, including my sister and our friends, George and Elsie Bowers. They were our neighbours in Liverpool, who had shown great interest in the Faith during the time I was investigating the teachings. They became Bahá'ís shortly after I did. The two Johns and I were invited to go in April 1966, just twelve days after our move to Southport. When we arrived in Haifa and gathered together in the shelter of that peaceful, beautiful spot, we felt far removed from the noise and bustle of the world. There were just twenty-three of us on that pilgrimage, and our little family were the only three from the United Kingdom. Looking back we realise what a privilege it was to be there at that time. We were given the most loving hospitality and we slept in the Pilgrim House, right in the midst of the beautiful gardens on the slopes of Mount Carmel. All our meals were provided for the whole nine days, and we were cared for with the utmost kindness and love.

Remembering those nine precious days, I feel the deep surging happiness that filled my heart each moment. I kept a diary of all that took place, and a record of the effect that the absolute peace had on my inner being. When we returned home, I wrote a full account of our pilgrimage, describing my feelings. A few of those glorious moments I must include in these pages, as their influence on my life has been far too deep to leave them untold.

I had never travelled by air before, and my excitement was increasing every moment. George and Elsie Bowers drove us to Speke Airport, in Liverpool. They had only recently made their own pilgrimage, and were filled with delight to see us embarking on this journey of discovery. It was Tuesday 12 April, 1966 with a heavy sky and drizzling rain. In London, we learned that our flight had been delayed, so we were given refreshments while we waited. Nothing could disturb our feelings of adventure, and even the delay seemed to be part of it all.

I could hardly contain my excitement when the moment came to board the plane, on the very first flight of my life. (I didn't know then that, in the years ahead, I would travel by air so many times, and that I would do it on my own!) Great was my delight to find myself seated next to the window, where I could witness the whole amazing panorama, and where I could feel that I was flying like a bird in utter freedom. I won't forget the sheer thrill of delight when the plane rushed along the runway, and soared into a new dimension. We had left the world far, far below, and were now being carried through the skies. With a thrill of joy, I marvelled at the cotton-wool white clouds surrounding us, and the brilliant sunlight gleaming on the wings of the plane. The dismal grey skies were left behind, and everything below was so minute. Cars looked like toys, and fields were little squares of patchwork in differing shades of green.

Upon our arrival in Israel, we spent the night in Tel-Aviv. None of us had much sleep because of our great excitement. Next morning I woke early with the full realization that we were actually in the Holy Land, and would soon be taken to the very spot where the most recent manifestation of God had walked. There was no way that I could imagine what this wondrous experience would be like. Oh, the joy that lay ahead of us! After a light breakfast we caught the bus to Haifa, on the last stage of our journey to the world centre of the Faith.

When I first caught a glimpse of the golden dome of the Báb's Shrine, I felt too full of wonder to look at it directly. I had seen pictures of this beautiful place on post-cards and photographs, and had marvelled at the sight. Now it was so close to me. It was right in front of me! We arrived at the door of the Pilgrim House and were lovingly greeted by Jane Kent. As she embraced us, we had a foretaste of the love that seems to fill the hearts of everyone in that heavenly place. We followed her slowly into the cool, restful atmosphere of the Pilgrim House. It was an oasis of peace and love waiting to enfold us, and I felt like a weary traveller reaching the end of a very long journey.

A large, life-like painting of 'Abdu'l-Bahá hangs on the wall. It seems as if He is actually present, a gently smiling host, bidding us to be happy and above all, to love one another. A sense of peaceful repose fills the room and I can't believe that we have really arrived at last.

At twelve-noon, Mr Paul Haney came to the Pilgrim House, to accompany us on our very first visit to the Shrines on Mount Carmel. Slowly, our hearts beating with expectation, we approached that beautiful building, the golden dome gleaming in the sunlight. We left our shoes and cameras outside, and stepped softly into the Shrine of the Báb. Time and again I have longed for returning pilgrims to tell me about this glorious moment. I have thirsted for descriptions but now that I am experiencing it for myself I understand so well that it can never be described. It is so beautiful, so utterly breath taking, touching the spirit and lifting the heart with a deep surging thankfulness to God. I have been blessed throughout my life and now He has brought a fragile little human such as me, to this momentous hour! Such a privilege! I felt very humble as I stood before that Threshold, absorbing the spiritual beauty of such nearness to God's Manifestation. Fragrant flowers and chandeliers, and lovely Persian carpets are a delight for the outer being while, inwardly, I was overwhelmed completely.

Many moments later we went into the Shrine of 'Abdu'l-Bahá, eldest Son of Bahá'u'lláh, known to Bahá'ís as the Master. My reaction was of purest love and tenderness. I felt 'Abdu'l-Bahá's own wonderfully loving nature surrounding us. It was as though He dried my tears and filled my soul with happiness. It was a most wonderful feeling. There in the Shrine were glowing pink lights, exuding a sense of warmth and assurance. Just as the Manifestation of God bridges the great void between the infinite, unknowable Essence of the Creator and His creatures, so does 'Abdu'l-Bahá reflect the love of the Manifestation, in a beautiful human way for us to understand.

On our second day of pilgrimage we were driven around the Bay of Haifa, to Bahji, where Bahá'u'lláh is buried, and the Mansion House where, in 1892, His Spirit winged its flight from this world. We walked very slowly along a tree-lined path. Our thoughts were far beyond our every day lives. I wanted to weep, as I tried to grasp more fully what was happening. Was I really treading that path, to pay homage to God's Great Messenger? When we reached the door, we stepped out of the bright sunlight and crossed the threshold into the Shrine of Bahá'u'lláh.

The immensity of spiritual power and the overwhelming sense of majesty and awe in that holy Place are indescribable. It seemed to be the nearest to God that anyone can be in this world. Powerful feelings encompass the soul and stir the heart. The grandeur and strength of the Blessed Beauty, Bahá'u'lláh, flowed into my spirit. Some of the Persian pilgrims knelt down and wept as if their hearts would break. Later, we had tea and delicious sweetmeats served in the Pilgrim House of 'Abdu'l-Bahá'. The warm, scented breezes blow so gently and refreshingly. I seem to be drinking in all the love and beauty with my whole being. Fragrant flowers and rippling breezes, warm sunshine, and peaceful harmony, all these surround us, within the loving shelter of God's glorious Faith.

We went by car to the headquarters of the Universal House of Justice, and were greeted so lovingly that each one of us felt really precious. Seven of the nine members of the House of Justice were present. They shook hands with each of us in turn. They combine great dignity and humility, a blend of beautiful human qualities that are so rarely seen. I was seated next to Dr Lotfu'lláh Hakim, who had known 'Abdu'l-Bahá for many years and had travelled with Him to Edinburgh (1912), during His Western tours. Dr Hakim advised me to write down everything that takes place during my pilgrimage, and to do this each night before I sleep, and then to start afresh, next day. He told me that this is very important, and will be especially so in the future. We were served tea, and the dear Japanese gardener, Fujita, handed round the cookies with gentle, quiet devotion. He had served 'Abdu'l-Bahá as well and had lived all the time at the world centre. Everything here is like a foretaste of the Kingdom of Heaven. I am beginning to glimpse the beauty of humility in all those who serve in this blessed Spot. This evening Mr Ian Semple dined with us and, later, took us for a walk in the beautiful gardens, while the warm, fragrant breezes blew gently over us. We walked up to the Archives Building, where we stood entranced, gazing at the glittering panorama of twinkling lights around the bay of Haifa. Tall cypress trees bent serenely in the evening air, standing like sentinels, dark silhouettes against a starry sky. Such incredible bliss and utter contentment rested in my heart. Words fail completely in attempting to describe the emotions that I feel.

Friday, 15, April was another glorious morning, and we had before us another precious day of pilgrimage. We all went into the Báb's Shrine, with members of the Universal House of Justice, immediately after breakfast. Mr 'Ali Nakhjavani told us the sad news that during the night dear Jessie Revel had passed to the Abhá Kingdom (heaven). She had been living in America during the visits of 'Abdu'l-Bahá to the western world, and He had invited her, together with her sister Ethel, to go to the Holy Land, to serve the Faith. We prayed for her wonderful soul in that peaceful Shrine. Her funeral took place at two-thirty this afternoon, and it was very moving to be there. The flowers were so very beautiful and everything was so simply and lovingly done. It is sad that I am now unable to bring her the message of love from my mother, who met her while on pilgrimage two years ago. I bought four red roses from the town and attached a note to dear Jessie, with our love. Her body was laid to rest in the Bahá'í burial ground where John Esslemont, Amelia Collins, Horace Holley and other devoted Bahá'ís, all of whom had served at the World Centre, were now buried.

From that very moving scene, the western pilgrims (nine of us) were driven straight to Bahji for our two-day stay in the Mansion of Bahá'u'lláh. After travelling through barren, sandy places, we arrived at this beautiful garden, so fresh and colourful, peaceful and welcoming. This is truly God's garden. And the Mansion House itself is such a blessed place. It vibrates with spiritual power and it is full of historic records of the Faith. All around the large, cool hall are tall pillars and many rooms. We were shown the room of Bahá'u'lláh, and very softly we entered into a deep silence. This is the very room where He slept. It was there that He passed from this world to the Abhá Kingdom (heaven) on 29 May, 1892.

What a calm and peaceful room it is, vibrating with a power that is not of this world. Everything seemed glowing in the soft light of a single lamp. One beautiful red rose was standing on the small bedside table. His slippers were there at the side of His divan. Oh, how tenderly they made me realize the human side of His wondrous life, and all the terrible agonies that were heaped upon Him.

I wakened today at ten past five, even though the closed wooden shutters over our windows made the room quite dark. Quietly, I left my bed and went across the hall to Bahá'u'lláh's room alone. There is no way of conveying the tumult of my soul, the breath taking wonderment of such close proximity to the Manifestation of God. Aware of my own smallness and insignificance, I was overwhelmed that God, in His mercy, had brought me to this moment, to so great a privilege and honour. How did this happen? Why me? There is no way of comprehending.

Next day we visited the Ridván Garden, outside 'Akka, a place of heavenly beauty. It was moving to be at the very spot where Bahá'u'lláh would sit, beneath the shade of a large mulberry tree. The whole garden was bathed in golden sunshine, and the little fountain sent sprays of cool, sparkling water into the air. We entered, for a short while, the room where Bahá'u'lláh used to stay, and our hearts continually turned to Him with such a deep, yearning love. I felt conscious of His awe-inspiring greatness while, at the same time, being aware of His suffering and sorrows.

We visited the Prison City of 'Akka on the next day, where Bahá'u'lláh was imprisoned for more than two years. I was deeply moved to see above the door of His cell, the words in English, 'Prison Cell of Bahá'u'lláh'. This was the actual cell where God's Manifestation was held prisoner. God sent His Spirit of Truth into the world and the world rejected it. I felt a great sadness for His years of persecution and imprisonment, but was assured by the knowledge that God's purpose would prevail. I know that inside or outside that prison-cell, whatever He reveals will be fulfilled and will flow out across the world.

I awoke to the dawn-chorus at five minutes to five on 17, April and as we had left our windows un-shuttered last night the room was beginning to get light. I washed and made my way quietly to the room of our Beloved. The red rose, beside the lamp, has opened wide and the gleam of the soft light shines on their delicate petals. It was here, in 1890, that Professor Edward Granville Browne, an oriental scholar from Cambridge University, had met with Bahá'u'lláh, as He sat on the eastern-style divan, which runs along the full width of the room. Granville Browne was the only Westerner to meet Bahá'u'lláh. Many moments later, after silent prayers, I came quietly out of that peaceful sanctuary.

From my bedroom window I can see the roof of the Shrine of Bahá'u'lláh, and many lovely cypress trees waving gently in the soft air. Of all the other dawns, for the remainder of my earthly life, I will not waken to the protective, love-drenched atmosphere of Bahji, nor will my physical form be able to go, in just a few steps, to the actual room where Bahá'u'lláh's spirit left this world and ascended to the 'Abha Kingdom.

21, April 1966 was the Ridván Festival. We were told that because it is Ridván (one of the holiest days in the Bahá'í calendar) both the Shrine of the Báb and the Archives Building on Mount Carmel, would be floodlit until midnight. We gathered there, waiting, and as the light faded into twilight both buildings were suddenly illumined. What a beautiful sight! Glowing lights, amidst the gathering darkness of the world, awakened feelings beyond the power of words to express. These things, of such wonderment and beauty, will surely remain with us forever. Gentle, warm breezes blew softly in our faces, and our spirits were stirred by the greatness of God's love.

We were escorted to the house where 'Abdu'l-Bahá' lived, in Haifa, and where He passed away in 1921. The Master's house was spacious and light, with beautiful flower arrangements. Everything was simple yet tasteful. 'Abdu'l-Bahá's bedroom has been kept exactly as it was when He was alive. The covers on His bed are white, as well as those on the wall-divans. It is peaceful and restful. We have read about the night He died, and here we were, standing in the very room where He asked His daughter to lift the curtains around His bed, as He had difficulty in breathing. We felt so close to Him and His life in this world. Our tears rose up and overflowed with infinite tenderness.

Finally we had our last visit to the Shrine of Bahá'u'lláh. Very, very slowly we all moved in procession towards that Most Holy Spot, so that we could pay homage to the Beloved. Resting our souls once more, in that most quiet, sacred Place, I lingered with deep longing, and gazed towards that dim portal of mystery, beyond the fragrant rose-petals and gentle lights, to catch the mystic accents of His Voice, which whispers, not from there, but from one's very heart. I thought of His words, *Thy heart is My home; sanctify it for My descent."* (Hidden Words, revealed by Bahá'u'lláh)

Breathing in the divine fragrances of Mount Carmel and Bahji greatly reinforced my love and devotion for the Báb and Bahá'u'lláh, and a growing desire to teach His

Cause. Our son, then eighteen, was given the honour of reading a prayer during the devotional programme at the Ridván Feast.

When the day of our departure came, I felt my heart would break. But, just before we left, a strong sense of resolve welled up in me. I must take back, into the world, where there is so much confusion and misery, some of the beauty and goodness that had been showered so bountifully upon us. We would renew our endeavours to serve the Faith as we returned to our new home in Southport.

4

THE CALL OF THE EMERALD ISLE

During those years in Southport, our son John left the Collegiate Grammar School in Liverpool to start his studies at the University of Cambridge. Before beginning this new chapter in his life, he spent five months in Iceland working on a building site. He stayed with Jess and Nick Echevarria, who had gone there as pioneers from Canada. In spite of freezing temperatures, John enjoyed it immensely. When he returned home, he had grown a fine beard, and with his blonde curly hair, looked like a handsome young Viking.

Throughout those years, my husband and I found the greatest happiness hosting fireside meetings in our home. Many Bahá'ís and their friends came to those gatherings, where we joyfully shared the message of this new revelation. Our days were gloriously full with weekend schools, conferences, public meetings and our regular Friday night firesides. We found ourselves uplifted and inspired in ways that we had never felt before. Our lives had been taken into a new dimension of service. For me, it was a blessing beyond anything that I had dreamed to speak about Bahá'u'lláh's Revelation at meetings all over the country. The phone would ring, "Lou, will you come and give a talk?" and off I'd go to share the liberating, wonderful truth that had brought me such fullness of life and purpose.

I was determined that our happiness in Southport would not prevent us from pioneering again, when the time came. Our life in Park Avenue was certainly a gift from God and it was not my wish to love that gift more than I loved the One Who gave it, by being too attached to it. At a Teaching Conference in Birmingham in 1970, Adib Taherzadeh appealed for pioneers to aid the work of the Cause within the UK and overseas. I remember him telling us, "Just say, I will go Bahá'u'lláh, I will go." My heart felt as though it was being drawn by a powerful magnet of love, and I was longing to jump up and say, "I will go, Bahá'u'lláh." A few minutes later I was standing with my husband and son on the platform, with about forty other Bahá'ís all eagerly offering to pioneer. Adib embraced my husband as he came towards him, and his face lit up with joy on seeing us, as a family, eagerly wanting to go. Many eyes were filled with tears in the moving atmosphere of love and devotion that filled the hall.

A few weeks later, we were invited to the Bahá'í National Office at 27 Rutland Gate in London to consult with the pioneer committee about where we should go. One of the most urgent goals of the nine-year world plan was the Republic of Ireland.

Above: Southport and Scarisbrook Bahá'ís – the last Nineteen Day Feast in June 1970, before we left for Ireland. Below left: Proud parents at John's graduation, summer 1970. Below right: First four-day visit to Ireland, 1 May, 1970

Two spiritual assemblies were needed, one in Limerick and the other in Cork. The formation of these two assemblies was of great importance, as they were to form the basis, along with Dublin and Dun Laoghaire Assemblies, for the election of the first National Spiritual Assembly of Ireland in 1972. (These assemblies were created by Bahá'u'lláh in His Book of Laws to channel the spirit of the teachings faithfully to the local level).

Although, in my heart I had the deepest longing to go to Africa, we set all our energies towards making a new home across the Irish Sea, in Cork. Young John had graduated from Cambridge that summer, and although he had been studying social anthropology, and was especially interested in West African culture, he immediately said that he wanted to join us in our pioneering to Ireland.

Settling in

On 18 July, 1970 we left the summer school in Dun Laoghaire, where we had spent a happy and inspiring fortnight and, with full hearts, drove down to Cork. We were about to open a whole new chapter in our lives. We were invited to stay in a small, furnished flat, while the two young pioneers, who lived there, Stephen and Shirin Ader, were on holiday in Turkey. The flat was at the top of a large house at 2 Strowan Villas. We had the use of one bedroom, a small living room/kitchen and a tiny vestibule where young John managed to sleep on a sofa. Our next-door neighbours, John and Doreen O'Callaghan and their four daughters, were extremely kind to us and did a lot to make us feel really at home. One of their daughters, Eleanor, became interested in learning more about the Faith, and to our great joy she later became a Bahá'í. I had no idea, then, that we would become so close in the years ahead. In fact I was to share one of the happiest times of my life with her in Africa!

Our little family stayed there much longer than we had expected, while looking at houses for sale within the city boundaries. It wasn't an easy time, especially for my husband, who had given up his work at Eric Bemrose, in Liverpool, and was patiently struggling to accept our new and vastly different life-pattern. I missed being near my family and friends at home, especially my sister Pat, and Hagar, my mother. We also missed our beautiful Boxer, Simon, who had made himself a much-loved part of our family. We had found a good home for him, following many weeks of effort, only to learn, soon after our arrival in Ireland that he had been put to sleep by his new owners. He had been pining for us so much that they thought it would be better for him. This sad news brought added grief, during this somewhat stressful period when we were trying to cope with so much uncertainty.

Towards the end of September, on a grey wet day, we moved into our new home, at 20 St Joseph's Lawn, in Bishopstown. I remember the feeling of relief and delight that swept over me when one of the removal men brought our large, beautiful portrait of 'Abdu'l-Bahá into the house. Through the years it had taken pride of place in our home, wherever we lived. In Southport we had called one of our rooms 'Abdu'l-Bahá's Room. Now, in Ireland, it seemed as though we had truly arrived, and the beloved Master was with us.

Young John was immensely relieved when he was offered employment in Cork County Hall. His work was to find suitable houses that would encourage the 'travelling people' to settle into more permanent homes. There were many families who belonged to the itinerant population, and John, with his gentle, loving nature, was ideally suited for this work. He converted a large mobile library-van into a schoolroom for the children, where he helped them to read and write, to enjoy painting and making clay models. He drove around the beautiful countryside of County Cork calling for the children at their homes. They looked on him as a kind and understanding friend, and he enjoyed this work very much. Sometimes, on fine sunny days, he would invite me to go with him, and it was a joy to be travelling through the lovely rural areas. My son was a delightful companion, and we were always very close.

For a few months, I ran a little kindergarten in the converted garage, which my husband had skilfully transformed for me. It had a sink with running water, electricity, and small tables that he made out of packing cases. The little children were lovely and this made it a very rewarding and happy experience. From a financial point of view, we needed more income and, very reluctantly, I had to give up my work with the little ones to look for employment outside the home. Sometimes, when I turned the corner into St Joseph's Lawn, one of my young pupils, Elena Hickey, would come running towards me, calling, "Here's my teacher." She had the cutest Cork accent one could imagine, and although so many years have passed, I can still recall her beautiful smiling face.

Because I had been at home all the years of my married life, it wasn't easy to think of going out to work again, but it had to be done. It wasn't very long before I found employment in a large newsagent in Patrick Street in the centre of the city. Among other things, they sold games and toys as well as sweets, which made it a very popular store for children. That first morning, as I left home to get the bus, my inside was churning. How would I cope in this new situation? The day stretching ahead would seem very long. I found myself walking into Eason's Store, feeling as vulnerable as a teenager starting her first job.

I had bought a plain grey suit, which all staff members had to wear, and I was given a name badge to fasten into my lapel. It was a pleasant relief to find that everyone was so friendly, and I soon lost my initial anxiety. It made me realise that the years had taught me a different outlook on life and given me a more confident approach to other people. Actually, I enjoyed being in the shop and speaking to the customers. Sometimes the days dragged slowly and I was relieved when it was time to catch the bus home. Clocking-on each morning and then clocking-off at night made it seem more like being in a factory than a shop. The hours were quite long, from nine in the morning until six in the evening, and eventually I decided to look for work elsewhere.

Historic visit of Mr Hugh Chance, member of the Universal House of Justice, to Strowan Villas, Cork in summer 1970. (From left) George Bowers, Patricia Hick, Zoë Backwell, John Turner, Mr Hugh Chance, Gillian Philips, Dr Keith Munro, Hortense Braederhorst (in front), Peter Trundle, John Turner (Sr), Shirin Ader, Mary-Lou Martin, Lou Turner, Mrs. Chance, Else Bowers.

Sorting out the garden at 20 St Joseph's Lawn – backbreaking work for the two Johns

John and I had started going to a small art class, which was held in the home of a friend, Jimmy O'Mahony. We thoroughly enjoyed those evenings, as it gave us a greater sense of belonging. We worked in oils, which I found fascinating, and each week we painted the portrait of one of his friends, who would come and sit for us. One evening, while we were enjoying a cup of tea and a sandwich, someone mentioned that a new baby-wear shop was opening in town and that they would be looking for employees. The prospect of working as a sales-assistant in a small shop seemed more appealing than a large store like Eason's. The shop was called Anna's, after the lady who owned it, and much to my delight she took me on right away, though I had no experience in baby wear. It was very interesting and I especially liked to dress the window, choosing attractive colour schemes, and arranging the lovely little garments in creative patterns. After a few months, the owner of the shop told us that she needed to cut down on expenses and would have to manage with just two assistants. As there were three of us, we knew that one of us had to go. The other two ladies were widows, and I felt that my situation was not as difficult as theirs, so I told them that I was prepared to leave and look for something else.

A short time after this, I was travelling by bus into town, when I saw a beautiful rainbow, which gave me a special sense of happiness. It seemed as though it ended directly over a large hospital called Our Lady's, and the thought came to me that it might be a good idea to see if they would like a visiting hairdresser. A few days later I applied and was pleased to be called for interview. The hospital, which was very old and rather grim-looking, cared for patients who were suffering from serious mental disorders. When I went inside, it was distressing to see how ill some of the people were. This was a bit too much for me and I was relieved when I was asked to work part-time in St Anne's Psychiatric Hospital, instead. I had taken a hairdressing course in Liverpool, four years before, as I thought it might help me to find employment if we moved to a new area. Now, all that effort was bearing fruit. I began work in a tiny salon, which catered for one lady at a time. While shampooing their hair I would pray silently for their healing. The patients would often confide in me, sharing their worries and anxieties. Those patients became very dear to me and they would look forward to my visits. We often talked about the spiritual aspect of life, which was easy to do, because they all held a firm belief in God. I thanked Bahá'u'lláh for giving me the blessing of such an opportunity. I had prayed fervently for an opening that would enable me to be of service to others in some way. This was the answer. It brought to my mind the words of Bahá'u'lláh, *"He is the prayer-hearing, prayer-answering God"*, *(Bahá'í Prayers p.145)*.

As pioneers in a Catholic country, we had been advised to be gentle in teaching the Faith and not too direct, which might bring opposition to our small community. It was important that we didn't provoke antagonism against the Faith, so that the spiritual assemblies could be brought into being. This was our most important task, and we lived accordingly. In the following year, two English Bahá'ís, Val and John Morley, moved from Dublin to Cork, to ensure the successful formation of the very

(Back row from left) Peter Trundle, John Morley, Stephen Ader, John Turner (Jr), John Turner (Sr). (Seated from left) Val Morley, Shirin Ader, Lou Turner. (The ninth member Maude Bennett was in hospital)

first spiritual assembly in that city. With great devotion, they took up residence in a modest house in John Philpot-Curran Street, off Shandon Hill, which they affectionately called "The Cabin". Never will I forget the day when we gathered together, and with a sense of excitement and wonderment, witnessed the birth of the first Spiritual Assembly of Cork. The bells of Shandon Church were ringing close by, and each of us knew that a great moment had arrived, and a new era had dawned.

In the days that followed we perceived a new spirit in the city, and felt a growing awareness of what it means to have a divinely ordained institution in our midst. We had already served on the local Spiritual Assemblies of Liverpool and Southport, and had known them to be of great importance, but during our time in Cork I felt that I had gained a far greater insight into their significance. One of the nine members of our Assembly was a pioneer, also from England, a young man called Peter Trundle who was the same age as John. He was a very devoted Bahá'í, with a radiant and happy face. His love for the Faith shone out, for all to see.

As I look back, I realise how much my husband must have felt the tremendous strain of no longer going to work each day, yet he quietly accepted it with his usual goodwill and patience. He was a very unselfish man as well as a wonderful husband and father, always ready to help and encourage us. We were a very close family unit, where loving affection was a natural part of our lives. For such a blessing I will always be grateful.

In 1972 there was great rejoicing, when the first National Spiritual Assembly of the Republic of Ireland came into being. Our son was elected as one of the nine Bahá'ís who was called to serve on that great institution of Bahá'u'lláh's administrative order. We knew that this was an immense privilege and we felt at each moment that we were being showered with blessings from every side.

We loved the Irish people, and my heart was in tune with them. Walking to St Anne's hospital beside the River Lea, I would find myself marvelling at our being there, and the realisation of why we had come, why we had crossed the Irish Sea, to make a new life in County Cork. It was that reason which made everything so beautiful. The swans on the river, the trees and the sky, everything was perfect. It all reflected a deep, inner gratitude to God for lifting me to a new awareness of the divine purpose in our lives. Our little family, which my mother called "The Turner Trio" had been granted the opportunity of serving, in some small way, the Plan of God. It was special just to be alive in the century that 'Abdu'l-Bahá' called 'The Century of Light'. Nothing was commonplace, nothing was ordinary; everything shone with the wonder of God's perfect creation. On my way to St Anne's, during those days of utter contentment, I can recall vividly how truly happy I felt. Crossing the little bridge that spanned the river Lea I would gaze at herons standing so peacefully in the water. Even the trees took on a special loveliness.

In the following year, the members of our new National Spiritual Assembly were called to the Holy Land for the second election of the Universal House of Justice, which takes place every five years. My husband and I went with young John to the airport, and, as the officials were taking all the necessary security precautions, I was thinking of his purpose in making that journey. He was helping to lay the foundation of Bahá'u'lláh's future World Order. The sacredness of the mission he was on and the purity of that purpose were hidden to those around us, as the security guards searched him for firearms and other destructive weapons. John and I stood watching the aircraft as it took off and soared gracefully into the vast sky. Our son was going to Haifa to play his part in the Divine Plan for mankind and, inwardly, we were humbly giving thanks.

He was married in the summer of that year to Zoë Backwell. Her father, Richard, had at one time been a much-loved member of the British National Spiritual Assembly. Dick, as he was affectionately called, was the author of a book called *The Christianity of Jesus*. He and his wife, Vida, had been pioneers to Northern Ireland since 1963, along with their three children. After their marriage, John and Zoë went to live in Hamilton in Scotland, where she was doing her teacher-training course. John was greatly missed in Ireland, and our home seemed very quiet without his delightful, loving presence, but we rejoiced with them in their happiness.

Lou and John Turner in their garden in Cork with John and Val Morley (1972).

Zoë & John's wedding day – 6 July 1973. Outside Adib & Lesley Taherzadeh's home in Monkstown, Dun Laoghaire.

5

ANXIETY FOR HAGAR

Earlier in 1973, we received the sad news from my sister Pat that our dear mother Hagar had been taken into Sefton General Hospital and was far from well. She had suffered a stroke in 1968. Now her condition had greatly deteriorated. Pat was in fulltime employment and unable to be at home with her during the day. This was a very difficult situation as we were not happy about her being in hospital. That year it was fortuitous that the National Bahá'í Convention for the United Kingdom was being held in St George's Hall, in Liverpool, so John and I decided to go to England and visit my mother at the same time. When we got to the hospital it was one of the most distressing experiences of my life to see her lying there. She had been placed in a psycho-geriatric ward that the doctors admitted was not the right place for her. They confessed to having nowhere else to put her.

At first, I hardly recognised my lovely mother, frail and thin, and looking so very vulnerable. My heart was overwhelmed with an awful sadness. Her sight was failing, but a most beautiful smile lit up her face as I came closer. With all my heart I longed to carry her in my arms and fly away to the safety of our home. The other patients in the ward were all confused and unable to speak rationally. It was a terribly sad place for her to be even for the shortest time.

We could see how isolated my mother felt, and what depths of loneliness she was suffering. I begged God to help us, and I beseeched Him for a miracle that would enable me to take her home. We had to return to Ireland, but in the weeks that followed, my mind was in turmoil. In spite of the doctor's warning that she could become a considerable nursing problem, I decided to bring her out of hospital and put an end to the dreadful ordeal she had endured for so many months. How could I leave her in such a lonely state? My heart was aching for our mother, who had looked after us in our childhood, and lovingly cared for us when we were sick. There had to be a way of bringing her home. The doctor tried to insist that I should leave her where she was, but I knew that this was utterly impossible for me. I could not rest, and every day I kept thinking, "She is still there, so alone and sad, in that room." At last, I made up my mind that no matter how difficult the situation was, I would return to Liverpool and bring her home to Ireland. It was her eightieth birthday by the time all arrangements had been made, and seemingly insurmountable obstacles had been overcome. God had truly brought about a miracle. I booked our flight and arranged with Aer Lingus to have a wheelchair at our disposal. The hospital doctors had agreed to her being discharged in early December.

First, there was shopping to be done, as she needed new clothes. Our thin little mother had lost so much weight that everything was now far too big for her. I went to Liverpool, on the overnight ferry, feeling excited and a little bit scared as well. First, I went to Pat's home, which was close to the hospital. That gave me time to pray, and to gather strength for what lay ahead. It was 6 December, my mother's eightieth birthday. What gift could I take, at a time like this? I went to the shops and bought a large box of assorted sweets. There would be many opportunities for the giving of treats in the days ahead. At the hospital entrance I braced myself, I needed to be prepared for whatever might be awaiting me. When I walked into the dayroom it was with such a flood of joy that I went towards her. My frail little mother clung to me, and tears flowed down her cheeks. We held each other close and wept with relief and happiness. She whispered to me, "It's been hell! It's been hell!"

She was being discharged around teatime so I spent the day in town, buying the clothes that she would need. I chose a dress, a coat, and a cardigan, in very small sizes. Instead of buying shoes, I decided to get slippers, as her feet were very swollen. Once back on the ward Pat and I got her dressed and my spirits soared as we led her gently to the waiting car. Elsie and George Bowers, our very dearest of friends, had offered to drive us from the hospital to Manchester Airport. The staff and officials were helpful and kind, and Hagar was quietly at ease. We all knew that she enjoyed flying. What a joyous feeling it was, knowing that she was coming home and that her dreadful ordeal was over. When we landed at Cork airport, John was there to meet us. He helped Hagar from the car when we reached St Joseph's Lawn, and carried her up the path and set her down in the middle of our living room. She was home at last. My heart felt at peace, after months of torment. My dear little mother soon began to eat and regained the weight she had lost. The Irish Bahá'ís in Cork showered her with love and affection. They thought it was marvellous that Hagar was a Bahá'í, when their own parents could not accept Bahá'u'lláh, and here was a grandmother who had so earnestly embraced the Faith.

To her joy, she served on the Spiritual Assembly of Cork, and one of our young Irish Bahá'ís, Noel O'Riordan, would sit by her side and hold her hand very gently. He would often say, "Be happy, Hagar, 'Abdu'l-Bahá said that we must be happy, and if you are happy, then I will be, too." It was an amazing time in Ireland, when large numbers of young people came into the Faith, especially in Limerick. They had such a pure devotion for Bahá'u'lláh. They wrote beautiful songs, and sang them with so much humility and love that we were all affected by the spirit they released.

In Limerick there were two devoted Bahá'ís, who had also moved there in 1970. Anne and Fred Halliday had come from Sheffield. We felt very close to one another, as we tried with all our hearts to teach the Faith in our new communities. We were more than happy to travel the sixty miles to Limerick to spend time with them and to pray together. When the first few people became Bahá'ís, it was in Limerick, and how greatly we rejoiced with them.

Farewell to Ireland

In 1975, John offered to help with the work of the Bahá'í Publishing Trust in Oakham. They were in need of extra staff, and he had experience in publishing. It was very hard to consider leaving Ireland, as we felt very close to that lovely community and had tender feelings for the warm-hearted Irish people. We had formed strong ties of friendship with John and Doreen O'Callaghan and Eleanor, who had a special place in our hearts. On our very last evening in Cork, Doreen arranged a surprise party for us, with lots of tasty dishes for all the friends to enjoy. She made us so welcome and to our great relief, she lovingly invited us to stay in her home overnight.

Our furniture had been sent off to Oakham on the previous day, and it felt very strange and sad to be leaving all our Irish friends. On the morning of our departure, Doreen drove us to the Airport where we were greeted by several of those dear friends, who had come to say farewell. Our hearts were very full, as we turned again and again, to wave to that little group. Slowly and tearfully, we walked towards the plane, knowing that we were closing a very special chapter in our lives.

Our new home at 8 Kennedy Close, Oakham, was a furnished, rented house, and that was yet another new experience for us. It felt very odd, having most of our furniture stored in the garage. That was a difficult time, especially as my mother's health continued to fail. I felt a deep sadness for her, as she had been active and independent all her life, with a very strong spirit. Now, she could no longer read nor write because of her sight. We registered her as being blind, and managed to get 'talking-books', as well as some Bahá'í tapes for her. I found it hard to bear, seeing her face light up whenever I went into the room while knowing that I couldn't stay with her all the time. As the days passed slowly by, she longed to leave this world to be with my father again. I sometimes asked her if she would help me to fulfil my dream of going to Africa when she was in the spiritual world. We spoke about these things quite freely as she had no fear of dying and just wanted to be released from the limitations of this world.

We had been in Oakham for less than eighteen months, when we responded to an urgent call to assist the Anglesey community in Wales. We knew how difficult this was going to be, especially as Hagar was now so very frail. There were many setbacks in our search for a new home, but eventually we found a suitable house in the market town of Llangefni. Young John and Zoë were a great help to us during that time. They made the journey down to Wales from Scotland, and were there in Anglesey when our furniture arrived. Meanwhile John and I saw that all our belongings had been taken out of the garage in Kennedy Close, before we started the long drive with my mother.

In Anglesey we became part of yet another caring, loving community, where all three of us were elected to serve on the local Bahá'í Assembly. It was the third time that my mother had served in this way, in the three years since leaving hospital. It was a wonderful bounty for her, and it brought a lot of joy to her life, as she loved the Faith so dearly. Once a week she attended a day-centre in Llangefni, which gave us a short break from full-time caring. John was always there to help, in his quiet, unobtrusive way. He never complained or sought anything for himself. My dear, dear husband was my close companion in every crisis. His presence was like a rock. He worked away happily in our new home and, as well, did a bit of digging and planting in the tiny garden.

We had been in Llangefni only two and a half months when Hagar suddenly became quite ill. She had a chest infection. A few days before the Holy Day of the Birth of the Báb, 20 October, the doctor advised me to stay at her bedside during the night, as he was very concerned about her. The following morning, he was greatly surprised to find that the immediate crisis had passed.

Bishopstown (February 1975). (From left) Hagar, Lou, Kay O'Neill, John Morley, Dolores Dowling, (front row) Peter Trundle, Dorothy Riordan, Eithne Earley, James McNamara ('Sykey')

6

THE CLOSING OF A CHAPTER

John and Zoë were planning to visit us for a few days, to see how we were settling into our new home. Young John was very anxious about his grandmother, so he was delighted to be seeing her again. We invited my brother Joe, who was living in Bangor, to spend the evening with us, and the memory of that lovely night will always be very precious to me. How relaxed we all were, oblivious of what was waiting round the corner.

Next morning I wakened early, and made some porridge for mother. She had not been well enough to eat for several days and I was pleased that she could manage just a little. I had spoken to John, briefly, while getting dressed, and he was looking forward to the company of the young ones. He and our son had a lot to share, in the few days that we could be together.

It is strange to think how suddenly and swiftly our lives can change without the slightest warning. When I went back upstairs, after preparing breakfast, I found my husband sitting on the bed looking very pale and ill. He said his chest felt terribly tight. To my horror, he suddenly fell back against the pillows and closed his eyes. With desperation and panic, I rushed to get my son, who hurried to his father's bedside. I ran to call the doctor as the surgery was just a few minutes away. It seemed my feet barely touched the ground as I panted down the lane. I blurted out my urgent, heart-breaking message to the receptionist. Then I turned and ran home, back to the terrible crisis that I knew was waiting for me.

John was at his father's bedside and, while overcome with grief, had given him the 'kiss of life' in a desperate attempt to revive him. I felt as if my own heart had stopped while we waited in an agony of suspense for the doctor. Meanwhile, my frail little mother had to be told what was happening, and this was an unimaginable burden for her, in such circumstances. To have to impart such awful news was one more grief to bear. My husband had left this world before the doctor came, and in some strange, unfathomable way, I knew in my heart he had gone. That day became a blur and I thank God for the numbness of shock, which protects us from that which is beyond our strength to endure. People came and went, and I felt their sadness and their sympathy. My son, with his own grief and pain, attended to all those things which had to be done and which relieved me of so much stress. That night, with gentle care and love, he made sure I was comfortably folded in blankets, on the living-room settee. My dear husband's body was in our bedroom where he had died those few short hours ago.

I dozed, but had no wish for sleep knowing that I would only waken to the painful realisation of our great loss. During those hours of darkness, lying alone in the silence, my memory unfolded all the joys we had shared. Thirty years of marriage with so much love and affection. Our deepest hearts' content was in being together through everything. I thought of his encouragement and support in every aspect of my life, and my heart was filled with thankfulness. God had blessed us in our marriage and had given us the most wonderful and loving son. We had all been guided to accept the teachings of Bahá'u'lláh, Who had transformed our lives with His healing message of love.

As the memories came flooding back, my gratitude increased and overflowed. The thing that most amazed me, in the midst of so great a sorrow, was that young John had arrived just the evening before, and had come three hundred miles to be with us. In my heart I whispered, "I didn't know that this was going to happen, but God knew, and He brought young John to us." The wonder of God's love overwhelmed me. He knew our grief before it happened and poured out His strength to comfort our hearts, making it possible to move forward with our lives.

If I had not found the Faith, and had not learned so much about the purpose of life in this world, there is no way that I could have survived. I would never have been able to bear the death of my closest companion, my beloved John. The strength given to me was simply amazing. In the depths of my grief it lifted me up and filled me with certitude and confidence. I had always thought that life without my dearest helpmate would be utterly impossible. Very often I had told my husband, "I don't know what I would do without you." One might have expected my mother to pass away but not my husband. How deeply I missed his ever-willing support and especially his care for my mother. Hagar was fragile and unable to do anything for herself. Struggling through those early days after my husband's death, I clung to Bahá'u'lláh and held fast to His love. The knowledge that our loved ones are released into a world far more beautiful than this one, and that one day we will be together again gave me great comfort and hope. John and Zoë stayed for the funeral, and several days longer than they had planned. Before leaving, they assured me of their decision to come and live in Anglesey. Never would I have asked them to do this, to sacrifice their jobs in Hamilton to support me in my hour of need. I could see, however, that this was their dearest wish, in their love and concern for me.

My mother lived for just three months after John passed away, and it had been a most heart-rending time. Having struggled to cope on my own, eventually I agreed, with an aching heart, to let her go into hospital. We arranged for her to spend three weeks as an in-patient followed by three weeks at home. It was a most difficult time, and God alone gave us strength to endure. On her last day in this world she listened to some passages from the Writings of Bahá'u'lláh, as I quietly read to her. Her face lit up with pure happiness and I could feel how much it comforted her.

Hagar passed away on 27 January, 1977, and her body was laid to rest in a grave beside that of my husband, in a small cemetery in Llangefni. John and Zoë left their home in Hamilton, and with absolute detachment, gave up their employment and their flat so that we could be together. It was far from easy for them, yet they never complained. How deeply I appreciate their spirit of total selflessness. Always will I be thankful for their sacrifice and love.

7

MY DREAM OF AFRICA COMES TRUE

The saddest part of becoming a widow was in having to make decisions and plans on my own. Now it was "I" not "we" after thirty years of sharing our lives, our aims and all our interests. My dream of Africa was still very much in my heart and I realised that now it was for me to decide what I wanted to do with the rest of my life. There could be no asking, "What shall we do?" or "Where shall we go?" I knew that I must serve the Cause and do it on my own initiative. The realisation that my mother no longer needed me to help her, and that my husband had left this world, spurred me to action. I wrote to the International Goals Committee and told them that I wanted to go to Africa on a two-month teaching-trip. [The IGC was a committee of the National Spiritual Assembly responsible for advising and assisting pioneers and travel teachers]

Looking back, I am quite astonished that I made no attempt to specify any particular part of Africa. I told my loved ones, "I don't know whereabouts in Africa Bahá'u'lláh wants me to be." I knew that God would guide me, and with absolute trust, I left it in His hands. Through the first year of bereavement it was the thought of Africa that helped me to move forward. During those painful moments, when grief was like a void inside me, I had only to remind myself that soon I would be on the continent of my heart's desire, teaching the Faith in Africa, with the message that will bring it peace and security in the years ahead. The Committee contacted me several times with various countries that I might visit, such as Gambia, Cameroon, Rhodesia or Ghana. My answer was always an eager "yes", without any hesitation or fear. Eventually, it was decided that I should go to Calabar, in Nigeria for a period of two months. It was just at this time we learned the most wonderful news, that John and Zoë were expecting their first baby. With all my heart I wanted to be home in time for this joyful event.

Irene Bennett, a Bahá'í pioneer in East Africa for many years, had recently moved to Nigeria. [a pioneer is someone who arises to move to another place, often another country, for the sake of assisting in the establishment of the Faith] When she heard of my proposed trip, she eagerly invited me to stay in her bungalow and make her home my base. It had three bedrooms, and was quite spacious. She also said I was just the inspiration she needed. There were so many delays in getting my visa, and in making all the arrangements for my big trip. I was kept very busy, going to Liverpool for my passport and making sure that I had all the essential inoculations. As a traveller, I was completely inexperienced, and, apart from making my pilgrimage to Israel eleven years earlier, I had never been abroad. The months passed, and I was very eager to start my exciting journey, but there was no way of hurrying things along. I tried to be patient as the days and weeks slipped by, until, at long last, on the 21 October, 1977, I found myself boarding a plane for Lagos, via Accra. It was amazing when I realized that it was exactly a year to the day since John had died, and on that poignant anniversary, with the help of God, I was on my way to Africa. I had never travelled on my own, and it seemed incomprehensible that I was going without my husband, on such a great adventure.

Just a few moments after I settled comfortably into my seat, the air-hostess announced that our late departure from Heathrow would probably cause us to miss our connecting flight in Accra. A wave of panic gripped me. How could I get to Lagos? Irene would be waiting in Calabar. What should I do? All my happy anticipation drained away and I felt a terrifying aloneness. There was no loving companion to share my plight, indeed no one to help or advise me. Tears began to rise, and I had a desperate longing to rush off the plane and head for home. Turning my face to the window, I struggled to control my fears and the overwhelming desire to break down and cry.

What happened next was remarkable, and it completely changed the tide of anxiety and apparent helplessness into a wonderful sense of calm. In struggling to control my panic I suddenly began to think, "I'm making this trip for Bahá'u'lláh. This is my whole purpose. It doesn't really matter whether I'm in Accra or Nigeria. I am in God's hands now, and there must be a special reason why I am delayed." With this affirmation of faith, I let go and a sense of perfect calm swept over me.

'Abdu'l-Bahá, the son of Bahá'u'lláh, explains that we can all speak to our own spirit. He said that when trying to make an important decision, we should ask ourselves whether to take a certain course of action or not. It is then that our spirit answers. I remember silently telling myself, 'Forget about times and schedules, place everything in God's hands. Your adventure has already begun.' I relaxed completely. Nothing had changed, outwardly, but something in my own attitude reversed all those feelings of panic, and from that moment until my return to England, through all the anxious times that lay ahead, I never again felt that level of insecurity and fear.

By the time we reached Accra I had so completely accepted the thought of staying there overnight, and feeling that there was a special reason for this, that it came as a little shock and even disappointment, to learn that the aircraft for Lagos was waiting for us after all. We were urged to hurry, and so ran quickly across the tarmac and scrambled breathlessly aboard. One of my fellow passengers was a young man from Holland, and we chatted happily. Once he realised that it was my first visit to Africa, he volunteered to help me when we eventually reached Lagos. He realised that I had no way of knowing that passing through that airport would be quite beyond anything I had experienced in the UK.

It was so totally different from the orderliness of Heathrow, and I was deeply grateful for my Dutch companion, who led the way through what seemed to be a thronging multitude. There were crowds of people, excited voices, and stern-faced officials. I produced my passport, my visa, and inoculation papers, with child-like obedience, whenever I was asked. I then proceeded to complete forms that declared how much money I had with me, both English and Nigerian currency. This became very embarrassing, as an over-zealous young airport boy, in his eagerness to earn a little extra in tips, was literally breathing down my neck. He was looking over my shoulder as I wrote. Perhaps, he couldn't read! The heat of Africa seemed to grow even hotter as I worked my way through all the necessary officialdom of arrival.

Suddenly, my Dutch companion had gone, and following the eager young Nigerian to the luggage collection, I was glad that I was not entirely alone. We stood there, waiting, but in vain, as my case had not arrived. The next hour or so was spent in trying to locate my baggage. It was nerve-racking but, thank God, I felt no real panic. Struggling to find an official who could help or advise me, seemed fruitless, and I began to understand that this was not England. I was where my heart had longed to be. I was in Africa. It was almost midnight when they explained that my luggage had been left in Accra. Someone thought that it might arrive next morning at about ten o' clock, but my flight to Calabar was leaving at eight o' clock. There was only one flight each day and Irene Bennett would be waiting. There was no-one by the gate when I dared to venture that far, and there I was in Lagos, late at night, without my luggage, and with absolutely no hope at all of getting to Calabar next day. I was on my own and my big adventure had really begun.

It was not only my son who had warned me to be careful in Lagos but the National Spiritual Assembly had also given specific guidance to Bahá'ís who attended a Conference in Enugu, just a few months earlier. They had advised them about excessive taxi-fares and exorbitant hotel prices. In fact they had urged the Bahá'ís to avoid staying in Lagos altogether, if possible. But here I was right there! I had no choice but to stay in the airport lounge all night, just holding onto my hand luggage that contained the warm clothing I had been wearing when I left England. Gradually, the crowds thinned and eventually very few people remained. Mine was the only white face, and I was the only female. One young man offered to get me something to eat from the counter, and I gave him some money for a few sandwiches and a drink of Malta. This was a cold drink, very dark in colour, almost like Guinness, but non-alcoholic. During the long night hours I lay down on a bench, tucking my arm through the handle of my bag and dozing fitfully. Opposite me sat one of the airport officials, and for a while we were talking quite happily. He told me that his name was J.J. Udoh, and that he worked in the Technical Records Department. He was interested in hearing about Bahá'u'lláh's message of universal peace. Each time I opened my aching eyes, he was there, reading a newspaper held in front of his face. In the midst of so much that was new and unfamiliar to me, I found it difficult to relax and to feel completely sure about his constant presence. On looking back, however, I feel that he was a sort of guardian angel watching over me as I slept. The long hours passed and, suddenly, joyfully, I realised it was morning. It was my first day in Africa. The thrill of this thought filled me with the utmost excitement. I longed to jump up and go outside to explore the sights and sounds of that land which had been calling me for so many years. The thought of breakfast didn't occur to me. I had no way of washing. I was just waiting for the luggage to arrive from Accra. There were several other passengers in the same situation, but being in their own country, they had spent the night outside the airport, in hotels. At last the baggage was there. It was easy to see my own case, even from a distance, a red suitcase that had belonged to my mother. When it came into view I was filled with relief. Crisis over - but immediately I was faced with another. What should I do now? It would be twenty-four hours before my flight to Calabar, and this was still Lagos.

Help appeared in the form of a fellow traveller from Worcester, a friendly young man in his early thirties who was a regular visitor to Nigeria, through business connections. When he realised my predicament, he immediately offered to take me to see a friend of his, Mr John Walters, who worked for British Caledonia. It was only a short distance to his office, but for me it was the most wonderful thrill. In those few moments I was catching my first glimpse of Africa. The sun burst upon us as we left the airport, and crowds of hopeful taxi-drivers and lots of young boys surged around us, pushing forward trying to take the suitcase from my companion's hand. He just pushed them away, quietly and firmly, and we escaped into one of the hovering taxis. I felt myself bathed in the heat and brilliant sunshine that is Africa, and it filled me with happiness.

John Walters was a tall and handsome Englishman, who was exceedingly helpful and understanding. I will never forget that little office and his kindly way of speaking. He looked at me, his eyes twinkling, when he said, "This is Africa. But remember, when you are in this room you are on British soil!" Despite my joy at being in Africa his words were reassuring. Mr Walters listened as I told him about my fears regarding the flight to Calabar next day, especially as the travel agent in London, had not given my ticket from Lagos the necessary okay. This last crisis, after many months of setbacks and suspense, had been thrust on me just the night before I left home. It had seemed almost the last straw in a series of difficulties, one after the other throughout the year. Once or twice I had been tempted to call it all off.

John Walters responded warmly and told me confidently that I would get on that flight. He then asked whether I had the address of any friends in Lagos. I showed him the only one I had, which was the Bahá'í Centre in Surrelea-Jones Avenue. He said that it was a very long way from the airport, and he called a boy to get me a taxi, instructing him to wait with me when we arrived, until someone had answered the door. If there was nobody in the Centre, then he was to see that we came straight back again. Mr Walters told him in a very firm but kindly way, "I want you to get a taxi for this lady, a good taxi mind you." I felt safe and in capable hands, but I knew with absolute certainty in whose hands I was being shepherded and guided. That subtle awareness of invisible help and protection was a tangible reality throughout the entire journey.

That taxi ride from the airport is one that I remember with nostalgia. The long stretches of dusty road, and the potholes that bumped us along causing the driver to weave continuously from one side to the other. My eager eyes scanned everything, absorbing with wonder, the sights and vivid colours of Africa. The sounds and the scents, all so new, filled me with the delight of a child on finding its dream come true. It was so bright and noisy, with a great sense of rhythm. I was totally entranced.

The hot wind brushed my hair into an untidy bush and I revelled in the scorching sun and the deep blue of the sky. The women with babies on their backs, walked with such grace, as though the large baskets on their heads were an extension of themselves. Tiny houses and huts with thatched or corrugated iron roofs. Little stalls displayed their modest goods, the owners with beaming smiles on their happy, radiant faces. Bursts of music and loud, strident motor horns filled the air. Every wagon seemed to have its own painted slogan: "God's Time is Best"; "He is King"; "All is not Lost" and many more in the local language.

Everything seemed so lush and colourful, the mango and palm trees, the bananas and oranges. The long, gaily-patterned skirts on the ladies added to this amazing scene of laughing children and beautiful black-skinned faces, amidst bustling and cheerful activity, under the vastest of skies. I revelled in the tempo. Its heartbeat and its entire atmosphere were so completely different from the orderly, cool restraint of life at home.

When we finally arrived at the Bahá'í Centre, it was a great relief to find two Bahá'ís present. One was a young man from Ghana and the other, a Persian boy, was on his way to Joss next morning. They met me with such warmth and love that I immediately felt relaxed and safe. There was a brief argument with the taxi-driver before my fare was paid, and I learned later that this was an everyday occurrence. They asked him to come back for me and for the Persian Bahá'í, at five-thirty the next morning, as we had to be in the airport very early. I was glad to know that I would not be alone.

By then it was late afternoon and suddenly I realised how hungry I felt. The boys showed me where I could wash, and then they went out together to buy some food. Water was a little trickle from the cold tap, but with immense relief I managed to have a wash. Only then did I become aware of my swollen feet and ankles. None of these things troubled me, everything felt perfect and my heart was singing with joy. How quickly it grows dark in Africa. Suddenly, the air was filled with the chirping of crickets and a chorus of croaking frogs. I listened, absolutely enthralled, as we sat in lamplight eating our very simple meal.

We talked together like old friends, so close in our shared love for the teachings of Bahá'u'lláh. The lamplight shone on their faces and gathered us together in its golden glow. I felt in those lovely moments, what I was to feel many, many times during that trip. Inwardly I marvelled at the peace and harmony that flowed between us. I marvelled how, although we had never met before, I felt utterly at ease and very happy in their company. All my life I had experienced homesickness when absent from familiar surroundings and my loved ones, even when I was in my own country. Now, on a far continent, away from family and friends, with no previous experience to guide me, I was walking an unknown path with confidence and joy!

I was given a little bed in a rather bare room, but it held everything I could have wished. The thoughtful care of those two young men was all the re-assurance I needed. They seemed to have anticipated my every need. They even bought mosquito coils that would protect me through the night. There was no light, as the electricity was off and, with only my torch to guide me, I took off my dress and sandals and lay down on the little hard bed. Amazingly, without difficulty I slept till five. It was still dark when I washed and dressed by the little circle of torchlight, with eagerness to start the day.

There was no time for breakfast or anything else, as the taxi had arrived. My companion and I scrambled in and were quickly speeding on our way to the airport. When we arrived we had to part-company as we were flying in different directions. We both knew that a hard, tough struggle lay ahead of us. It was fairly quiet at first, but very soon the crowds gathered and then the usual complete chaos erupted. Everyone seemed to be pushing and talking loudly, and the clerks at the counters kept saying, "Only okay tickets allowed."

I sat there and watched. People were reaching over the heads of those in front of them, offering sums of money in their desperate attempts to get a flight. What would happen now? How could I get on that plane with no okay? It came to my mind what was said about 'Abdu'l-Bahá when He visited America. They said that He seemed to be at the centre of a whirlwind where all was calm and still. Far from being gripped by panic and anxiety, in the midst of so much noise and struggle, I felt as though I leaned on another source of power entirely. I found myself waiting to see what would happen next. A lady had advised me to put my suitcase in the queue for Calabar and all around me people were being refused tickets, and arguing fiercely.

Slowly, we moved forward, advancing towards the little window, and still I had not the slightest idea what I was to do. In a moment I was there before the angry-looking clerk, and I heard myself saying, very calmly, "I should have been on the flight yesterday, but my luggage was left in Accra. Mr John Walters of British Caledonia said that I would get on this flight today." I will always be convinced that the clerk who stamped my ticket did so without knowing why he did it. His companion, working beside him, looked surprised and extremely annoyed. I could see that he was remonstrating severely with him, and in great relief and happiness I turned away. It gave me a deep sense of humility, and utter thankfulness for all the unseen blessings that were being showered on me.

My luggage disappeared from sight and I walked away to the small departure lounge. Seated there with his newspaper, was my friend of the night time hours, Mr Udoh. He greeted me with a huge smile and when it was time for my departure, he carried my bag to the aircraft. When I tried to offer him a tip as a token of my appreciation, he looked embarrassed and uncomfortable. I regretted very much having caused him such discomfort, and I apologised sincerely. He smiled and waved me goodbye, like an old friend. It was not the last I saw of him, for when I returned, more than two months later, we met again. On that occasion, as well, he proved to be an extremely kind and helpful friend. I settled myself in the small `plane and I was able to look down over the tiny villages and the minute houses, as we flew over Cross River State. Brown earth and lush, green fields, swaying palms, all the entrancing features of West Africa. I was nearly there.

Among the small group of people waiting when we landed, there were no white faces, and neither was there anyone looking for me. They had evidently given up on me, after the long delay in my arrival. Once again, someone came to my rescue. This time it was a young boy, about twelve years old. He had been on the same flight, and when his parents eagerly came forward to greet him, they realised that I was on my own. When I explained where I was going, the boy was delighted to tell me that he was a pupil at Hope Waddell Training Institute and Miss Bennett was one of his teachers. The boy's parents kindly offered to drive me to Irene's bungalow, which was on campus. It was wonderful to be taken right to my destination. The long journey was safely over, and it had all been quite amazing for a totally un-travelled person like me. I think that those experiences, and that whole episode, created a firm base upon which I was to build those other wonderful journeys that were to follow in the years ahead.

Strange as it may seem, had my trip to Nigeria been completely free from mishaps, and everything had gone smoothly, I am sure that it would not have given me the confidence that I gained from that unforgettable first journey. It had shown me that help was always at hand, and that I could call on that great unseen Source of Power, at all times and under all conditions.

Irene was so thrilled to have me with her, in the three-bedroom bungalow that was close to her school. It was a delightful surprise to find that she had another visitor staying with her, Aresteh Katamzadeh, a lovely young Persian girl, who had wanted to come and help the Bahá'í community in Nigeria.

Sadly, she was prevented from staying, as she was not granted a residents' permit. I went with her on several occasions to the Immigration Office to plead for an extension to her visitors' visa. When this was not forthcoming and she had to leave the country, she was heart-broken. She struggled to hold back her tears when the time came for us to say goodbye at the airport.

Before Aresteh had to leave, we did quite a lot of travel-teaching, to share our Faith with others, and we were accompanied by Mike Effiong, who was Irene's houseboy. He came every day to clean and cook, and to shop in the market for fruit and vegetables. He was about twenty-six years old, married, and the father of a lovely baby boy called Muhajar. Each morning I wakened to the thrilling realisation that I was in Africa, and to the brilliant sun and the warm, humid air. We were usually without water until late in the evening. Then we would collect as much as we could for the following day. Irene, Aresteh and I would wait for its welcome sound, as it came trickling into the bath. We were unable to do very much before that wonderful moment: feeling so hot and sticky, and limp with exhaustion. The sound of that water was always the signal for us to leap into action. Apart from collecting this precious water in as many bowls, jugs and utensils as possible, it was bath time. We took it in turns and each of us was strictly limited to a couple of inches of water. There was always the fear that it might cease at any moment, so we had to be quick. There was no luxuriating, no lingering in a long hot scented tub. Yet, those hurried bath-times in cold water were the most wonderful moments imaginable. The dust and intense heat of the day just melted away. It was utterly refreshing. Shortage of water was accompanied by a very erratic supply of electricity as well. This meant that not only were we without light, but we were also minus our precious, cooling ceiling-fan. We just melted in the heat. Those shortages were a daily test to those who, like Irene, had gone there to live and work on a long-term basis. Those difficulties could in no way spoil the inner happiness that filled every moment of my first African trip.

Aresteh and I went to the big market amidst the jostling crowds, scorching sun and a myriad flies. I loved it all. My eyes opened wide at the mounds of colourful vegetables and fruits, and so many babies sleeping on their mother's backs. Everyone seemed much happier and more relaxed than they are at home. They seemed to smile much more, despite the obvious hardships in their lives.

One day I made some bread, watched by a curious and smiling Effiong. I placed the dough in tins on a small stool outside the house, and left it to rise in the strong tropical sun. Effiong was an enthusiastic teacher of the Faith and often made trips to other areas. Several times I asked him if it would be possible for me to go with him. He was always most agreeable and he seemed to enjoy my love for his country and my longing to see more of it. Sometimes, I would stand, looking out across the river, close to Irene's house, and ask Effiong about the distant little place that could be dimly discerned across the water. It was Creek Town where the Christian missionary, Mary Schlesser, had so bravely lived and taught, and where she eventually died. It was known, in those days, as 'White Man's Grave' because of the dreadful conditions, which resulted in malaria and other tropical diseases.

I expressed my desire to visit Creek Town, and Effiong did his best to make arrangements for us to go there as soon as possible. When the day came, I was naturally very excited and delighted that Aresteh was eager to come as well. A taxi took us to the river and there we hired a small speedboat that was shared with several other passengers. Transport was always crowded. Whether it was a bus, a lorry, a boat or a taxi, they were all without fail crammed to overflowing. At home, we are used to having a certain amount of space around us, and many people dislike being crushed or having another person so close that they touch us. But I have since learned that in many parts of the world it is perfectly natural to lean against a fellow-passenger. This is in no way objectionable or embarrassing for them.

Our little boat, crammed with happy people, sped swiftly across the water. The wind in our faces was sheer joy as we travelled smoothly along, not far from the bank on our left, with its rich vegetation. Occasionally, we passed slower moving fishing boats. It was a fairly short journey, and as we drew closer to the little mooring place we could see the shining black bodies of the children who were swimming there.

As soon as they glimpsed us they began waving eagerly, jumping up and down with great excitement. Visitors, and especially strangers, are a very rare happening for

Bahá'ís of Cross River State

Wearing an African dress outside Irene's bungalow

Making bread under the African sun

*With Irene Bennett
at Kwa Falls*

Effiong with a dead python

the inhabitants of that small town, in the heart of the Bush. They very quickly came out of the water and clustered around us with huge smiles and wonderment in their dark eyes. This was something that occurred in all the villages during my travels, the trusting, happy expression on their faces, with a really open friendliness. No wonder I felt such pleasure and delight. All my life I have loved children and babies and, in later years, after becoming a Bahá'í, my heart yearned to do some work for children in Africa. There in Nigeria the children were everywhere, running towards us calling out a greeting. They possessed so few of the world's material goods, but without doubt they seemed contented. I had as yet to visit India and other parts of Africa, to see the agony of poverty and despair.

None of that injustice was to mar my first trip to Africa, and on that never-to-be forgotten day in Creek Town there were many treats in store. I recollect the sheer intensity of the sun with its noonday fervour, as we slowly wended our way through the sandy dust. Effiong greeted those who passed us and eventually we arrived at a little group of stores under a veranda. There was a lady sitting at her sewing machine making dresses, and on a small table at the front of the wooden house next door, there were some bottles. A sign stated: "Good Medicine Made Here". An invitation was given to us to sit down and talk about the Bahá'í Faith. A stool and some wooden boxes were eagerly provided. Thankfully, we were able to sit under the shade. A funeral had just taken place, and we respectfully watched as the coffin, covered with flowers, was taken to the church. This started a conversation between a gentle little lady and myself. She told me that her mother had recently died. She said that her name was Offiong Essio Ayo the Second. Her face seemed rather sad and I spoke to her about the loss of my own mother earlier that year.

We were very happy to be joined by Mr Cobham, the Headmaster of a Boys School. As we started talking about Bahá'u'lláh, he leaned forward and spoke in a very dignified and kindly way. I cannot forget his words and the effect they had on me. "All my life I have taught my boys from the Gospel," he said, and I thought that he was now about to tell us that he didn't want to hear about a new Faith. To my astonishment and joy he said, "But this should not prevent me from listening to your message." Surprise and admiration flooded my heart, that this mature and open-minded attitude should be his response. Deep in the African Bush, far from home with all our intellectualising and materialism, these qualities in this man touched me deeply. I found myself thinking of a little book revealed to us by Bahá'u'lláh called 'The Hidden Words'. One of its verses reads:

> *"Noble have I created thee, yet thou hast abased thyself.*
> *Rise then unto that for which thou wast created."*

Many times while in Africa my heart echoed those words, for I saw much that was noble, and which seemed far removed from our western view of life.

Mr Cobham listened thoughtfully, as we shared our message with him and dear Offiong Essio Ayo. He was clearly very interested and warm in his response, and it seemed a good idea to offer him the only book we had with us, as a small gift. This book was an Indian publication called 'The New Garden'. He accepted our offering with obvious delight, but we were in for another surprise. Our frail-looking, gentle Offiong Essio-Ayo turned to us, so mildly and quietly, and with what can only be described as an innocent, child-like quality, she asked, "Please, where is mine?" Once again, we had glimpsed this quality of simplicity, of heart-to-heart openness and purity. With a real sense of regret and sadness, we explained that we had no other books with us, but promised to return and bring one especially for her.

We returned the following week. This time we were a larger group. Several of the Calabar Bahá'ís came with us, and they were all eager to meet our dear friends in Creek Town. When we arrived, we were sad to see that Offiong-Essio-Ayo was not well. We found her sitting outside her little house, looking even more frail than she had before. She offered us a pineapple as a gift, and despite her poor health she was very happy to see us. We sat with her under the scorching noonday sun, limp and perspiring targets for the mosquitoes, but feeling an indescribable inner peace and happiness.

I handed her the book we had brought for her, and in a slow deliberate way, she began to read aloud. We listened and were enthralled. Each single word was spoken separately and distinctly. We were from different backgrounds entirely. Irene and I were from England, Arasteh from Iran, Mr and Mrs Ekpe from Calabar, and Offiong Essio-Ayo had never moved beyond that tiny spot in Creek Town: slumbering and sheltered by its tall, thick trees, so remote and far-removed from the life-style of our western world. The words came clearly and slowly, and melted our hearts, "God-has-a-plan-for-mankind." She was reading about the great Plan of God for the unity of humankind, the bringing together of all people, from every race and nation. It was a poignant moment, for we realised that its fulfilment was even then taking place in that little corner of our planet. We came away, eventually, after embracing that dear soul. Although I never saw her again, she will always remain a very precious part of my African experience.

The Calabar Bahá'ís would take me with them on their regular trips to the villages of Ikot-Efanga and Akansoko. It was fascinating to hear Mrs Ekpe speaking in her own language, which was Efik. The words rolled off her tongue so fluently, until she would suddenly say, "Lou-Lou, <u>YOU</u> teach!" I was always happy to do this, but it felt very strange to have someone else translating for me. It seemed as if my sentences were stilted, and that I wasn't communicating properly.

One of the great highlights of my visit took place in November, on my birthday. Effiong had gladly agreed when Arasteh and I had begged to accompany him on a four-day trip to a place called Ugep. This was a great adventure. We took food and blankets and our close companions, the anti-mosquito apparatus! Travelling was so exhilarating, in spite of the red dust that coated our skin and hair and roads full of huge potholes and ditches. It was great fun, and it touched a place in my heart that had never been touched before. Teaching, and sharing the Message of Bahá'u'lláh with those who want to listen, brings a kind of joy that nothing else can bring.

Calabar Bahá'ís and villagers from Akansoko

With Aresteh ready for our trip to Ugep

Teaching in Ugep

Lou at the back of a bunch of excited children in Ekori

Meeting with the Bahá'ís of Ugep was a wonderfully warm and loving experience. They had so very few possessions, yet their desire to share what they had seemed a natural part of their lives. Bananas or oranges, a coconut drink called Malta, these were offered with deep humility and generosity. Patrick was a lovely young Bahá'í who worked as a taxi-driver. He readily offered us his one and only room, during our four-day visit. Very quietly and humbly he said that he would move in with his 'junior brother' so that Arasteh and I would be comfortable. When we retired for the night, we draped our mosquito-net around the bed, while Effiong, our self-appointed guard, slept outside the door.

We had a small oil lamp to help us in the dark, and because of the intense heat we slept fitfully. Early in the morning I woke and lay in the grey half-light, listening to the shrill crowing of a cockerel in the distance. It was always amusing to realise that if we needed to find a toilet during the night, we had to ask Effiong to escort us, as it was some distance away from the house. When this happened we would follow him, like two small children, and wait while he obtained the necessary key from a neighbour. We were then taken to a tall hut-like construction, which had no windows and, needless-to-say, was dark inside. The first time we went on our little trip to the toilet, Arasteh was really nervous, and on seeing huge beetles and a lizard on the wall, she squealed. In her sweet, Persian accent she begged me, "Please! How did you manage?" Afterwards, we laughed heartily, and always saw the humour in every situation that happened to come along.

In the mornings, we managed to get ourselves dressed, but without water, how could we wash, or even clean our teeth? Effiong was always ready to help, and he assured us that he would obtain some water for us to bathe. After a while, he returned, carrying a small plastic pail, which he set on the floor. When he had gone we gazed in consternation and amusement at the few inches of water in front of us. There we were towels and toilet-bags at the ready, each of us having come from a background where showers and an endless supply of running water are taken for granted. We giggled at our own absurd expectations – and got on with our washing from the one small pail.

One day in Akansoko, the children were sitting on wooden benches and listening to our stories as well as learning Bahá'í songs. One little girl, probably about two or three years old, could find no room on the bench. She began to cry quietly and looked very forlorn. I took her on my knee and she lay there quite happily. In a short while she had fallen asleep, her little curly head resting so naturally against me. Suddenly a childhood memory came flooding back. As a little girl I had had the greatest longing for the gift of a black doll. I wanted very much to have one for my eighth birthday. When the day finally arrived, my parents gave me the most beautiful doll I had ever seen, and I loved and cherished her for many years. I called her Jacqueline, and my Mother made her some lovely little dresses that exactly matched the ones she made for me. Now, the eager smiling faces of those African children filled my heart with tenderness, and linked me with that little girl I had been so very long ago.

The weeks flew by so swiftly, each day unfolding a new adventure, a new challenge and a deep fulfilment. I recorded the happenings of every experience in an exercise book, so that nothing would be lost or forgotten. It held a treasury of memories but, sadly, the physical record was not to be. Upon my return to England I left it in a telephone booth in Cromwell Road Air Terminal, in the excitement and flurry of the moment. The written details have vanished but the sweetness of the experience will never fade.

I had lived to the full every moment of each day, hardly believing I was actually there. Opportunities for sharing our wonderful message were everywhere, in the villages, in the lorry parks, even on the river while travelling. During the hot, humid days or the black of night, under the starry sky, with an oil lamp, and our friends the moths and mosquitoes, those wonderful people were listening closely. They wanted to hear about this wonderful person, Bahá'u'lláh, Who had come to earth to rescue humanity from its ills. Was there anything more perfect? The most surprising thing was my sense of inner security. I never had a trace of loneliness, no sign of that homesickness which often dogged me in the past. I felt that 'home' was everywhere – not somewhere many miles away. Perhaps I was slowly beginning to understand that we never leave the spiritual dimension in which we have our true reality. It is all around us, and it is where we are connected and linked with our Creator.

This realisation holds us in perfect tranquillity and peace.

8

JOY AND GRIEF EMBRACE

My whole time in Africa was filled with endless happiness, and when I returned to my loved ones in Anglesey, we had only one week of waiting before Zoë and John's little daughter was born. She arrived in this world several days earlier than expected, as though eager to be alive in this New Day of God. Now I was a Grandmother, happy and proud, and deeply thankful for such a beautiful blessing. They named her Anisa Louise. In Arabic, Anisa means 'life'. It was wonderful to hold this precious baby girl and to sing the African Bahá'í songs that I had learned in Nigeria. She would gaze up at me with such wide, blue eyes as I sang:

> Bahá'u'lláh loves those who are pure in their heart,
> He will give them a blessed crown.
> He will give them, oh, yes, He will give them, oh, yes,
> He will give them a blessed crown.

I felt that somehow she understood what I was singing or, at least she felt it in her spirit. The first year of Anisa's life passed swiftly as she delighted us all with her beautiful smile and lovely chuckles. She made wonderful progress. John and Zoë were thrilled and proud of their baby daughter. Indeed they looked forward to increasing their little family in the years ahead. John was, as always, full of gentleness and loving concern. He took great pains to assure me that being Anisa's Grandma was of vital importance to her life. This helped me to feel confident and positive about myself. His expression always encompassed me with a sense of warmth and tender understanding. He missed his dear father, and he knew with deep compassion to what extent my own life had changed.

Our lives since becoming Bahá'ís had always revolved around service to the Cause of God. We wanted to share the divine message with others so, after consultation, we decided to move to the area of Colwyn District, where a Spiritual Assembly was to be formed on the following 21 April, 1979. Meantime, during the summer, I rented a tiny bedsit in Mostyn Road, Colwyn Bay, where I lived for a few months. I thought I might be able to do some teaching, in preparation for our move. Though being in Colwyn Bay had been exciting at first, I began to feel a void of inner loneliness. This was totally unexpected. No matter how I tried to reason it away, the pain and the sense of aloneness just wouldn't ease. I knew in my heart that I had to leave and go back home to my family in Anglesey. Several times a week I drove Zoë and Anisa to Colwyn Bay (while John was working), and there we carried out a vigorous house-hunting campaign. It wasn't easy to find a four-bedroom house with a good-sized garden, within our price range. We were eventually guided to a lovely house in the centre of town, up a steep hill called York Road. We all fell in love with it and nego-tiations began.

John's work as a Research Officer in the Department of Social Theory at the University of Bangor involved a lot of driving. He visited and interviewed elderly people, who were living in remote, rural places. This was part of his research to investigate the delivery of social services in those areas right across North Wales. This, of course, included Colwyn District, and living there would be helpful for his work. We had just celebrated Anisa's first birthday when I was asked if I would make a trip to Pembroke Dock, in South Wales. Several people from the Spiritualist Church had become interested in the Faith, and the Bahá'ís wanted someone with an understanding of their philosophy to help them. I was eager to be actively serving the Faith and gladly accepted. Inwardly, I felt a sense of trepidation. This trip would be quite different from my exciting trip to Africa. To be staying in a guesthouse, without the close companionship of my husband, seemed more difficult than going far away overseas.

It was a bitterly cold day in January when young John drove me to the railway station in Bangor. I could see in his eyes, the loving concern he was feeling about my going alone. He made me promise to take care of myself and, with a gentle smile waved me off saying he would meet me in two weeks time. I could have no way of knowing that I would never see him again, in this world. It is a blessing that future events are veiled from us and we can be happy right up to that moment of grief.

The following days in Pembroke Dock were filled with joyful activity. I was mak-ing new friends and sharing the beautiful teachings of Bahá'u'lláh with other souls. There is nothing in the world to compare with this special, precious happiness that fills the heart. Two letters arrived from John, asking about my comfort and health. Was I warm? Had I enough money? He ended his second letter by saying, "Take care of yourself dearest Mum, for all our sakes." He wanted to know the time of my arrival in Bangor, on my return home.

On my last evening in Pembroke Dock I spoke at a public meeting where several interested people were present. At the end of my talk I remember saying something about the bird of the soul being freed from the cage of the body at death, and taking its joyful flight into the spiritual realms of God. Happiness enfolded my whole being as I returned to my guesthouse that night. It was very aptly named Harbour Lights, as it had a warm atmosphere with a feeling of welcome and safety. I had become close to the lady who owned it. Her name was Marion John, and she had asked me quite a lot about the Faith, during many little talks we had together.

Next morning, this lovely lady wakened me quite early and called me to the tele-phone downstairs. My sister Pat was on the other end of the line. She was talking about my homeward journey. She asked whether I would be going through Chester. I was puzzled, because of her concern that someone should meet me on route. It was then that she told me the shattering news that my son, had been seriously injured in a road accident and was in hospital in Rhyl. He was suffering from head injuries and on a life-support machine. It had happened the previous morning and they had not been able to contact me. This couldn't be real, this terrible thing. I remember crying out, "I've only got one son, Mrs John, I've only got one son!" The long, slow journey home had to be faced. I was numb with shock, as I boarded the train for Swansea. There are no words to describe such a nightmare. The fields and countryside flashed by and I remember watching a flock of seagulls, wings outspread in graceful flight. A small part of me began to think of that other world, beyond this physical one, where the spirit is free, like those circling birds. Clutching at a single ray of hope, I thought that perhaps my dear young John would catch a glimpse of that other world, as people sometimes do, in a near-death experience. Deep inside I really didn't think that this would happen.

When I reached Cardiff, after my second train journey, I found that the next connection was in three hours time. Oh God! Three hours to stand in that station and wait. My John was seriously injured. There was no way I could go straight to him. My armour of self-restraint was shattering. I felt a captive, so alone on that station platform, while my only son was in a hospital many miles away. No one seemed to care, as I spoke to polite but busy railway staff. I telephoned Gwen and Mary Prince, where Zoë and the baby had been staying overnight, and I learned from them that the hospital had called her urgently. Everything inside me seemed to snap. Despair and grief washed over me. A porter took me by the arm and led me to a room where a kindly policewoman listened to my agonising tale. She was the angel who got me there.

I was transported to Colwyn Bay by a series of police cars. It was a long, long journey, through the icy snow, with the sirens shrieking. It all seemed totally unreal. When we reached the home of the Prince family, many hours later, Zoë was there with several other people, looking shocked and grief-striken. As she put her arms around me, she quietly whispered, "He's had a wonderful welcome, Mum."

At the moment when the doctors told her that John had died she had vividly felt that his Dad had said to him, 'Come on son!' I clung to poor, dear Zoë and sobbed from the innermost depths of my heart, for her agony as well as my own. His lovely, radiant spirit had winged its flight. He had brought only love and joy from the moment of his birth, and it felt as though all the sunshine in our lives had slipped away. I felt old and very, very tired as someone guided me to a chair. A number of people were coming and going, and I remember my sister arriving from Liverpool. She walked into the room, and came rushing towards me. Vaguely, I was aware of being still in my outdoor coat and boots. Someone had called the doctor, who gave me a tablet when she arrived. As a result I was later able to sleep. What a great mercy is sleep, but waking to that awful realisation of loss, all over again, is one of the deep and painful sorrows of bereavement.

However devastating our grief and however paralysing our sorrow, the days continue to pass in spite of us. Eventually, though we don't really know how, our lives move slowly forward to embrace new challenges. All our strength was drawn from the teachings of Bahá'u'lláh. Thankfully, our dearest ones who leave this world are still alive and active in the spiritual worlds, and we know that we will meet again. All our fondest moments are not lost and all the love we have shared can never die. Our loss is only temporary and I knew, in my heart, that I must now respond to everything in a positive, creative way. Zoë was so brave, as she struggled through those sorrowful days. Our sweet little Anisa was just thirteen months old, and many times I heard Zoë say, "Thank God for Anisa!" Although she was so young I have not the least doubt that she suffered the loss of her Daddy, who had loved her so dearly.

We went ahead with the whole difficult process of selling our house in Llangefni, eventually moving into our new home at the end of May. We were given enormous help and support from the Bahá'ís of Anglesey and Bangor, and one or two Bahá'ís lovingly suggested that I should apply for a pilgrimage to the Holy Land. They knew what a comfort this would be for my spirit, and although I couldn't feel any eagerness about it, I sent a letter of request to Haifa.

In a remarkably short space of time a reply arrived, and those nine days of spiritual bounty were due to commence on the 11 June. Viv Povey, a Bahá'í from Bethesda, was making her pilgrimage at the same time, so we arranged to travel together and to spend the night before our flight with her parents in London. When we arrived in Haifa, it was wonderfully uplifting to be once again in those holy shrines, kneeling at that sacred Threshold. I felt the nearness of all those loved ones who had made their own pilgrimage and who were now in the spiritual worlds of God.

I recall my thoughts as I walked along the path leading to the Shrine of Bahá'u'lláh. My husband and son had been with me in 1966, sharing those unforgettable days, and now I was here on my own. I thought, 'All through our lives we walk our own individual path to God. No matter how closely and lovingly we share our journey with others our path in this world is our own personal experience. Sorrows and joys are borne by each one of us, and all our decisions spring out of our own hearts and not from the heart of another.'

The path to His Shrine stretched before me, a symbol of my lone journey to God and I felt an inner contentment and acquiescence.

With Mr Furutan, Hand of the Cause of God, in the pilgrim house.

Outside the House of Justice building (under construction).

With George and Elsie Bowers in Ákká

With Bahá'ís from North and South Dakota and Mr Baghdadi

61

9

INDIA BECKONS

Towards the end of my pilgrimage, Dr David Ruhe, one of the members of the Universal House of Justice, showed us a film about New Era High School, in India. He explained that teachers were needed there in Panchgani and especially someone who could care for the children as a house-mother in one of the dormitories. For many years and especially during my pilgrimage, I had felt a great longing to look after orphaned children. In my imagination I always saw myself in Africa, but when Dr Ruhe spoke to me later that evening he thought I would make an ideal matron at the school. I felt a deep happiness at the prospect of doing this work in India. We stood outside the Shrine of the Báb, in the holy atmosphere that surrounds this precious Spot, and he gave me the name and details of Dr Ray Johnson, who was the school principal.

When I returned home to Wales, Zoë encouraged me to write to the school, as she understood how I felt about working with little children. So my plans to spend three months in India gradually began to take shape. It was an enormous step for us both and so soon after John's tragic death. I found it terribly hard to consider leaving her. My granddaughter was just two years old, and going away from her was going to be an agonising wrench. The call to serve the Faith was very strong and that aim alone made it possible. The Bahá'ís of North Wales were overjoyed and excited about my new venture. It was the Bahá'í New Year (Náw Rúz) and we held a party shortly before I was due to leave. It was overwhelming to see the response of the friends who came to our home, eagerly bringing their gifts, and cards full of love and good wishes. It was all very exciting. Ruhi Behi, who was living in Anglesey, eagerly offered to drive me to Heathrow Airport. And so it happened. As we rolled along he regaled me with stories of New Era School, which he had attended as a boy and where his parents were still working.

I travelled on Iraqi Airways and arrived first in Baghdad, where Bahá'u'lláh had been cruelly exiled for ten years of His life (1853-1863). Although we were not allowed to leave the airport, I found it moving, just being there. It was a wonderful feeling of relief to be met on my arrival in Bombay, (renamed Mumbai), the following day and to be taken to the home of one of the Bahá'ís. It was sheer luxury for me to wash and rest a little, and to have something to eat before continuing my journey. The same dear Persian lady drove me to the station where I would catch my train to Poona. This was yet another big challenge, when I realised that the train was scheduled to arrive very late that night. In Bombay I had glimpsed my first overwhelming sight of extreme poverty. I felt a deep heartache at seeing people, even small children, begging all around me with such desperation. It was an aspect of life in India that I just couldn't get used to and it made me very unhappy.

Sitting on the train that night was like an unbelievable dream, that I should be travelling completely on my own in India. Even now, it amazes me to think of this experience and to recall the trust and confidence that I felt. Even arriving in Poona in total darkness did nothing to shake my serenity. I will always believe that help from the unseen world was the power that shielded me from fear. Shortly after alighting from the train I found myself surrounded by three excited ladies, greeting my arrival with such happy enthusiasm. Irene Tafaaki, Head of the Primary Department at Panchgani, whom I had known several years earlier, in England, was now embracing me joyfully. The other two ladies were being introduced as we hurried towards a small station café for refreshments.

Beverly Millar and Millie Howe, from the United States, were also teachers at the school.

I remember very little about that midnight journey by car, except that we seemed to be travelling continuously upward, winding slowly round and round like a spiral. Panchgani was once a hill station and is situated at 3500 feet above sea level, over-looking Chicklee Valley, which is a particularly beautiful spot. Excitement and fatigue from my long journey flowed over me. It was well after midnight when we finally arrived at the Bahá'í *Bhavan* (Centre) where Irene lived with her husband and two little girls. I was to stay in their home initially, until the principal decided in which dormitory I should serve.

I slept very late next morning and kept surfacing to near-consciousness and then sliding away into sleep again. Voices would come and go, and gradually I became aware of strong sunlight filtering through the sides of my window-shutters onto my closed eyelids. Eventually I wakened fully and sat up, gazing around the room, which was the family's living room. I was on their divan-bed and certainly very comfortable. There were sounds from just outside my window of goats and birds. Suddenly the ex-citing realisation hit me: "I'm in INDIA," with a great uplifting sense of adventure.

The Tafaaki family had a lovely Hindu lady called Bismillah, who cooked for them. Suddenly her head appeared at the open door, and her kindly smile enfolded me in greeting. Apparently, the children, Janie and Munirih, had been very anxious to see me before they left for school. They had been peeping into the room to see if I was awake. It was now almost noon. My journey had taken two full days and a night. With added jet lag no wonder I slept so long.

The Bahá'í *Bhavan* was within walking distance of the school, comprising a large main building with classrooms, a library and offices. There was a smaller building which had a spacious new dining room, kitchens and a modern gymnasium. There were several small houses where members of staff lived, and a number of dormitories for the children and their house-mothers. The setting was stunningly beautiful, with

Panchgani overlooks the Chicklee Valley

Teachers and children of New Era School, Panchgani

Gloria Ekpe from Nigeria and Afshid from Iran – on the steps of the school

Bahman and friends with Mrs Lewis, one of the dormitory Matrons.

the Krishna River flowing peacefully below. There were trees and terraces with scores of large flowerpots trailing their brilliantly coloured blooms. Sometimes I had the thrill of seeing a grey monkey running swiftly up a tall tree or leaping along the ground.

Children from many parts of the world were studying and living together like one big international family. There were Hindus, Buddhists, Muslims, Christians as well as Bahá'ís, all learning and playing together in unity. Everything was so new to me: the blazing sunshine and intense humidity, the unfamiliar food, and water that was unsafe to drink without being boiled. We had huge red melons and mangoes and rice dishes every day, and tea that was made by boiling the leaves of the tea with the sugar and milk, all in one pot. Gradually, I got used to its sweetness and syrupy thickness, though still wishing for a homemade 'cuppa.'

As I strolled through the school grounds, I kept meeting new people, and being introduced to members of staff, as well as children of all ages and from many parts of the world. At times the experience was quite overwhelming and I would wander away, on my own, feeling far from home and everything familiar. Dr Johnson and his wife, Linelma, allowed me several days to acclimatise myself to life in India, and to recover from the effects of my long journey. I knew that in a very short time my work would be assigned to me in one of the dormitories.

Three or four times, during those first days, Mrs Johnson had spoken to me about their need for someone to help in two dormitories, both having older boys living in them. This was disappointing as it had been the thought of working with very young children that had attracted me to serving at New Era School. One day I was taken to see these dormitories while the children were in their classrooms. One of them catered for thirty ten-year olds, while the other had twenty boys aged between twelve and thirteen. The idea of being matron in a dormitory of older children, especially boys, filled me with great apprehension. I certainly didn't feel competent to fulfil this role and although I didn't express my fears to anyone, I felt very nervous about it. My prayers, during the next few days, that somehow I might be spared the approaching ordeal, were fervent and heartfelt.

One evening Dr Johnson and Linelma invited me to dinner, along with several other teachers, so that we could consult about my work. The meal was lovely, but inwardly I felt like a child whose fate was being determined by its elders. My mouth was dry and I felt a little vulnerable. I was sure that I would be completely inadequate for the task that was being assigned to me. Very weakly I protested my feelings of inadequacy and inexperience in coping with boys in a situation like that. The moment passed while it was being explained to me how urgently the boys in Hadden House dormitory were in need of a mother figure. For the next few days I was in a state of nervousness and dread. I remember lying awake in the middle of the night, praying for Bahá'u'lláh to 'take this cup from me'. But it was not to be answered in the way that I wanted and there was nothing else to do but to go forward into another of life's difficult experiences, *'clinging to the hem of His Robe'*.

Meeting My Boys

At last, the dreaded day came and, after our evening meal in the huge dining room, Dr Johnson and Linelma escorted me to my dormitory in Hadden House. They began to introduce me to the students. There were beds down both sides of the long room and very little space for anything else. Mrs Johnson began speaking about me in the most glowing terms, which was very embarrassing, especially since my own feelings were of the deepest inadequacy. Inwardly I groaned, as she told them how fortunate they were to have me in their dorm. "Mrs. Turner has come all the way from England to be in Panchgani, and aren't you the lucky ones to have her here, in Hadden House?"

I was imagining what their secret thoughts would be. I was convinced that they would react very differently after the principal and his wife had left. Oh, how I longed for a large hole in the floor to appear and swallow me up. Mrs Johnson was saying, "Tell Mrs Turner your name each in turn, so that she can get to know you." I struggled to take in the list of totally unfamiliar names as they called them out. Marshallah, Vafa, Bowman, Monojh, Payman and Kelly. This last name sounded so delightfully simple to my western ears, and the little Canadian boy gave me a wide, knowing grin. His was the only white face in the dormitory, apart from my own, but after that initial observation, any sense of differences completely vanished away. The boys were marvellous, and I quickly became very fond of them. Certainly, they never took advantage or tried to make things difficult for me, as I had expected they might. This was quite a surprise and such a relief. As for learning their names, it was much easier than I had imagined. The boys would test me to see how many I remembered. "What's my name, Miss?" Or, "The boy over there, Miss, what's his name?" They were always delighted when I got it right. One lively, happy-looking boy said to me, "Just think about Batman, Miss, because my name's Bahman." For this and many other reasons, I will never forget him.

One day as I was standing outside talking to one of the teachers, Bahman went by and, as he passed us, he said, "Remember, Miss, we love you." I was amazed and very moved by these few words, which are now engraved on my heart. It emphasised my surprise at these youngsters who came from other parts of the world. I wouldn't imagine a thirteen-year old schoolboy at home, making this comment in such a loving and unselfconscious way.

Later, I was given the privilege of having a much deeper insight into Bahman's life and feelings. It happened one Saturday morning, when the students were not having formal lessons, and two or three boys were in the dormitory, not doing anything in particular. As he half-reclined on his bed, Bahman suddenly started to tell me about his life at home in Iran. He was much quieter and more serious than usual, for he always gave the impression of being very cheerful and happy-go-lucky. He began by telling me that his mother had died of cancer a few years before. As I was trying to express my sorrow for this event in his life, he went on to say that only the previous year his father had been killed in a road accident. This young boy had lost both his parents, and his usually bright demeanour was subdued and full of inner pain. I was so saddened by this news, for it would never appear to anyone that this bright, impish boy could have experienced such a depth of bereavement at his tender age.

I have no idea what it was that prompted him to share these feelings with me, and I cannot even remember how the conversation began. I remember saying, "You <u>are</u> a Bahá'í aren't you, Bahman?" "Yes, Miss." We spoke of the comforting teachings of Bahá'u'lláh about life after death. I also shared with him my own, personal sorrow of when my husband and my mother died, and how, just two years later, my only son had passed away as the result of a car accident. To be able to feel with another soul, when they are passing through such heart-breaking experiences, and to help them to know that we also feel the same pain can bring a measure of comfort and release for both. Age did not seem to matter.

We talked about the spiritual worlds of God and how Bahá'u'lláh has told us that we will meet our loved ones in that world of Reality, when our life in this world has ended. Bahman listened quietly. Two other boys, who were also there, made comments from their own experiences of losing grandparents and other relatives. Then Bahman said, "Perhaps my mother and father are here now, Miss?" And I felt so happy to hear him say this. That Saturday morning brought us very close in a wonderful way, and I know that I will never forget him.

Many lovely friendships were made with the children, often from other dormitories. One little girl gave me a small bunch of cornflowers, when she met me in the school grounds. She was Indian, and had such large, dark eyes, gazing at me very shyly. This loving gesture affected me because my father's favourite flower was the cornflower. It had been very much a part of his lovely gentle nature to give flowers. I told this little girl about him, and after that she often stopped to say, "Hello, Miss. I remember that your father loved cornflowers." She would then hand me a lovely little posy. The boys in my dormitory invariably called me "Miss". I remember telling them that I had learned all twenty of their names and they had only to remember one. We would laugh about this, but it never changed, and perhaps I grew to be fond of being called "Miss".

My own little room, where I slept, and where I spent most of my time when the boys were in their classrooms, was at one end of the dormitory. It consisted of a high single bed, a metal wardrobe and a small wooden table and chair. I put out my few photographs and personal items to give a sense of home. The school bought a kettle and a small electric ring, so that I could make myself drinks. There was a small adjoining area for bathing, with a stone floor, a washbasin and a bucket. That single tap, with its cool water, was a heaven-sent luxury in the extreme humidity and heat. In the mornings, my first duty was to waken the boys and see that they dressed and washed in time for breakfast. It was my responsibility to gather them together for prayers, each morning and evening. I thought it would be nicer to go outside for morning prayers, surrounded by trees and flowering shrubs, in the early sunshine. It was a lovely start to the day and we would say individual prayers in turn. I tried to encourage them to learn new ones.

The children were taught through the English language, but Hindi, French and Persian were also spoken. From an early age they had the benefit of learning traditional Indian dancing. Their instructors were two very talented professional people, Mr and Mrs Gopolakrishna, who were very dedicated to their work. It was wonderful to see even the very small children dancing with such perfect ease and grace. The costumes were beautiful and always made in rich, vibrant colours. Sometimes the older girls were taken in the school jeep to remote villages, where they gave a thrilling performance for the local people's enchantment. For me, it was always moving to see the very poor women, who worked so hard, sitting on the ground with their babies and children, gazing in wonder at this magical scene. There, under the wide sky, as dusk was falling, small lamps had to be lit by the dancers. The show would then continue as the darkness quickly closed in. How different from our life at home, with its theatres and cinemas and their comfortable seats. There is no way we can measure the depths of pleasure and joy felt within the hearts of those people as they watched these beautiful dances.

Mr and Mrs Gopolakrishna and their daughter – teachers of Classical Indian Dancing

The climate was difficult for me to cope with. Adjusting to the spicy food and the water was also difficult. All water had to be boiled. It was not surprising that for several days I became quite ill. I lay on my little narrow bed, feverish and with stomach pains making me feel weak and faint. This made me more than a little homesick. There were moments when I wished with all my heart that I could wave a magic-wand and find myself at home, in my own little bed. I wrote in my diary.

'How deeply and sadly I miss my beloved husband and son. Many situations since I came to India have enhanced and increased my aloneness. Bahá'u'lláh is leading me through the fire of tests once more, and I cling to His mercy to bring me out of these shadows into the light. In the fevered heat of my tired body, my spirit feels imprisoned, and I feel a deep sense of loneliness, like "Ruth amid the alien corn", so poignantly expressed by the poet.'

Only now, on looking back, do I realise how short a time it was (a little more than a year) after the loss of my son, and just three-and-a-half years after the passing of my husband. And I see how brave it was to have ventured forth, on my own, to spend three months in India.

Eventually, one of the Bahá'í families on campus took pity on me, and invited me to stay in their home until I felt stronger and would be able to return to my dormitory. This was such a blessing and comfort for me, and in utter relief I lay down to sleep. During the night the mosquitoes began having a field day, and in my helpless state, I was their unconscious victim. Next morning, I was completely covered with large red bites, especially on my face and arms. Everyone was very kind and they assured me that I would soon be feeling well again, as tummy-trouble was quite common for people who had newly-arrived from overseas.

Vafa's Birthday

When I was feeling a little better I returned to Hadden House. The boys were delighted to see me. This was reassuring, and it did a lot towards raising my drooping spirits. It happened to be Vafa's fourteenth birthday when I returned, and they all gathered round me, full of smiles and warmth in their enthusiastic welcome. "Isn't it good that you came back on my birthday, Miss?" Vafa beamed his delight and proceeded to show me his birthday 'tuck'. This was his party-food, which included orange squash, and an assortment of buns and tasty morsels that the school provided for the students' birthdays. Most exciting of all was the birthday cake.

The boys spread everything out at the end of the dormitory and placed the large, iced cake in the middle. They all surged round him, eagerly thrusting their plates forward, as Vafa began to cut into it very carefully. It was rather a large piece he was slicing off, in fact it was a great wedge, and I was thinking that he could never give a piece to everyone if the portions were all going to be like that. Then, ignoring all the plates that surrounded him, Vafa thrust this wedge towards me saying, "This is for you

Miss." I gasped. My diet had been extremely simple for several days, and my stomach was still feeling a little uncertain. Vafa piled our plates with crisps, biscuits and nuts, and then filled our glasses with orange juice. Seeing the happy excited faces of the boys around me, I was glad to be back.

Sometimes a small convoy went to the villages to see the Bahá'ís, and to teach the Faith. That was exciting for me. The children in these villages were full of eagerness to learn as much as possible. Just as in Africa, people were very hospitable. It would have hurt their feelings, for example, to refuse to share a meal with them. One night I noticed that while we had been talking together, some of the women had been mixing rice in huge buckets, with their hands. Later, when we were invited to stay and eat with them, the rice was shared out, along with a small amount of meat and bones. It was served with a very hot sauce that really burned my lips. I was still recovering from my bout of stomach pain and dysentery, and one of the teachers, Vinney Raj, saw my predicament and surreptitiously took a large portion from my bowl and transferred it to her own dish. She was from Malaysia and she said that she was used to hot food. I can tell you I was mightily relieved.

Journey to Ooty

My three months in India were fast coming to an end, and I felt that I would like to see a little more of that great sub-continent before returning home. I spoke to Dr Johnson and asked if he could arrange some travel teaching for me. We had a lengthy consultation with one of the special Bahá'í Counsellors, Mr Afsheen. Eventually, it was decided I should travel to Bangalore and visit a place called Coimbator, before finally making my way to Ootacamund, known locally as Ooty. I was asked to visit an ancient tribe called the Toda people. It was explained that Ruhiyyih Khanum had spent some time with these lovely people, nearly twenty years before, and that their chief had become a Bahá'í. Dr Johnson gave me a letter of introduction for Mr and Mrs Akhdakavari, a Bahá'í couple who owned the Iranis Hotel in Ooty. I was taken by car to the bus station in Panchgani at six o'clock that evening and was fortunate to share a taxi with two of the teachers from the school, all the way to the National Hotel in Poona. We shared a room in one of the small, hut-like buildings, in the grounds of the hotel, for ten rupees each. These ladies, Mrs Copeley and Mrs Beale, had some business to attend to very early next morning, and they assured me that they would return before 7.30 am. In their kindness, as a safety precaution, they locked the door of the little building from outside, so I settled myself to a quiet time of prayer, and a leisurely preparation for the day. Having washed and dressed and meditated, they still hadn't returned. It was then almost ten minutes to nine and I was becoming very anxious. I was now getting stomach pains and the toilet was outside the locked room. You know what that means! I began to rattle the doors and bang as loudly as I could, as my panic level rose steeply. I felt so helpless. Thankfully someone heard me and, eventually, in what seemed an eternity, they brought a second key to let me out. My two companions had been unavoidably delayed and were most concerned about my plight once they got back and learned of my ordeal. Throughout the day they were extra kind and caring, and Mrs Copeley accompanied me everywhere. We travelled by three-wheeled cabs called auto-rickshaws, to and fro across the town. They were black and yellow and reminded me of buzzing wasps. We went to the State India Bank and the hairdressers, as I was badly in need of a perm.

The bank manager was courteous and helpful, allowing me the money I needed with my chequebook and Barclay card. It was the same in Trade Winds travel agents, where the young man I spoke to was extremely kind. He booked my train and air tickets, and I heard him speaking on the `phone, saying, "A foreign lady travelling alone". He was able to arrange everything perfectly for me. Mrs Copeley and I were, by that time, extremely hot and thirsty, and our helpful young assistant spontaneously and generously sent for two bottles of mango juice for us.

At the hairdressers we were told that we could both have our hair permed in the Chinese Salon. It turned out to be a hot and lengthy process, and when thirty lovely Indian ladies came surging in, wanting their hair dressed for a marriage party, it became even more wearisome and even hotter. In the end the result was quite pleasing and it turned out a real bargain, costing less than a third of what I would have paid at home.

After many little adventures and delays I boarded the train for Bombay. I had never seen so many people on a railway station before. It was bedlam. A berth had been reserved, but I discovered with a jolt that there were four bunks – two lower and two upper – and that the other three passengers were men. There were no blankets or pillows. I quickly clambered up to a top bunk, spread my cotton sheet-bag beneath me and rolled up a woolly shawl for my head. Miss Jagada, the Montessori teacher at Panchgani, had insisted that I should take her shawl, as the nights were very cold in Ooty. I hadn't thought it would end up being a pillow. It was incredibly noisy and unbearably hot, and though I tried to catch some sleep, it was virtually impossible. The train stopped noisily and with a great jolt, at every station. At five in the morning we reached Dadar station, Bombay, and it cost thirty rupees for a short run by taxi to the airport. On arrival I learned that the flight would be more than four hours late. During that time I went twice to the restaurant, first for tea and toast and then for cucumber and tomato sandwiches. As always, I really enjoyed the `plane journey and was seated beside a very nice Indian gentleman from Bangalore, which was where our journey ended. To my dismay, the flight to Coimbator had left at noon. It was a blessing indeed that some Bahá'ís were there to meet me on arrival at Bangalore. I was warmly invited to stay overnight with Neda Motlagh who made me very welcome in her home.

The following day I set off for the airport again and this time travelling by auto-rickshaw. My flight was at noon. It was a short journey of fifty-five minutes, and quite soon I made friends with the lady sitting beside me. She was travelling with her husband and two teenage daughters, and it was comforting to know that they also were taking the bus to Ooty. We shared a taxi in Coimbator, which helped a little with expenses for this costly trip. Crowds of people were waiting for buses to Ootacamund and we learned later that they were going to the annual Flower Show.

It called for great patience and endurance to stand in that intense heat, the air thick with flies, and for more than two hours. When at last I settled on the bus, the journey was most enjoyable. The scenery gradually became green and lush, with an abundance of trees and mountains that could be seen in the background. Higher and higher we climbed – the road twisting and turning continuously. It was quite magnificent. A young man turned round, from his seat in front of us, to point out the coffee plants and tea plantations. We chatted happily.

My Indian family alighted before I did, which made me feel alone again. It was growing dark, and several more people had boarded the bus. I felt rather uneasy. Two men beside me enquired where I was going. I felt a little nervous, so I asked my friend in front to let me know when we reached Ooty. After some time I realised that we were passing by the Iranis Hotel and Restaurant. The bus continued for some distance and I was greatly relieved when my young companion got out at the same stop, and kindly offered to carry my case. He walked beside me, and I felt even more thankful for his company when, just at that precise moment, the electricity failed. Suddenly we had been sunk into total darkness. This was quite a feature in India, believe you me! I wrote in my diary of that event: "How clearly I see that God takes care of us at every step of our journey through life."

It was wonderful to meet Mr Akhdakavari at the hotel, and his loving Bahá'í greeting, "Allah'u'Abhá", was like music to my soul. A Bahá'í named Vahid escorted me to the centre where ten Iranian children were staying. They had been sent to India because of the revolution in Iran the previous year. Sixteen other children were accommodated in a nearby school run by a British lady, Mrs. Momart, who had made her home in India. A lovely, young Persian girl looked after these children, and they called her "Miss Mary".

During my stay in Ooty I was showered with kindness by the two dear ladies who had taken on the task of mothering the children in the Bahá'í Hostel. Mrs Athari did all the cooking, while Mrs Laghari taught them prayers and gave classes in morality. She slept in the girls' dormitory and I shared a small bedroom with Mrs Athari. Accommodation was very limited with a tiny kitchen and one other room where we had our meals. In the two washrooms there were large containers of water and a few buckets for bathing. It was very basic. Those two ladies impressed me greatly, with their total selflessness in caring for the children, while being separated from their husbands who were still in Iran. Despite so many hardships, they were happy in their devotion to the young ones in their charge.

An Indian professor came every day to teach the children English. They also had maths lessons in a small room adjoining the two bedrooms. On two or three occasions, when the professor was not able to come, Mrs. Laghari begged me to give them an English lesson. Feeling more than a little inadequate I agreed, and was pleasantly surprised to find it a most enjoyable experience. Dear Iran Laghari came to me afterwards, and hugged me. "Very good English you teach them!" she said, and her eyes glowed with happiness.

Ooty was a lot cooler than Panchgani and at night it felt decidedly cold. They shared their food so generously with eggs, bananas and bread for breakfast. The great test for me was in coping with the flies, yet again. They literally covered the table like a blanket, and the food underneath could scarcely be seen. This had to be ignored. There was no alternative. After all, I had to eat! So many lessons to learn as my horizons continued to open. What a different world this was. The streets and markets were crowded with a multitude of beggars, which saddened me greatly. They were everywhere, and though I tried to give what small tokens I could, it was deeply painful to see their plight. Crippled, lame and blind, there were men, women and children, all in the most desperate state of poverty. One morning on my way into town, a man with leprosy was lying on the ground, ignored by the crowds. He just lay there in the scorching sun, moaning pitifully. We had to walk around him, almost stepping over him. It was totally devastating, and on account of these things, I knew in my heart that I would never be at peace in India as I had been in Africa.

Mrs. Momart, of Elkhurst School, became a firm friend and we shared some happy times together. She was very warm in her response to the Bahá'í teachings, and was eager to accept a book I offered her, which was about Bahá'í education for children. One day, when I was posting a letter, I met a beautiful Indian lady who invited me to her home for tea. She lived in a very attractive bungalow, quite near to the Bahá'í Hostel. She had been married to an Englishman but was now a widow. Her name was Mrs. Pearce. After showing me several photographs of her family, to my surprise and delight, she asked if I would like to sleep in her lovely bungalow at night. She was very concerned for my comfort, as I was so far from home and family. She gave me a front-door key so that I was able to come and go as I pleased. There was warm water for washing, and the privacy of a small bathroom all to myself. It was like a five-star hotel compared to the somewhat rigorous life I had been living. We sat together each morning, enjoying our eggs and buttered toast and marmalade. I felt a surge of happiness when my kind hostess poured our tea into delicate china cups, while we added our own milk and sugar. My bed was soft and welcoming each night when I returned. It was a quiet, restful haven for body and soul. A gift sent by God.

One day, a Bahá'í called Ahmad arrived from Madras, (Chennai), to help me in the travel teaching I was so eager to do. It was the busiest time of the year and everyone seemed to be fully occupied with the Flower Show and horseracing events that were taking place. Crowds of tourists were flocking into the area, all with the intention of enjoying these events. But opportunities to speak about the Faith opened up in unexpected ways. Mrs. Pearce invited me to visit her school, Blue Mountain, and we spent a very happy morning there. Mr Dave, the School Principal, was very keen to learn more about the Faith, and he asked me how we approached the subject of training the children spiritually. We talked of many things that Bahá'u'lláh and 'Abdu'l-Bahá taught us about the education of children. He seemed very pleased and excited by these teachings. When we finally said goodbye, he took my hand saying, "Mrs. Turner, we are kindred spirits!" I left a book with his wife, called *The New Garden*, while we were enjoying a cup of tea together.

When I was travelling by coach one day, a young Catholic priest started talking about religion. He seemed very open-minded, and scribbled his address on a scrap of paper. He asked me to send him some literature to his home in Goa. As my circle of friends widened, the Bahá'ís begged me to stay in Ooty, to continue teaching. It would have been lovely to stay longer, but my time was limited.

An Ancient Tribe

One of the highlights of my visit to Ooty was the day I spent with the Toda people. Five of us went together on this most unusual trip. The first thing we did was to seek out the Chief whom Dr Johnson had suggested I visit. He had met Ruhiyyih Khanum, the widow of the Guardian of the Faith, many years before.

We meet the Chief of the Toda people

Their traditions and dress, and their whole way of life have remained unchanged through long periods of time. The women wore their long hair in ringlets and both men and women appeared very colourful in their loose, flowing robes. The little houses of the Toda were unique and looked very picturesque, set in the midst of rolling green plains, with a backdrop of beautiful mountains. We were invited to go inside one of their homes. To get through the doorway we had to bend down, almost onto our hands and knees and scramble our way in. I was thankful for a supple back.

Once inside, there was a lovely sense of calm and peace. We found it strangely humbling to be welcomed with a graciousness and warmth that is rarely seen in our western way of life. As an expression of their hospitality, they handed us a container of delicious golden honey, with a spoon, which was passed to each of us in turn, starting with me. I felt that I was receiving the most wonderful, precious gift in the world from our lovely hostess.

So many times in Africa I experienced this same indescribable quality of deep sincerity, and a generosity of spirit that bears no relation to the material value of the gift that is being offered. We ate our honey in an atmosphere of gentle quietness before we came outside again.

Outside one of the Toda houses

A Difficult Journey

It was soon time for me to return to Panchgani. Trying to make arrangements for this was fraught with difficulties. The thought of making that journey alone gave rise to further feelings of anxiety. There was the long bus ride to Bangalore and the uncertainty about whether I would be met on arrival. It was a further cause of distress to learn that the bus would reach Bangalore very late at night. The whole prospect was quite daunting. Communication by letter or telephone was very slow and unreliable. How wonderful it would have been to travel with a companion. Being on my own was still a new and strange experience for me, and it was in situations like this that it became acutely painful. It would take too long to describe the many events and challenges that I encountered on my journey back to Bangalore, and the enormous feat it was to make a reservation on the train to Poona. Here are some glimpses of my adventure.

It cost 160 rupees for a first class compartment (that I managed to book, after a long, difficult struggle.) At about five o'clock next morning I arrived at the station with my kind hostess, who guided me to the correct compartment. Imagine my shocked surprise as I entered the carriage, to find it already occupied by an Indian couple with their five children and an enormous amount of baggage. The ages of the children ranged from five to fifteen. Somehow, all eight of us were to share the compartment's four berths. The long, hard journey lasted more than twenty hours. Hot, dusty air blew through the windows of the train, turning my hair into a bush, while my dress gradually became more and more crumpled and soiled. I was hot and dishevelled and felt so limp. My travelling companions chatted loudly and happily to one another, in Hindi. Sadly we were unable to communicate throughout those long hours.

As we stopped at the various stations along the way, young boys and men would run to the windows, eagerly calling, "Chai, Chai!" as they offered cartons of tea, spread out on the trays hanging from around their necks. In the middle of the day a porter brought us some food, described as mild curry. To my dismay it nearly stripped the skin off my lips! What on earth the hot variety would be like I just couldn't imagine. In the immediate situation it seemed a very minor thing to trouble about. I had been informed that we would arrive in Poona at three o'clock in the morning. I felt more than a little alarmed at this news, although I was able to manage my panic. The long hot hours of that journey passed very slowly, and all the while I was trying to imagine how I would cope when we finally reached Poona. Within myself, I prayed continuously for help.

I clung with all my faith to that invisible assistance which, alone, enables us to bear these difficult things. My mouth was dry with apprehension when I found myself totally alone on the station platform. It was dark, and I was a stranger. I felt utterly defenceless. Picking up my bag, I found my way to a small office where three or four railway officials were sitting together talking. In a voice as calm as possible, I asked them if they would telephone the hotel for me. It was a shock when they totally ignored my appeal for help. I began to feel desperate. They refused blankly, although I begged them to contact the National Hotel and let someone know that I would be arriving shortly. They still refused with cold indifference. So I turned away, wondering what on earth I could do. A few minutes later, I realised that the hotel was very close to the station, as it could be seen from an upstairs balcony, where I had hoped to find a waiting room as a safe place until daylight. I gazed longingly at the Hotel - my refuge. Then, as I glanced down, I saw several rows of bodies lying on the ground all wrapped up like mummies. It was one of the most distressing aspects of India to see the homeless and the hungry lying in the streets, or just sitting begging for food. Now, in the middle of the night, it was eerie and frightening. To walk out of the station I would have to step over those prostrate forms. I couldn't stay where I was because the waiting room was locked, and my only alternative was to get an auto-rickshaw and trust that I would reach the hotel in safety. No sooner had I decided on my course of action, than a man approached me, and I took him to be a railway porter. He was, in fact, the driver of a little three-wheeled cab that I wanted. It was the most wonderful relief, just a few moments later, to be standing there, in front of the National Hotel. However my relief was short-lived. The front door of the hotel was closed and locked and, to my shock a man was seated in the entrance porch, wrapped up like a beggar. He sat cross-legged on the ground, with his long robe wrapped around his head, half covering his face. There was nobody about in that silent and lonely darkness. The little auto-cab had buzzed off and disappeared into the distance. I felt trapped. Having left the station, I felt that I had leapt from the frying pan into the fire. It was an awful feeling, until I realised that he was only a watchman guarding the hotel! He intimated that the door was locked and that I would have to wait until it opened in the morning. I pleaded to be allowed inside, explaining that I was a Bahá'í from the school in Panchgani and that I knew the owner of the hotel. Finally, I realised that he could do nothing about it because he didn't have a key. The only thing I could do was to find somewhere to sit for the next few hours until morning.

There was a bench just a little distance from the entrance to the hotel, and very gratefully I sat down. I was extremely tired and weary, having travelled for nearly twenty-four hours and I had never felt so dishevelled and dirty before. I longed so much for a glorious bath or shower, and just to quench my thirst and go to sleep. I sat there in the dark, gazing into the black sky, dotted with beautiful silver stars. God was certainly teaching me patience as well as an ever-greater dependence on His help. At about six o'clock in the morning I was surprised, and oh, so happy to see Vinney Rahj, one of the teachers from the school, walking towards me. She had been staying overnight at the hotel, not in the main building, but in one of the little outhouses which I had shared with Mrs Beale and Mrs Copeley on my previous stay in Poona. Apparently, there were many members of the school staff staying there, following a wedding reception the day before. When I explained what had happened to me on my return from Ootacamund and Bangalore, she eagerly suggested that I should go to the room that she was vacating, so that I could wash and rest for a little while. Oh joy!

Vinney was leaving very early so she handed me the key to her room. Just one room but to me it was heaven. Oh, the luxury of privacy and a hard little bed to lie on. The cold water tap and bucket appeared more wonderful than the most beautifully fitted bathroom in the world.

After a wash and a short rest, and the wonderful opportunity to change my clothes, it was time to have breakfast in the hotel. They served boiled eggs and toast, and it was one of the few places where tea was made in the way we are used to at home in England. It was delicious and so refreshing although I still had a deep feeling of exhaustion and weakness. A Bahá'í from a small restaurant in Panchgani kindly offered to escort me to the bus depot. I was so thankful to him. He helped me to get my ticket (a rather difficult feat without knowledge of Hindi) and at last I was on my way back to the school and the dormitory. I was so eager to see my boys again.

When I arrived they were immensely happy to see me. This uplifted my spirits and cheered my heart. Several young, smiling faces met me, and with a joyful greeting, "You came back to us, Miss!" I felt I had come home. As I was sitting in the dining room, Bahman came in, and when he saw me his eyes lit up in glad surprise, "Oh, I missed you, Miss." And he walked across the room and clasped my hand. Tears welled in my eyes. I had so much love for that child. Now, so many years later, I often think of him and wonder where he is now. Some years ago I did write to him, just before he left school, and his moving and beautiful reply I will keep always. In it he called me his mother.

In July, the students and staff were taking their summer vacation, and the monsoon was expected shortly. My flight to India had been booked for a three-month period, but I had left the actual date of return open. Before making my trip down south I had asked the office staff at New Era, if they would contact the travel agents in Bombay, and book me a flight home shortly after the school term ended. It was disconcerting to learn that this had not been possible, and that there were no flights available now until September. This was a great shock to me, as almost everyone would be leaving, and my money had almost run out. Worst of all, my loved ones at home would be expecting me.

Eventually, I travelled to Bombay on a coach with the children who were flying home for their vacation. It was with the loving help of Ridván Khanum, who had founded the School in the 1940s, that I found somewhere to stay. The rains had come in great torrents and we were all wading ankle-deep in the streets. I was given shelter and hospitality from the Persian lady who met me on my arrival in India. She lived very simply, on the fourth floor of a large block of apartments. There was a tiny corner in her one room, which had a plastic curtain across it and this was used for bathing. There was no shower of course, but we managed with buckets of water for which I was very grateful. She cooked on a two-ringed oven that was near her small sink. We shared her double bed and ate at a very small table close by. The toilet was outside her room along the passage, and she shared this with several other families. Her home was a refuge for me, while I waited and tried every day, to get a flight to England that I could afford. Ridvan Khanum offered to lend me the extra money for my fare, otherwise I would have been stranded there. After almost a week, we managed to book a seat on the Polish Airline, Lot Airways. Homeward bound at last! India was great, but home was even better!

I remember the uplifting feeling of love and joy on seeing my family again. The great leaping of my heart at the sight of Anisa, then two and a half years old, was overwhelming. Engulfing waves of tiredness overcame me. At last I had the sweet relief of sleep, safe and sound in my own little bed. I was now very much thinner than when I had left the UK. During the first night back, I woke with intense stomach pains and a good deal of nausea. In the morning Zoë called the doctor. When she arrived she walked straight across the room and stood by the window. She then wrote a prescription and left me in no doubt that she suspected I had contracted a serious illness in India. No physical examination was forthcoming, but, thankfully this was not the case. I quickly recovered, and soon regained full health and vitality, ready for my next adventure – well not just yet!

10

AN INVITATION FROM CANADA

Before leaving New Era School in India, Irene Taffaki had expressed her desire that I should return in the autumn to teach the Knowledge and the Love of God to the primary school children. My heart's desire! How dearly I longed to do this, but I couldn't be parted from Zoë and Anisa on a full-time basis. When I told Irene that Zoë was a trained primary school teacher, she suggested that all three of us should go to India and work at the school together. Zoë and I talked at length about this, and finally we agreed that it might be a good idea to go when Anisa was a year or two older.

A few months after my return from India, I received an invitation from Jessie and Nick Echevarria who were living in Ajax, near Toronto. They suggested I spend several weeks with them during October, a beautiful time of year in Canada. Our friendship had spanned the years since their emigration during the 1950s. We had shared those unforgettable days in 1963 at the World Congress in London, when we all stayed in the same hotel and shared the amazing joy of that historical occasion.

What a contrast, after three months in India, to be visiting a country of great material plenty, where every kind of food is available in overflowing abundance. I was very much aware that the exciting trip ahead would be different in every way from my Indian and African adventures. I smiled as I started my packing. No need for insect-repellent or anti-malarial tablets, and no call for Flip-Flop sandals or thin cotton dresses for this trip. I set off to Manchester Airport feeling very excited, even though my expectations were completely different. I had a very comfortable flight, travelling by Wardair Airline, and was pleasantly surprised to find, in addition to the excellent food being served, that we had china plates and cups and very fine cutlery as well. At the end of a long flight it was a most wonderful feeling to be greeted by my two old friends, and to know instantly that the closeness we had shared for 30 years was as warm and affectionate as ever. After I arrived and settled in, Jessie and Nick took me to meet many of their friends and to speak at some of the fireside meetings in their home. Wherever we went, we were greeted with generosity and loving hospitality. Jessie delighted in seeing the look of amazement on my face, at the outsize portions of gorgeous food that were served to us when eating out. I never ceased to be astonished at this, although it evoked such sadness, having seen the hunger of so many in India.

The two great highlights of my trip took place in early October. The first was a farewell party in Hope Township for Mr William Sears, Hand of the Cause of God, and his lovely wife Marguerite. ("Hand of the Cause" is a title given only to 50 people throughout the history of the Faith. They were very special people and played a very vital role in spreading and protecting the Faith). Many eager friends attended that gathering, held in the home of a wonderful Bahá'í family known affectionately as "The Haddons". The afternoon's activity started with a barbecue of beef, with beans and salads of every description. There were sweets, cakes and crusty rolls in abundance. Then Mr Sears spoke to us. As always, he evoked a burning love for Bahá'u'lláh in all those who heard him. Competitions, games and workshops, carried us along on wings of joy to the end of that memorable day.

The second wonderful event was a beautiful trip across the border to the United States. We travelled with a close friend, Ernie Ruche, who very kindly drove us in his luxurious car. The colours of the autumn leaves were just breathtaking. Trees of lemon, copper and gold, with orange, lime and flame, stretched for miles and miles along the highway. What a glorious sight! We had made an early start at six in the morning on 12 October, 1980 and then had breakfast in London, Ontario around half past nine. We crossed the border and drove through Detroit. It was very exciting to be in the United States for the very first time. After a long drive it was good to get

William Sears and Marguerite at a farewell gathering in Ontario

out of the car and do a little walking. Ernie took us to a lovely spacious restaurant for lunch where I had a New York steak, French-fries, salad, coffee and a sweet. It was a huge meal! The waitress was intrigued by my English accent. We were treated with kindness and warmth wherever we went.

We arrived in Niles and found a nice motel where we washed and changed, ready to be off again. After walking a short distance, I saw to my utter joy and amazement, we were standing in front of the Bahá'í House of Worship in Wilmette. It was unbelievable to be looking at that wonderful temple. It is open to all the peoples of the world from whatever race or religion. It simply took my breath away. A great spiritual power surrounds it and I felt very much as I did when entering the Shrine of the Báb in Haifa. It is totally beyond expression in words.

Tears blurred my eyes with a deep thankfulness to God, and for the kindness of Jess and Nick who had brought me to that very special place. There were fragrant roses in the gardens surrounding the temple, and the whole atmosphere just radiated peace and tranquillity. We entered the glorious Mashriqu'l-Adhkár (The Dawning Place of the Mention of God) the Mother Temple of the West, with the utmost devotion. My soul was bathed in love and absolute wonder. Sacred verses from the Pen of Bahá'u'lláh adorned the walls, high up beneath the majestic dome. We stood, entranced. It was as if the essence of a spiritual reality had been crystallised into visible form on earth. I gazed upwards, reading those sacred Words:

"By My life! The light of a good character surpasseth the light of the sun and the radiance thereof."

Those words were so powerful and it seemed as though they were filled with life. In my heart I was saying, "This is the Tabernacle of God." It was an unforgettable experience. We prayed silently, and then sat for a while in the room where 'Abdu'l-Bahá had laid the foundation stone for this House of Worship in 1912. Later we visited the Bahá'í Home for the Elderly, which was near the Temple itself, and talked with Ruth Walker, the lady who ran it.

We lingered in the tranquillity of the gardens, admiring the beautiful design of trees and flowers, before taking a walk to the edge of Lake Michigan. Impish little squirrels crossed our path, and we took a few snapshots as tokens of an inspiring and unforgettable day.

Next morning, we learned that it was Columbus Day in America, and we stayed for a few extra hours, enjoying the glorious sunshine. After a little sightseeing, we enjoyed a late lunch in a restaurant known as 'Pancake House', before starting our long journey home. What a sleepy little foursome we were, when finally we arrived back in Ajax at half past four next morning. We had driven over 600 miles. But what a memorable journey it had been.

Jessie and Nick took me to so many places of interest and enjoyment during the weeks that followed. We visited an exhibition in Ottawa called "Science of Man". We

Outside the Bahá'í Residential Home at the Temple

then went to the Art Centre and Parliament Buildings, staying overnight in Kalada. Next morning we drove through lovely countryside to Haliburton, where we visited several Bahá'í friends and the following day we experienced the world-famous Niagara and Horseshoe Falls. On Sunday 20 October it was a Holy Day – commemorating the Birth of the Báb in Shiraz 1819 in Persia. We visited Jess and Nick's daughter, Lynn, and had a delightful time with her and their young family.

Another memorable occasion was being taken to downtown Toronto, when we travelled again in Ernie Ruche's luxurious car, gliding smoothly along the highway. He took us for a meal in the Organ Grinder restaurant, after which we set out for the Planetarium, striding along in strong wind and sunshine. For the next hour we felt that we had been transported far above the world, and lifted into another dimension. Gazing upward into that vast dome of the night sky, I was filled with awe at the greatness and grandeur of God's creation. It was breathtaking, and it made me feel like a tiny ant, so puny and insignificant. But then I remembered one of the verses of Bahá'u'lláh that gives us a glimpse of our station in the sight of God.

"Out of the wastes of nothingness, with the clay of My command I made thee to appear, and have ordained for thy training every atom in existence and the essence of all created things."

The Bahá'í Temple at Wilmette

Such an amazing thought, it made me feel even more humble. After that thrilling experience in the Planetarium, we drove to the Town and Country restaurant where we had arranged to meet two more friends, Pat and Bob Smith. For ten dollars each, we could select whatever we wanted, from a bewildering array of dishes. We talked and laughed and enjoyed each other's company. But, in my heart, sadly I thought of India. Bahá'u'lláh came to change the imbalance and injustice in the world. He told mankind that we should, *"...eat with the same mouth and drink from the same fountain."* It was a sobering thought in the midst of all that plenty. I wrote in my diary: "We must not wait passively for that day, but try, with all our might, to work for its speedy fulfilment. It cannot come too soon".

At one of the meetings, where I was asked to speak, I met a lady and gentleman from India, who were visiting their relatives in Ontario. During our conversation we discovered, to our amazement, that they lived in Bombay in the actual district where I had so recently stayed. But, as we continued to talk, we realised, to our utter astonishment that they actually lived in the same street and in the very same building. It was too incredible for words. The size of India, and the size of Canada, yet we had been brought together on both those great continents. It is difficult to imagine a greater coincidence. Each day with Jessie and Nick abounded in warmth and humour, and I was filled with thankfulness for their gift of friendship. The days sped by, and my lovely time in Canada came to an end. I felt refreshed and renewed by all the loving care that had been showered on me. Returning home to my small granddaughter and Zoë was, as always, so delightful and a tonic to my heart. Their loving and wonderful welcome always brings me a deep sense of inner joy and thankfulness.

Nineteen-eighty had been a wonderfully challenging and eventful year, when I had tasted both pain and joy on my travels to those diverse continents. Early the following year I felt that my heart was being drawn irresistibly back to Africa, and when I consulted with the International Goals Committee, they suggested my going to Ghana.

I was overwhelmed with happiness.

11

RETURN TO AFRICA

My excitement was great indeed, as I prepared for a two-month trip to the land of my heart's desire. To be going back to Africa was a source of immense joy. Just before I was due to leave home, the National Spiritual Assembly of the Bahá'ís of Ghana asked if I would prepare a series of lesson-plans for the children during my visit there. My heart was rejoicing at this wonderful opportunity. For many years, long before I ever became a Bahá'í, I had wanted to write stories for children, something that would help them to understand the world and give them a spiritual perspective on life. Although I had been blessed with a good home and loving parents, it had not been easy to adapt to life at school and the large crowded playground. Children can be so unkind to one another, sometimes making them feel vulnerable and alone, and I was a rather sensitive child. When our childhood is over, we are able to understand much more about human nature, and generally see things from a different perspective. When John was a little boy my desire to write stories for children increased greatly. I wanted to tell them that we are guided and cared for by a loving Creator and that our prayers are heard and understood. In fact I wished to impress upon them that we are never alone. When we were living in Cork, I was asked to serve on the Committee for the Bahá'í Education of Children. At one of our meetings, we decided to send the Spiritual Assemblies a Nineteen Day-Feast Newsletter especially for children. We called it *The Little Circular*. The adults in the community were already receiving their own Newsletter on a regular basis. My joy was complete when the privilege of writing the articles and stories was given to me. It was exciting to do this work, and even more rewarding to find that the grown-ups were enjoying them as well. During those years in Ireland, I decided to take a correspondence course in the Montessori training of children. This had fulfilled, to some extent, my dream of earlier years.

My lovely friend Eleanor O'Callaghan was pioneering in Ghana and was also serving as a member of their National Spiritual Assembly. Knowing that I would see Eleanor again added an extra measure of excitement to what promised to be a most memorable teaching-trip. To be once again on African soil and to be able to contribute something towards the spiritual training of children was a beautiful gift from God. My travel arrangements were made on wings of joy. I decided to travel by Aeroflot, the Russian State Airline, because of the low cost at the time. I realised that it meant flying to Moscow where I would have to stay for at least one night, before resuming my journey to Ghana. When we arrived in Moscow, our passports were taken from us and we were escorted by bus to a large hotel close by. After queuing at the desk, sleeping accommodation was allocated, and I found myself sharing a two-bedded room with a Ghanian girl in her early twenties.

It was exciting. There were people from many parts of the world, quite an international gathering in fact. Meals were served in a large dining room with tables that seated six to eight people. The food was plain and quite unusual, and many of my fellow-passengers complained about it. As everything was included in the price of the air ticket, I felt it was expecting too much to want better food. Those of us, who wished, were allowed to go on a bus trip during the afternoon. Apart from this guided tour we were strictly kept indoors. Inside the hotel there was nothing to do. Everything was bare with no amenities. Our guide was a lady with an extremely stern manner, in fact almost a military bearing. The little single-decker bus was in no way luxurious, not even comfortable, but it helped to give us a small glimpse of life in Russia. I gazed out of the window, wishing I could go inside the shops and mingle with the people. On that occasion we had to remain on the bus but on my return journey, two months later, we were allowed to get out for a few moments in Red Square. I didn't know then, that one day I would go to Poland and stay with a Polish family, who would take me shopping with them, enabling me to move about quite freely in their country. The shops in Moscow looked very drab from the outside, and in the small windows there was scarcely anything on display. It was a sobering thought to reflect on life at home where we all have so much.

My journey continued next day, and I felt the tremendous exhilaration of boarding the aircraft, of rising high into the air and leaving the world far below. It seemed to me like the flight of the spirit when freed from the body, leaving all our earthly cares behind and soaring into the realm of the spiritual worlds. It was lovely to be on my way to Africa again. My heart was light. After a very long flight with numerous stops, which included Budapest, Tripoli and Mali, we touched down in Accra. The heat and the many distinctive scents of Africa enfolded me, and I revelled at being back on that great continent once more. After passing through official channels, often difficult and harrowing in a developing country, my lovely Eleanor appeared as if by magic. Standing in the hot sunshine, she welcomed me in her gentle way. It was like coming home. I so much admired her ability to handle the situations that confronted us. Taxi drivers appeared like raindrops from the sky, and clamoured around us, talking and shouting, trying to pick up my luggage in their eagerness for custom.

The economy in Ghana was so dreadful and the people were suffering greatly. Yet they laughed and smiled with good humour. Eleanor spoke firmly to the throng of drivers who were crowding about us. At last, we scrambled into a taxi that took us to the Bahá'í Centre. There, she made tea, which I relished. I had a refreshing wash and was thankfully able to rest on a comfortable bed. Blanche Musa came to see us. I remembered meeting her four years previously, on my way home from Nigeria. Blanche drove us to her own home and cooked a delicious meal of chicken and rice with vegetables. Eleanor and I shared a bedroom, and it was a wonderful feeling to stretch out and finally get a deep sleep. As the final part of my journey had taken seventeen hours, I really needed it. Blanche's little boy Baba was very cute and he loved to sit on my knee while I showed him pictures of Anisa, who was then almost three-and-a-half. Next morning we had our breakfast in the garden. It was a restful feeling, to sit beside a beautiful flowering tree with large red blossoms, under the wide blue African sky. I felt wondrously contented. Later, Eleanor and I took a taxi back to the Bahá'í Centre, where we packed a few necessities to take with us to Aplaku, a village about ten miles from Accra.

Just as we were leaving, another of the local Bahá'ís, Ben Norty, called at the centre and asked if he could go with us. We were delighted and the three of us went outside to try and get a lift. Transport was always a great problem in West Africa, and getting from place to place difficult and hazardous without a car. After some time, a passing driver stopped to help us, and went out of his way to take us to our destination. When he let us out of the car he refused to accept any payment. Eleanor said that he did it for me, because of their respect for someone a little older. During the journey we enjoyed a very interesting conversation with him. When he spoke about his family and children, we gave him a leaflet entitled, *Love that Child*, as well as the address of the Bahá'í Centre in Accra.

Outside the Bahá'í Centre in Accra

We arrived at the lorry park just in time to get a ride on what is known as a Mammy-Wagon, or Tro Tro. The only way to get in is by clambering over the side of the wagon, which is quite high. There are no steps or doorways except for the driver's cab. How I managed to climb up I do not know, as I was wearing a long green dress that was not very full-skirted, and this made it especially difficult to stretch my legs. I almost threw myself in, much to the amazement of my fellow passengers. All I really noticed were the rows of startled brown eyes, on seeing my pale-skinned face suddenly heaving into sight over the side of the lorry. I giggled to myself and smiled broadly to all the astonished spectators who were always ready to laugh. We rumbled along the bumpy roads full of dust and potholes, all the way to Aplaku. We then began our walk towards the village. For protocol, it was important that we should meet the chief first. He greeted us very cordially and introduced us to his interpreter, and to several other people. They appeared happy about my being there, especially when I told them how thrilled I was to be in Africa. Eleanor spoke and Ben interpreted, trying to encourage the Bahá'ís there to elect their Spiritual Assembly. It was the Riḍván period when Bahá'ís all over the world would be forming their local Spiritual Assemblies. The Riḍván Festival commemorates the twelve days when, in 1863, Bahá'u'lláh announced to His followers His station as a Manifestation of God. It was exciting for me to be playing even a small part in this great event. We sat talking in the fading light until quite late, and they took us with such kindness to the little house where we would be staying. There is very often a natural, quiet dignity about the African in his village, and I love and admire them so much. I wanted to go to the toilet, and one of the ladies led me by lamplight for quite a distance across the fields. This was not to a hut of any kind, but to a trench with planks of wood across it! Later we were greatly surprised to find that Eleanor and I had the luxury of a bed each. I had fully expected to be lying on the floor. Everything was spotlessly clean, and we were very touched by their kindness and hospitality.

Early next morning we were able to wash at an outside tap in the lovely morning half-light. It was five o'clock and the cocks were crowing loudly and earnestly. I felt so happy and free. A few of the Bahá'ís, including the chief, began to gather under a huge tree. When they saw us coming they brought seats for us with eager anticipation. A group of children sat listening, and they watched us so intently, with big round eyes and shining faces. I cannot imagine anything more wonderful or more rewarding than to speak about the coming of Bahá'u'lláh, especially with people who are open and eager to discover new spiritual truths. There is deep contentment and quiet joy about such an experience. Afterwards, we sang songs and Eleanor encouraged them to hold the election of their Spiritual Assembly on the following day. Fortunately it was Friday, when they would not be going to the fields to work. We shook hands with the chief and said goodbye to them all with warm and loving farewells.

A lorry came rumbling by jammed full of people. They offered us a lift and once again, I didn't know how to get in – but I did! What a journey it was, with almost nothing underneath me, as the strip of wood that was supposed to be my seat was very, very narrow. In order to support myself, I clung to a post in front of me, mile after mile, smiling at the ludicrous situation and wondering how we all endured it. That hazardous journey was followed by a much easier one, this time in a crowded taxi. When we arrived back to the Bahá'í Centre we ate a bean and rice mixture that we bought at the roadside, with lots of delicious tea. It was particularly wonderful, as we hadn't had anything to drink since the previous day. There were many times in Africa when we went without water or food during our visits to the villages. The water looked totally unfit to drink on those occasions when it was offered to us. On looking back it seems a miracle that we survived at all! We packed the few things that we would need in Kumasi, where the National Bahá'í Convention was being held that weekend. Travelling by mini-bus, we experienced a lot of shouting and haggling from the crowds of people at the public transport depot. The driver insisted on my sitting in the front next to the driver's seat, with a passenger on my other side. It was three o'clock in the afternoon when we headed off. We travelled continuously until eight o'clock that evening, except for a ten-minute stop for a drink. It was so good to get out and move our legs again. We walked in the dark, weaving among the little stalls on the sidewalk with their tiny oil lamps glowing like fireflies in the night. When we finally reached the university campus, where the Convention was taking place, Eleanor asked for a lift from two professors who were travelling by car. Under Eleanor's directions, they took us to the home of a lovely Iranian family who were pioneering in Ghana. Mrs Najaf-Toumrai and her two teenage daughters and son, Mitra, Maryam and Mehran, were doing wonderful work for the Faith in Kumasi. They were studying at the university, along with their cousin, Flora. Maryam who was fifteen, gave up her bedroom for me during the whole of my stay with them.

When we arrived, they served eggs, bread and tea, followed by bananas and oranges sliced into large pieces. My feet were very swollen from the intense heat and all the travelling. Mosquitos had bitten me on my legs, arms and back, causing huge, red blotches that itched continuously. Inwardly, I felt radiantly happy to be in Ghana and to have met such lovely people but how I hated mosquitos! Many of the Bahá'ís, who were attending the Convention, had travelled to the Northern Regions, helping the believers to elect their assemblies and to understand the teachings more deeply. The faces of those pioneers were alight with happiness and it was wonderful to be with them. I felt a special blessing to be in Ghana for their National Convention. Dear Eleanor was elected once again as one of the nine members of the National Spiritual Assembly.

During the weekend, I was invited to consult with the National Assembly, when they expressed their pleasure at my being there as a travel-teacher. It was explained to me that one of the goals for that country was the spiritual education of children. I was asked if I would prepare a series of lesson-plans for children's classes and then travel to the village areas to find people who were interested in teaching them. They also requested that, at the end of my time in Ghana, I should arrange an Institute for the guidance of those who were going to teach. This was a responsible undertaking as well as a great privilege. My heart was rejoicing.

Happy days teaching the children

With the Najaf-Toumrai family outside their home in Kumasi

Also, during the weekend, an "American Auction" was held, and a beautiful picture of the Shrine of the Báb was the most cherished prize. One young man, a Bahá'í of only a month, did most of the bidding and put quite a lot of money into it. I was hoping he would get it and, after three 300 Cedi had been given for the Bahá'í fund, he won it! Then, to my complete astonishment, he came and placed his lovely gift on my lap. I was really overwhelmed, and while thanking him for his loving gesture, I begged him to keep it. He spoke to me with such kindness and gentle love that it brought tears to my eyes. I was reminded of my own son.

Bahá'í Convention – May 3, 1981 with National Assembly
members including Eleanor O'Callaghan

There was a wonderful spirit and everyone was happy and aglow with excitement. Such a strong sense of fellowship and unity was felt by all. We had our meals in the dining room on the university campus at Republic Hall. For breakfast we had a very thin mixture, rather like porridge, and thick slices of unbuttered bread with a teaspoon of jelly marmalade. Lunch and evening meals were identical, consisting of large pieces of yam and a small amount of black-eye beans with sauce. Meals in Ghana were much simpler and with far less variety than at home. Food was really hard to obtain and terribly expensive.

A few days after Convention, I had a thrilling experience. Fred Darko, a Kumasi Bahá'í, offered to take me to one of the village schools, where the headmaster was also a member of the Faith. Apparently, he was teaching the children some prayers of Bahá'u'lláh, and Fred thought that he would welcome an overseas visitor. At first we had great difficulty in getting any form of transport, after which we had a very long walk in really intense heat, along dusty, winding roads. On reaching the school we learned that our headmaster friend was absent, so we went straight to the primary class. We received a very eager response from the male teacher who was in charge, and I was invited to speak to his pupils. There were more than forty children between the ages of four and seven years. They sat so attentively, watching me with their large, dark eyes as I spoke to them. Fred translated for me and it was a most wonderful experience. Previously, I had always found it difficult to speak when translation was necessary, but talking to those little African children I felt we were communicating directly. There seemed no barrier of language, as I spoke about the special time in which we are living. I gave the illustration of God's Messengers being like lamps, each One bringing the same beautiful light from God, and now God has given us Bahá'u'lláh.

We talked about knowing God and loving Him, and how all people have the same sort of feelings. We cry when we are hurt or sad, no matter what colour our skin might be. I touched my arms and my hair, and spoke about our physical differences, and then explained that within us we all have the same spirit from God, which is the most important thing of all. It was wonderful to be sharing the teachings of Bahá'u'lláh with those eager, smiling children. We talked about trying to make this inner part of us as beautiful and bright as we can. We start as little children and gradually grow up until we reach old age. We don't stay in this world forever, but God has created lovely spiritual worlds for when we leave here. We can't see them with our physical eyes, but they are very real. We talked about 'Abdu'l-Bahá's description of the soul being like a bird in a cage, and its joyous freedom when once it has been released.

How wide-eyed they looked when I told them that God has brought a great plan for the world and could they guess what it might be. As Fred interpreted for me they gazed with such intensity, it was marvellous to see their eager anticipation. They really listened and seemed to understand. I told them that God has a plan for everyone in the world to live in unity and peace, and to love one another. It was a scorching hot day, and perspiration trickled in rivulets down my face as I sat there, but how light I felt in my heart. There was so much to share, and their teacher was really delighted.

He thanked us for visiting the school and said that it had been wonderful to hear about the spiritual worlds of God. As we said goodbye to the children, they waved and smiled so lovingly. It was a joyful feeling that we took with us, as we walked quite a long distance to another school. When we entered the room where the teacher was sitting, we discovered that he was having his lunch break and that he was actually talking about the Bahá'í Faith. I could scarcely believe it. The three ladies who were with him welcomed us eagerly and immediately asked me to speak. Such was the unexpected opportunity. We had a really long talk together about Bahá'u'lláh, and they were so responsive and warm. They thanked us as we came away, and I in turn thanked Bahá'u'lláh for the opportunity to teach. We returned to Kumasi at about three o'clock. Neither of us had eaten anything since breakfast at 7.45am. It was wonderful to be able to take a shower and wash away the heat and dust of the day. The delicious lunch that Mrs Najaf-Toumrai set before me completed my sense of thankfulness. Meat and bean stew, with rice and salad, and lots of glorious clean water made everything complete. Ghanaians mainly drank water and seemed hardly ever to drink tea or coffee. But my loving Persian family prepared delicious tea for me, and I even enjoyed it without any milk or sugar.

Eleanor asked me if I would like to visit two Bahá'í pioneers from Cameroon. They were David and Esther Tanyi. He had been given a great honour many years ago for being the first Bahá'í to live in a country. This honour was given the title Knight of Bahá'u'lláh. His face was always radiant, reflecting a pure and selfless heart. They were delighted to see us, and Esther started to prepare a meal for us, straightaway. She talked as she bustled about her tiny kitchen. We sat down to a satisfying meal of plantain and egg omelette, with tea in dainty little cups. Time passed swiftly, as we had so much to talk about, and when we left we were caught in a huge downpour, but we didn't mind one little bit. Thankfully, we managed to get a taxi. When we alighted we had to run very quickly from the car, wading in water that was by now several inches deep. We abandoned ourselves to the elements. Our clothes and hair were quickly soaked, but we walked in high spirits, hand in hand. We sang as we waded, like children in perfect happiness let loose in a giant paddling pool. When we eventually arrived on the doorstep of the Najaf-Toumrai's house, we looked like two bedraggled urchins soaked to the skin. A warm wash soon restored us and I was able to shampoo my hair at last. The family gathered us lovingly into its bosom as they plied us with hot drinks and eager questions all at the same time. How much at home I felt with those lovely people, who were so courageously and selflessly pioneering in a far-off land. Mr Najaf-Toumrai was still living in Iran and it was no small sacrifice for them to be parted from their loved ones.

I was invited, next day, to meet with the Spiritual Assembly of Kumasi, to consult about what I might do to help them in their work. They asked me to follow the guidelines of the National Spiritual Assembly by visiting the surrounding villages and schools to speak to the children, and to be on the lookout for Bahá'ís willing to take children's classes. This was a thrilling project for me.

Esther and David Tanyi's daughter, Baroh, was married to an American Bahá'í. Knowing of my great desire to go to the villages, she enthusiastically offered to go with me. We set off for Traboum in scorching heat which was overpowering. Transport, as well as the heat, was unbelievably difficult yet again. After walking a good distance from the bus park we were unable to get any form of transport. During this time, however, we had actually taken part in three spontaneous discussions. The first of these was when a young man offered me his seat on the bus. He was delighted when I showed him a picture of the Bahá'í Temple in Wilmette, after I learned he would be going to America in a few weeks time. We talked at length, quite oblivious of heat and flies and forgetful of all signs of tiredness. Then, while waiting in the thickly crowded market place, I spoke to another eager enquirer who had already heard of the Faith. He asked us to go to his village and teach there. We discovered that the Chief himself was sitting beside us, and we asked him if he would mind our going. His remarkable answer was, "If it is God's work, it is alright." Opportunities for teaching the Faith in Ghana are endless.

Life seemed such a struggle for the people as physical conditions made it a constant battle. The tremendous effort just to survive, to find money for food and basic things, absorbed everyone in this struggle. How the women worked? They carried their babies on their backs, their little limbs dangling, with beads of sweat on their foreheads as they slept contentedly against their mother. The women balanced large bundles on their heads, walking gracefully among the crowds, selling their fruit, corn, or bread. I was moved especially by those beautiful little babies – amidst the continuous harsh noises, fumes and scorching heat. There seemed to be little compassion for the mothers and their children, in all the pushing and shoving, the bartering and struggle of daily life.

I wrote in my diary at the time:

> "My heart feels the pain and shame of what life has become, and I think of the Blessed Beauty (Bahá'u'lláh) and His vision for mankind. This will be a world where justice, peace and brotherhood will reign supreme. O, God! Hasten the day. Take us swiftly through this time of universal discord and confusion. Chaos has overtaken every land, and consternation, fear and greed has taken possession of the human heart. The heart, which Bahá'u'lláh told us was designed by God for His love, and is destined to be His home:"

Baroh led me through the market and looked at the dresses. I felt that my legs would scarcely hold me or take me forward any longer. We had been out for more than five-and-a-half hours in great heat, and it was more than seven hours since my breakfast. The longing for cold water and a chance to sit down, was overpowering, but, even in the midst of this discomfort, I felt it was good to experience these things. It was after four o'clock when we finally returned to base. There was just time to have a short rest before getting ready for the study evening on Bahá'í marriage, which was being held on the university campus in Independence Hall. There were about twelve students present for a very interesting discussion. Before going to bed that night I managed to catch that troublesome mosquito that had disturbed my sleep the night before.

In the morning I started writing my lesson plans for the children. My thoughts flowed freely. My heart was singing in praise to God for making it possible. The work that I had longed to do for years and years had now begun. How richly blessed I was. I now prayed that it would go forward in pure love for Bahá'u'lláh and for the children of Ghana. All my life I felt that the spiritual training of children was so vitally important and I always yearned to help in some small way. Now the door had suddenly opened, and ushered me onto the path of Bahá'í education in Africa. Through the years, a number of my stories for children had appeared in children's magazines in the UK and the Republic of Ireland. Now this dream had been linked with my other great love – Africa. My cup was full. During the morning, as I worked, Mitra brought me tea and a very special and unexpected treat of chocolate pieces. They were always so kind and loving, and made me feel completely at home. I washed a few items of clothing, and Mahnoz called to ask if I would speak at her open meeting that evening. I decided to talk about the Master, 'Abdu'l-Bahá, which has always been a very special subject for me. What a marvellous evening it was! There were about twenty people, Bahá'ís and their friends, gathered in an atmosphere of unity and love. It started at eight o'clock and continued until well after midnight. During that time, five of our enquirers wanted to become Bahá'ís. The atmosphere was vibrant and charged with spiritual energy, so beautiful to experience and impossible to describe. One talk followed another, as these young people wanted to know more and more about the Faith. Fred Darko explained some of the basic teachings, so lovingly and so simply, and then he called on me. Later, when the questions came, I found that the words just poured from my heart, as if it opened to those radiant, eager people and the purity of their search.

It was such a great joy that night to be able to share the story of my own experience and my twelve years searching for truth. I wrote in my diary, next day, about that unforgettable evening.

"I know, with all my being, that the unseen world was bringing heavenly inspiration to that gathering. Each time it seemed that the Fireside was over, more questions were asked, and, as if by magic, inspiration continued to flow. I know, for certain, that I was not alone. With my own strength alone, this would have been impossible. But, in one of our prayers we are told that God has the power to 'change a gnat into an eagle'. How wonderful, beyond all description, is the feeling of that tiny gnat when it spreads its wings in flight, for the glory of teaching His Cause. It seemed to be not of this world. These souls are so receptive and they respond so readily. One may speak about the Faith almost anywhere and everywhere. Zoë often describes our efforts to teach at home as being like sowing seeds in concrete. I think about her and our little Anisa, and I wish that we could be together serving the Cause in this thrilling and wonderful way, without these separations. Eleanor said something that comforted me. She told me that one of the Hands of the Cause expressed the thought that we should not be afraid to let our children sacrifice! She also said that my teaching-trips would be an example for Anisa and that it would help her, spiritually, to see her grandmother doing these things, and that the bond of love between us will be strengthened, and will have an effect on her soul! …Oh, how much I hope so!"

At every opportunity I pressed on with my lesson plans, starting with the theme of God's love, and the reason for our creation. I wrote about the purpose of our lives and the great Messengers that are sent into the world to guide us. I wanted children to be assured of the love of God and to know that His Spirit is within us, and that His Presence is everywhere. The lessons explained why people quarrel about religion, and how the Messengers are like lamps in the world. People look at the lanterns, however, and see differences, instead of looking at the flame, which is one.

As the lessons progressed I shared them with Eleanor who thought they were beautiful. I was thankful that I seemed to be getting it right, as I wanted with all my heart to share with the children the wonderful truths that I had been so blessed to discover. Eleanor took the first few lessons to Accra to show them to the National Spiritual Assembly. Mahnoz invited me to stay with her for a few days. She arranged a meeting and this time I spoke about 'Abdu'l-Bahá. There was a calm, beautiful atmosphere that seemed to settle on the gathering. Two interested people commented on this. By the end of the evening to our intense delight one of these two young men wanted to become a Bahá'í.

A few days later, Baroh and I travelled to a village called Apuatuga, where we spent several hours in the scorching sunshine. The children gathered around us, eager and curious. We talked with them and took some pictures. Soon, the women came and we sat in a circle, completely at ease and filled with happiness. There was a wonderful sense of oneness, without any feelings of strangeness, even though our backgrounds were so widely different. One elderly lady reminded me very much of Miss Offiong-Essio Ayo, whom I had met in Nigeria, and we shared an immediate sense of closeness and understanding. She was sitting beside her grandson, who was involved in Christian Missionary work, and he agreed, after many searching questions, that the Faith of Bahá'u'lláh is a continuation of Christ's teachings.

On our travels one day, we met a Chief who begged us to go to his village. He said, "There is not one Christian there. Please go and tell them about Bahá'u'lláh". These opportunities seemed endless, opportunities that rarely occur at home and which create an incredible inner happiness. I felt as if my whole being was fulfilled and was somehow releasing its highest expression.

Something very sad, however, happened that day. A little black goat was hit and badly hurt by a passing truck. Two boys carried it quite casually and laid it on the ground. Its jaw and mouth were injured and bleeding and its head had been damaged. The flies were swarming around and into its mouth. My heart ached to see its obvious distress and pain. I tried to waft the insects away and shield it from the hot glare of the sun. Twice, it tried to scramble to its feet, bleating pitifully, and then it fell across my legs, leaving smears of blood on my shins. It was an awful situation and there was no possible means of relieving its agony. My eyes filled with tears and I was praying for its release. Baroh told me that the villagers were surprised that I should feel so sad about an animal. I asked our interpreter to explain to them that animals feel pain and injury as much as we do ourselves. I think that the boys took the poor little goat away to kill it, and I felt a pang of anguish for all the suffering in this world.

When we returned to the market, Baroh said that she would leave me there, as she had an errand to make. I was a bit surprised and felt not a little inner trepidation. I didn't know my way about and wasn't sure how to make my way home as there was no actual address for the Najaf-Toumrai's house. I took a deep breath and uttered a silent prayer for help, before taking a taxi to the Tech Junction where we usually alighted. I walked slowly along, and then asked a young man if he could direct me to the Bonso Gate. That much I knew. He was very kind and continued walking with me until at last we arrived at the house. What an immense relief to reach home safely, and I had done it all on my owneo!

Next morning, Baroh's husband arrived and asked if I would meet her so we could make another visit to Apuatuga to see the secretary of the local Bahá'í community. He very kindly drew a little map for me, which made me feel more confident about getting to town on my own. She and I had a wonderfully happy and satisfying day. We began teaching the Faith even on the Tro-Tro wagon, where one man insisted on keeping a postcard I had shown him of the Shrine of the Báb. In the village, the children always came running, and when I started to take snapshots they came flocking from all directions. We taught them Bahá'í songs, and they sang with great enthusiasm, clapping their hands as I gazed around at their smiling faces. Eventually we saw the Bahá'í we had been waiting for and he took us back to his home, where we sat outside, talking. I explained my mission regarding child education and the Institute, and the need for teachers to hold the classes. He was deeply interested and promised to help us if he could. We hadn't eaten or taken anything to drink for many hours, so we asked him for some water. When he returned with a large enamel jug, we found that the water was distinctly yellow. In spite of our great thirst we knew how unwise it would be to drink it. We could not hurt his feelings so we pretended to drink, and Baroh rinsed her mouth and then poured some on her hands. In this way we avoided offending his heart.

From there, we agreed to travel on to Pramso village to try and meet the Chief. It was disappointing to discover that he was away in Accra. This meant that we were able to sit and talk with several other Bahá'ís, all men. One of them invited us to his home and we were given water. Although still careful about drinking polluted water we saw that this water was clear. It tasted rather like coconut and was so wonderfully refreshing. One of the Bahá'ís, an ambulance driver, offered us a lift to where the buses stopped. When we arrived they bought us four large oranges that were juicy and sweet. It was teatime, and we had not eaten since breakfast. By then it was almost dark, and the members of the Kumasi Assembly had already started their meeting when we arrived home at seven o'clock. Radiant with happiness, although perspiring and dusty, I felt a deep sense of achievement, and we thanked God for such blessings.

Eleanor had come back from Accra and it was lovely to see her. I bathed very quickly, as the Spiritual Assembly had invited me to meet them. We talked about the work I was doing, and they asked me to send a report to the National Assembly so that they would know how things were progressing. It was suggested that I should try out my lessons in the villages to see how suitable they were. I asked Eleanor if she would read them and give her opinion. She encouraged me so much and inspired me to continue. Eleanor seemed to have the necessary vision for the work to go forward, and I pressed on with renewed vigour. Sometimes the heat was overpowering, and my back would ache from the constant bending over the table to write. I loved the task before me, and all the discomfort in the world would not have deterred me for one moment. When finished, it would help many children to learn about God's love for us, and to know that He has sent Bahá'u'lláh to guide us in this great age.

Eleanor joined us when Baroh and I went again to Traboum. We were very fortunate that morning to get transport straight away and we arrived in the village quite early.

Baroh with ladies from the village of Pramso

Most of the people were away working in the fields. We were led to a small clearing under the shade of a large and beautiful tree. Some small wooden seats were brought for us and many children, together with several adults, gathered around us. Eleanor taught them a prayer in their own language, which was Twi (pronounced Chwee) and then we sang some lovely songs. I told the happy group about 'Abdu'l-Bahá, and I held up His photograph for them to see. They listened with such wonder and intensity, both grown-ups and children. One lady expressed her happiness at our visit, saying how wonderful it was that we, who came from a faraway country, would spend so much time with them. The Chief and his brother asked us to tell them about the Faith. They listened carefully and asked many questions. The brother, whose name was Edward Reynolds Brenyah, told us that their mother was dying, and they asked if we would visit her. This was a great honour for us and I felt very humble as they led us to their home, where she was lying on her bed, very ill indeed. Her name was Monica Ampansah. I spoke to her, though her eyes were closed, and her son told her that God has sent another Messenger to the world. He leaned over her bed and in a low, soft voice he said, "His name is Bahá'u'lláh" and, to our amazement, she repeated, "Bahá'u'lláh." It was so deeply moving that I could scarcely speak, and tears rolled down my face. In response to his request for a prayer I recited the short healing prayer. The intense power and quality of those words created a spiritual atmosphere in the room. It was an unforgettable and inspiring moment in that little house in the heart of Ghana.

Eleanor told Mr Brenya and his brother that my own mother was in the spiritual worlds, as well as my husband and son. She assured him that they would greet his loved one when the time came. Slowly we emerged from the dark little room into the brilliant, hot sunshine. We were filled with a sense of wonder at what had taken place. One of the friends very thoughtfully brought some bananas and an avocado for us, which we ate with relish.

After a very long wait, a bus came to take us to Kejetia Market and, once again, we were able to share the Faith. We saw two young men with a United Nations booklet in their hands, and I said to Baroh that I thought they would surely be interested to know about the coming world peace. Soon, we were deeply engaged in sharing Bahá'u'lláh's message of unity and peace for mankind. Several other passengers became interested, and they eagerly involved themselves in our discussion. The day had been successful and rewarding in every way, as we had also found a volunteer to take some children's classes. Her name was Grace Amankwoh, and she looked very gentle and seemed to be truly suitable for this work.

When we finally reached our home base I could scarcely make my legs move forward. It was extremely hot. The time was four o'clock, and we had been out since 7.30am that morning. In the evening we all went to a meeting on 'Life after Death', on the university campus. During our discussion my throat began to feel sore and, by next morning, a full head and chest cold had developed. I felt extremely weak and really quite ill. Mahnoz Shapiro invited me to stay at her home, so that she could look after me. She gently rubbed my back with Vick, and brought out a lovely warm nightdress of a delicate shade of green, which she gave me as a gift. Her loving care was very comforting in my weakened state. I am sure it speeded my recovery.

Some days later, I attended an inspiring Nineteen Day Feast where twenty-three Bahá'ís were sharing a devotional service. We had readings from Buddhist and Muslim holy writings, as well as the Christian Old and New Testament. These were followed by passages from the writings of the Báb and Bahá'u'lláh. During the time of our consultation, Barry, who was a member of the National Spiritual Assembly, informed the friends that they had decided to ask Lou Turner to remain in the Ashanti Region for the whole of my time in Ghana. They requested me to hold the Teachers' Institute at the end of June. We all enjoyed the refreshments of fruit, biscuits and cold drinks. Still feeling rather unwell, I went for a short walk with the children but had to return when I felt rather faint. Several days later, thank God, I regained my full strength.

There was so much to be done, and my eager heart was longing to fulfil the many joyful tasks that lay before me. A day was set aside when the friends asked me to speak on three different subjects. The committee arranging the programme had planned to invite some of the professors and lecturers to a special lunch and discussion. This was to be held on the following Saturday. I was somewhat overwhelmed, when they expressed the wish that I should speak to them about the Faith.

It was a source of joy to me that the National Spiritual Assembly warmly and enthusiastically approved my first lesson-plans, declaring that they were "just right for the villages". They went on to say that they were simply and clearly written and conveyed much love. There were fifteen more to be planned and written out, as well as preparing for the Teachers' Institute. Meanwhile, I continued going to the villages each day, to find Bahá'ís who would make suitable and willing teachers. I was conscious of my total reliance on God's help, and the power of prayer that sustained me through those wonderful days of service. Informal gatherings continued where the local Bahá'ís brought their friends. One night there were people from Iran, Germany, United States, Spain, England and Ghana. Surely, it was a gathering of the Kingdom, when we were completely at one in heart and spirit. There was laughter and singing following the talk and an animated discussion. Once again, we were entertained by a mixture of Persian and African dancing. Those days were so precious. We decided that, at one of the meetings, we would share stories about some of the heroic Bahá'ís from the early days of the Faith in Persia. Several of us spoke, relating tales about Mulla Husayn, Quddus, Vahid and Bádi. I was asked to speak about Tahirih and Zaynab, those unique and marvellous women, whose names will be remembered and extolled for ages and centuries to come. The Africans were so receptive and open to all facets of spiritual truth. It was that which contributed to the happiness I always felt in Africa, away from the soul-destroying atmosphere of an excessively materialistic part of the world such as Western Europe.

12

RETURN TO AFRICA – PART II

Eleanor returned happily from her work in Accra, and she suggested that perhaps we could do a little travelling together. I responded eagerly to this, and to her idea of visiting Bill Brown. Bill was a Liverpool Bahá'í from my own home city. He had come to Ghana a few years previously and had married a lovely girl called Paulina. They were living in a small place called Begoro, with their young son Hans and their lovely baby Jeffrey, just ten-weeks into this world.

Travelling was always something of an event, exciting and full of struggle. We waited a long time for a lift, before a young German couple picked us up and took us the two-hour drive to Bamsu. From there we caught a small bus for part of the journey. At the end of it, the driver wouldn't take any money. Alighting from the bus, again we waited patiently, hoping for some further sort of transport. We ate a little rice in full view of all the interested villagers. They watched us with a look of happy surprise, on seeing two white-skinned visitors sitting there, relaxed and eating a simple meal by the roadside. Bill and Paulina were delighted to see us and welcomed us eagerly to their home. Bill was engaged in a building project to provide a clinic for crippled children. It was very sad to see so many little ones wearing leg-braces and trying to walk on crutches. Mostly they had been paralysed as a result of polio. All the staff were doing wonderful work. Bill was thrilled that I was in Ghana, because he had a special affection for my sister Pat, and he looks on her as his "spiritual mother".

At night I slept in a nice little room in a double bed. I made sure to burn mosquito coils, as there was no mesh on the windows. The mozzies were there in great abundance! It was lovely to be in Begoro, where there was more breeze than in Kumasi, and the scenery more lush and green making it very attractive. During the few days there we met two German ladies who were friends of theirs. They were working in a mission of some sort, and teaching Domestic Science. They seemed really pleased to see us and were very hospitable. They gave us delicious cool drinks of pineapple and orange, while we sat talking outside, on a small veranda. All was calm and peaceful under the night sky, with its twinkling, beautiful stars.

As we were leaving I felt something stinging between my toes, like a sprig of thistle. Quickly I scrambled into the van and I could see at once there was a small swarm of black ants scrambling all over my foot and between my toes. As I stamped and tried to brush them out, poor Eleanor squealed. She felt them crawling into her underclothes.

"Get out! Get out!" she shouted, and we both began to laugh hysterically. We continued to giggle as we finished the journey on the outside of Bill's truck, being jostled and thrown about, clinging to the sides and thoroughly enjoying our unexpected adventure. It was great fun.

From Begoro, we travelled to Tafu, where we called on a young Canadian called Wendy Stringer, who was teaching biology at the university. She lived in a small, single-storey dwelling. She had no running water until the evening, so we had to forego our much loved shower. Poor Wendy was suffering from a painful eye-disorder known as apollo, which seemed very widespread at that time.

Mark, the young man who had taken part in the auction during Convention, called to see Wendy, and his delight knew no bounds when he saw us. "O, Mamma, I was hoping to see you again!" His eyes were shining with happiness and that purity of heart which so impressed me in West African people. Wendy told us that they were planning to hold a meeting in the University and were expecting about six or seven people. I readily agreed, when she asked me to be the speaker for this discussion and to act as a spearhead.

To my astonishment, students began to arrive several at a time, then more and more in a seemingly endless stream. The expected half-dozen grew to more than sixty young people, all gathering around to hear about Bahá'u'lláh. I caught my breath with great excitement and, praying for guidance, shared what I felt in my heart. There were many questions, and then some enthusiastic singing of Bahá'í songs. Africans just love to sing, and it was a wonderful way to end such a marvellous evening.

We are promised divine assistance when we 'arise to teach,' and to serve the Cause of God. When experiencing this assistance for ourselves what we receive is infinitely greater than anything we can ever hope to give. We went to bed, utterly contented and filled with a wonderful sense of peace. Eleanor and I shared a double bed, while Wendy took herself quietly to her single room. Refreshed and renewed, we set off next morning for Koforidia, making the journey by Tro-Tro.

Eleanor took me to visit an English couple who were teaching at the University. We were greeted very warmly and to our pleasant surprise were given cups of tea and large slices of chocolate cake, a very rare treat in that part of the world. During the afternoon, we went into a beautiful school called Madonna High School, which was surrounded by magnificent gardens. Walking there we met Sister Maria, a Catholic nun. She had come from Austria and had made her home in Ghana. We spent a happy and interesting time with her. Eleanor spoke about Zoë and Anisa. She wondered what the prospects might be if they came to Ghana, Zoë being a trained teacher. Salaries paid in Cedis would be very low she told us, and accommodation would also be very difficult. Because of my great love for Africa, and the seemingly limitless opportunities for teaching and child education, dear Eleanor felt that I should consider staying in Ghana on a long-term basis. But she knew that I wouldn't stay there without my two loved ones.

We went to the bus station, amidst the crowds and noisy panic of getting tickets.

After a terrific struggle and a weary wait, the bus arrived. We managed to squeeze inside. There was a great fuss and a lot of shouting and angry words going on. Someone had crept in by the door at the back, and the driver took us all to the police-station to have him taken off. Feeling somewhat tired, hot and very grimy, I longed for us to reach Kumasi, to return home to a lovely shower and to put on some fresh, clean clothes. A long journey still lay ahead of us, and I was trying hard to be patient. Suddenly, Eleanor cried out, "I think this bus is going to Accra!" I groaned with dismay. "Oh, no!" But it <u>was</u> and it <u>did</u>! Back we went, right into the heat and city atmosphere of Accra. We made our way to Blanche Musa's home for yet another night away. When we arrived there was no water, save a small amount in the tank, and I had to content myself with a meagre wash and the same dress for yet another day. Eleanor went to the Bahá'í Centre for a few hours and, as Blanche had a visitor, I sat on the bed and looked at my lesson-plans. I shared a room with Lorraine, a sweet and gentle Bahá'í, who was also staying overnight. It was the Holy Day for the Ascension of Bahá'u'lláh, which is commemorated at three in the morning. I wakened at half-past two and joined Eleanor for prayers. It was a lovely experience, sitting by candle-light in the stillness and silence of that hour, when everyone else was asleep. We recited prayers for the Blessed Beauty, Bahá'u'lláh.

Although we had fully intended returning to Kumasi as early as possible, next morning, we found ourselves enjoying a leisurely breakfast of fried egg, with bread and cheese. Then Eleanor washed her hair, and by the time we left for the centre it was noon. We went out and were strolling along, deep in conversation, when a lady drove past in her car. Eleanor told me that she was the wife of a lawyer who was helping the National Spiritual Assembly with their negotiations about the Bahá'í Temple land. We were introduced and she gave us a very warm invitation to her home. She was charming and her home and garden were so beautiful. We sat out of doors on a lovely patio, talking with great animation, while enjoying large glasses of Coke with ice. Bliss! She had two small children and was very interested when I mentioned the spiritual training of a child. We had a long discussion and felt in total harmony. Afterwards Eleanor and I caught a taxi. By the time we reached the transport-yard it was five-thirty, and we began the difficult task of trying to board a vehicle going back to Kumasi. We set off, eventually, in a small van, for our long and exceedingly bumpy ride, over broken roads. Somewhat sweaty and weary, we arrived back home at eleven-fifteen. We had just one short break during that long journey, when I relished two cups of tea and a small sponge cake. Luxury indeed! Next day, Eleanor was exhausted and had a good sleep during the afternoon while I washed clothes and shampooed my hair. I struggled to write notes for the two talks. Tiredness almost overcame me, however, I knew that I had to press on in readiness for the following day.

It turned out to be a very successful gathering with a beautiful spirit. Talks were given by Eleanor, Mitra and Mahnoz. Mitra looked particularly lovely in her long African dress. Between sessions and discussions we sang and had a lot of fun. I tasted my first dish of Kenki, (pronounced Kinkey), made of ground maize. It was a little bit different to Garri, which had been the main food in Nigeria, but they are definitely an acquired taste.

After the weekend, I worked hard at my lesson-plans until lunch-time and then Eleanor took me to the market. What a chore it always seemed with its unbelievable heat, dust and flies and hordes of people everywhere. The crowds and scorching sun made it an intense struggle to even think and function at all. Grit and tiny stones soon became embedded into the soles of the feet, and perspiration clung to every inch of the body. The Cedi notes that we were handling were old and filthy, and we felt incredibly limp and dirty by the time we had made our purchases, before cramming ourselves into a taxi. Four of us sat in the back, with all our bundles of shopping and baskets, pressed firmly against each other, scarcely able to breathe. Once we tumbled out of the taxi, we still had a considerable walk ahead of us. On the way, we bought two delicious oranges each from a tiny roadside stall. We drank the juice as we stumbled our way home. Then we realised that we had been out of doors for more than four hours during the greatest heat of the day. "Mad dogs and Englishmen go out in the midday sun." Once back home, I bathed... such incredible bliss! We drank tea which was quite heavenly.

The following Wednesday, June 3, 1981 was something of a red-letter day. I had been asked if I would cook dinner for the family. They requested a typical English meal. In Ghana, how would I obtain the necessary ingredients for such a dinner? Added to this slight complication was having only one burner on a very ancient cooker with no oven. I didn't want to let the side down so, with a stiff upper lip, I went to survey the little kitchen. Although it was quite a feat I actually enjoyed the challenge, and managed to have a meal on the table bang on one o'clock. I created meatballs with minced meat, onion and tomato; creamed potatoes, green beans, salad and roast potatoes (par boiled and deep fried). Without herbs or stock cubes I had been in a quandary about how to flavour it, and give it some colour. Suddenly I remembered that Zoë had put two small packets of powdered soup in my luggage. These were beef and tomato flavour. I was thrilled and dare I say relieved to find these, and everyone seemed to enjoy the meal immensely. My satisfaction was total.

The following day, Mrs Najaf-Toumrai together with Maryam and Eleanor, set out for a trip to Upper Volta to attend the wedding of a relative. I had been looking forward to getting on with my work in a steady unbroken flow. Barry and Mahnoz, with great thoughtfulness, insisted that I should go and stay with them, rather than remain on my own. Time was getting very short and I was anxious to finish the preparation of my lessons. I prayed earnestly for Bahá'u'lláh to help me. My hope was to be able to visit Lomé before returning home, as everyone seemed to think that I should go there. My thoughts were being drawn irresistibly towards home, Zoë and Anisa, as I didn't want to stay away too long.

On the Friday of that week we all attended the Nineteen-Day Feast of Nur (Light) which was held in Mahnoz and Barry's home. Unfortunately there was no electricity and the room was wrapped in the lovely soft glow of candle light. Altogether there were twenty-five Bahá'ís, and it was a most joyful gathering. They called on me to say something about the children's classes and the Institute, which was to be held on June 28, a special day for me as it was my Wedding Anniversary. Nana, Richard and Fred, three devoted Bahá'ís, said that they would like to go to the villages on a regular basis, to help with teaching the children. The evening ended with everyone dancing. It was lovely to see the Persians and Ghanaians demonstrating their different styles of dance. There was a lot of laughter and pure happiness at this wonderful gathering.

As the days passed by, my back was giving me a lot of pain. This was due to long hours bending over the table doing my writing, added to the joyful but bone-shaking rides on the mammy-wagons. At times, it was impossible to continue with the lessons, and I would have to go and lie down until the aching had eased. My spirit was so eager to fulfil the sacred task that had been set for me. How glad and radiant was my heart to be doing this special kind of service for children. The body alone showed signs of weakness and made me clearly realise the distinction between the physical and the spiritual.

At one of our exciting firesides, we had with us two lovely young people, Annalisa Ben-George and her brother Michael. He had brought his parents with them. Their mother was Spanish and their father Ghanaian. They were exceptionally good-looking and full of charm. I was asked to speak about the proofs of Bahá'u'lláh, and the unique aspects of His mission. It was always very clear to me how much I was assisted and inspired on every occasion, when I was called upon to teach. How could I do it otherwise as I always felt lacking in ability? After our refreshments of tea, sliced oranges and popcorn, we all started dancing and as always thoroughly enjoyed ourselves. It was after one o'clock in the morning when we said our farewells, and I was driven home on the pillion of Mehran's motor-bike! I can tell you that a few silent prayers were said quite rapidly, as we bounced and swerved along those uneven, dusty roads in the darkness. It was two o'clock before we sank happily into our beds. I wakened as usual about six, but almost immediately drifted back to sleep again. When I woke at nine it felt extremely late to be having my bath, as everything starts very early in Africa. After a light breakfast, I was told that Mahnoz was coming, and that she would bring her car. She was planning to take me to a village called Kokadea. I recorded a few notes in my diary as I waited for her arrival:

> "Am waiting for Mahnoz.
> Have spent a little time in my bedroom, turning to God and praying.
> Feel so thankful for everything He has given to me throughout my life.
> Am thankful for His guidance and love, and for kind and caring parents.
> For a devoted and wonderful husband, and the gift of so gentle and loving a son. For leading me to His Pathway, through the love of Bahá'u'lláh!
> My heart wells up in joy and gratitude for so many blessings that have surrounded me."
> Thought of the great burden of suffering in the world. People who die of hunger. Those who have never had a home, and are compelled to live on the streets.

Thought of children who have been orphaned and are so sad and alone, and left without love. Of those who live in fear or squalor and those who are imprisoned. And I thought about the Bahá'ís in Iran who are dying for their Faith, suffering persecution in so many ways.

Thought, "How can I choose to live in the comfort and peace that I enjoy, at home? How can I be so selfish? Burdens of grief and sorrow are engulfing the world. Bahá'u'lláh has come to bring justice, to end all these inequalities and tribulations. How can I be sincere, and call myself a follower, if I choose any other path than service to the Faith, which is service to mankind?

"Serving at home, in Colwyn Bay, or anywhere in the UK. cannot have a fraction of the effect such efforts can have in a country like Ghana.

"Must return home and see my closest loved ones, Zoë and Anisa – my precious, only grandchild. We must talk and consult and pray that God will enable us to be together in our service, for that would be wonderful."

Little girls taking care of the babies

My diary notes expressed something of my longing to continue working in Ghana, while, at the same time, wanting to remain part of our little family of three. When I look back to that time, I feel a great happiness about my travels and I am also thankful that Zoë and Anisa have continued sharing our close, loving relationship. Bahá'u'lláh has helped me to keep the balance.

On Sunday morning, a thunder storm with torrential rain swept over us. After so much heat, I was thankful for the strong wind that lifted the net curtains with a refreshing draught throughout the large room where I was writing. None of us had felt well that morning. Flora had a head cold, and Mitra felt dizzy, and the pain in my back had been intensifying, making writing impossible, most days. There was a continuous, aching pain around the lung area and Mitra had kindly rubbed my back with a heat producing cream. After a short rest on my bed, I took a shower and struggled to pen a few more pages of the lessons.

In the following days we visited the villages of Kokodei and Swedro, gathering many of the little children together, singing and talking happily. On one of our trips along the way we saw people taking part in a funeral ceremony. The ladies were wearing either black and red, or black and orange, and both men and women were dancing very gracefully. We stayed in the car and continued our journey into the village. It had been many hours since our breakfast, but we managed to buy some hot plantain and avocado. The rain continued very heavily, bringing great relief from that intense heat and ever-scorching sun. Eleanor with Mrs Najaf-Toumrai and Maryam, had arrived back safely from Upper Volta, where they met with quite a few adventures, especially in connection with the journey. Eleanor told me that she had prayed, and called upon my two Johns, when they had been facing a very difficult situation on their return. They tried in vain to get some form of transport, for the long, hard journey back to Kumasi. After she asked my husband and son, both in the spiritual worlds beyond, to help them, everything worked out miraculously. A whole series of circumstances opened up, and they actually came back by air, instead of that awful ride by Tro-Tro, which they had been expecting.

June 12 was my nineteenth anniversary of becoming a Bahá'í, and I scribbled happily in my note-book:

"These have been wonderful years, and how swiftly they have flown away – like a bird in its joyful flight! I thank God for those years as a Bahá'í, learning and growing and venturing forth, going ever more deeply into the vast ocean of His love. It has been a tremendous blessing to be a pioneer in the UK and then across the Irish Sea. Travelling on the great continents of Africa, India, Canada and, now, back again to beloved Africa. What bounties? What blessings? And what love."

I was travelling with Barry Shapiro to Accra that day, and because I was feeling rather unwell, it was a relief to have him as a companion. It was an added bonus to go by car. My insides, as well as my back, were troubling me, and I had the oddest sensation in my diaphragm which was hurting all the time. I just wanted to be fit and strong so that I could get on with the lessons I was preparing. I was looking forward again to meeting with the National Spiritual Assembly to talk about this work. It was an immense relief when, at last, I had finished writing a complete set of eight lessons. I had written them in a simple style, and expressed in them much love. Always, I kept in mind that they were to be used by African children, whose lives are spent in their own small villages. How far removed they are from the experiences and environment of children in the Western world. It had been an intensely happy and rewarding experience to write for those children. Our journey of almost five hours passed more quickly than I expected, and was quite enjoyable, eating biscuits and drinking cold sweet tea. It had been necessary for me to support my back as much as possible, as we were bounced and jolted from side to side over the many potholes.

We drove to Blanche's home, where Barry was also staying. Later that evening he took us out for a meal in a luxurious restaurant. That was a happy surprise. We had a delicious meal with thick soup, asparagus, cauliflower and green beans, followed by a scrumptious Chinese dish with chicken, beansprouts and tasty sauces. We enjoyed a gorgeous sweet of fruit and chocolate ice-cream. It was a glorious feast indeed. It seemed far removed from Accra. Next morning, Blanche had a hairdressing appointment, and she invited me to go with her. I needed a trim and was glad of this unexpected opportunity. Afterwards we went to the market for Blanche's shopping. We wended our way between the various little stalls, so colourful and bright. There was a glorious assortment of plantain, peppers, avocado, white egg-plant, tomatoes and all kinds of fruit. Smiling, curious faces gazed at us in the usual friendly and open way. An older lady, standing behind her stall, was positively beaming at me. Another lady said, "She wants to be your friend." I smiled back at her, returning her lovely warmth. We saw one another a little later, exchanged a wave and a happy greeting. We had both found a friend.

During the afternoon Blanche asked me if I would make a bread pudding. While I was eager to fulfil her request, I was again somewhat disconcerted on account of the shortage of ingredients. My recollections of a bread and butter pudding held visions of thinly sliced bread and butter, with sugar and dried fruit, in layers, with egg and milk poured over it, and a little mixed spice or nutmeg sprinkled on the top. Blanche placed in front of me a huge, stale loaf of bread, and she told me that they had very little milk and only one egg. Certainly, there was no fruit. I had no choice but to get started. I cut up about half the bread and spread each slice with margarine, dabbed a little marmalade here and there, with a smattering of sugar, and poured in two small tins of evaporated milk and a beaten egg. I found a little box of cinnamon to sprinkle on the top, and the huge dish went into the oven. Blanche made a delicious dinner of roast beef with lots of vegetables. At one point the pudding looked very dry when we opened the oven door. Without any hesitation Blanche poured a large quantity of water over it. I was horrified, but didn't utter a word. Amazingly, it tasted very good, and everyone seemed to love it. The children wanted second helpings and there wasn't a scrap left after the meal. I suppose you could call it a little miracle!

All evening I wrote my lessons, but my back just pained unceasingly. At ten-thirty, exhausted, I was about to get ready for bed when Barry returned from the

National Assembly meeting and handed me a large envelope which was bulging with letters from home. What a thrill? There were twelve altogether. It was an absolute feast of news from my loved ones. Dear Eleanor had booked my return flight and had sent a cable to Zoë. I would be leaving on July 1, arriving in Moscow at 3am and departing from there at 6pm on the Thursday. This meant I'd be at Heathrow by 5pm British time. Then I began to feel a little anxious when I realised that I'd have to spend a night in London. Where would I stay? I found it difficult to sleep as I turned it over in my mind.

Next morning I didn't feel well, quite apart from my lack of sleep. There was a very uncomfortable sensation in my solar plexus that drained me of energy completely. Barry drove us to the Bahá'í Centre where I was to meet with the National Spiritual Assembly. It was very heart-warming to know that they were delighted with my work on the Lessons. David Tanyi, their Chairman, spoke warmly about my visit to Ghana and the love that I had brought. Kubana said that they would have been lost with re-gard to the goal for Child Education, if I had not gone at this time. I was overwhelmed by their response, and felt very humble. Edward Larbi enthusiastically volunteered to translate the lessons into Chwi, their local language. This was wonderful news and I felt relieved and content.

There was a study evening taking place in the centre and we enjoyed a lively discussion on passages from the Writings of Bahá'u'lláh. Thelma Kelghati, a Bahá'í Counsellor from Togo, arrived as we were in the middle and took part. The spirit of happiness in that room was marred for me because I felt so ill. It hurt when I walked, and I decided that it would not be wise to travel to Togo. I knew that it would be wiser to return to Kumasi with Barry and David straightaway.

What a difficult journey it was, with an overpowering aching and tenderness throughout my whole body, and a tiredness that made me feel so very weak. My greatest longing was to be able to reach there in safety, without feeling any worse. When we finally arrived, I managed to crawl into Maryam's bed. On top of it all I was suffering a burning headache. I slept almost immediately and when I woke Maryam brought me tea and two small marmalade sandwiches. David, Barry and I had bought fried yam, oranges and bananas for lunch, to be eaten in the car as we travelled and I had tried to eat a little of these. I was thankful to be back and to rest and enjoy the luxury of reading my wonderful letters from home. We had been invited to Anise Shapiro's seventh birthday party. Although feeling very wobbly, I didn't want to decline her lovely invitation, so managed to get ready in time. I took several pictures of her with lots of her little friends. They played and danced and there were all sorts of goodies to eat, with fruit drinks and birthday cake. She opened her presents, and I was glad to be able to give her a little necklace of multi-coloured beads that I had bought in Southport. Anise was very thrilled and I was just thankful to have been well enough to go.

Time began to pass more quickly, and gradually my health was restored somewhat. My trips to the villages gained momentum much to my delight. It was always comfort-ing to have someone with me. Esther Tanyi enthusiastically offered to be my escort. I met her one morning at nine in the Kejetia Market. Esther was happy we were travelling together and both of us had an enjoyable day. Travelling by Tro-Tro was, as usual, an unbelievable experience. Although it was already packed to full capacity, it kept stopping to take even more people. Even Esther was flabbergasted. Women with babies on their backs would climb in and then have nowhere to sit. They had to stand, with their bodies bent forward, at an angle, as there was insufficient height to allow them to remain upright. They just stayed in that position, jogging and swaying, mile after mile, packed like dates in a box and in the most incredible heat.

We were greatly concerned when a mother with a very young baby scrambled on, and had to remain at the back of the wagon. The baby's tiny head, so vulnerable, was against the hard wooden edge of the opening. The least jolt could have crushed its little skull. Esther and I kept our hands stretched out, as a protection. The mother seemed quite unaware of the potential danger, but for us it was really distressing. One great jolt nearly put my back out of joint, and I had given a startled little ouch, grimacing and smiling at the same time. This caused a lot of amusement in the other travellers. By the time we reached Traboum we had travelled nearly twenty miles over very bad roads. We were greeted enthusiastically on every side. The chairman of their Spiritual Assembly came to meet us and kindly offered water and groundnuts. A little while later he brought a dish of cooked corn on the cob with the outer coverings removed. However swarms of flies were crawling over them. My appetite faded, though I ate a little so that he would not feel hurt. What was left I transferred unobtrusively to the larger bag that I had taken with me.

Communication that day was limited because Esther is from Cameroon and was not able to speak the local language very well. I left a note for Grace Amankwa, telling her about the Teachers' Institute, and I fervently hoped that she would attend. We learned that the Chief's mother had passed away, that frail and wonderful old lady whom we had visited on our previous trip to Traboum. After a lovely hour of teaching the Faith we gave a few pamphlets to the eager souls who asked for them with outstretched hands, and we managed to catch a bus with unexpected ease. On our way, Esther asked me to call in for a brief visit to her home. She said that we could go shopping next day instead, after our trip to Asamung.

When I agreed, I had no idea what an adventure would follow several hours later. When we reached her home, Esther suggested that I should lie down and rest a little. I was glad to do this, as my legs felt weak after such a long time travelling and walking in the hottest time of the day. I rested for only a little while, as I was anxious to leave for home before it grew dark. It was about three-thirty, and dear, kind Esther cooked a delicious meal of rice for us. Not having eaten since morning, except for my mouthful of corn, I was extremely grateful for her hospitality. My anxiety, however, increased as time passed. Esther was waiting for some water to boil, so that we could have tea. The delay dragged on and on, and suddenly I caught a glimpse of a bus flashing past the window. To my dismay, Esther told me that the next one would be in another hour. Slight panic seized me. I needed to reach Kejetia where I would try to get a taxi, after which I must walk from the junction. It would be really dark by then and rain was now falling in torrents.

We stood together in the road, waiting for what seemed an interminable time, for my bus. Inwardly, I kept repeating the little prayer called the Remover of Difficulties. When I told Esther that I hadn't taken a torch with me, she hurried back home to get one. But before she returned, the bus trundled into view and I quickly scrambled on. The journey seemed unbearably long and my anxiety was growing. Rapidly it was getting dark and the rain kept lashing down relentlessly. To be an 'O Bruni' (a white person) travelling alone on public transport was a bit of a risk so my prayers intensified at every moment. Eventually we reached Kejetia and I found myself paddling in deep pools of water, while the rain soaked me through to the skin. Rushing across the road, I kept stepping into holes and I was not sure where I should stand, to get a taxi. It was an awful experience. The taxi-drivers took full advantage of the situation. The rain meant, of course, that they were in great demand, in a place where public transport was totally inadequate to meet the needs of so many people. The desperation of their passengers gave them an opportunity to charge an outrageous price for their services, especially for an 'O Bruni.' As I approached each cab, the driver would insist on charging forty Cedi, for what was normally a three Cedi journey! It was going to be very costly. I had the money to pay for it, but a strong resistance to the injustice made me refuse. I was frightened and felt very much alone. Water was streaming from my hair and my dress, as I ran from each taxi to the bus queue, anxiously calling, "Are you going to the Tech-Junction?" And in the scramble of people to get on the bus, I suddenly looked down and saw that the zip of my large bag was open. Before leaving the previous bus, I had put my handbag inside the shopping bag, so that I would be less encumbered, and I was holding the fare in my hand. I glanced up startled by the group of teenage boys who were the culprits. "You're opening my bag," I cried, feeling amazed and indignant. Then, I swept away towards another taxi, but the driver was already squeezing his quota of wet passengers inside. Someone from the bus queue called out, "Tech! Tech!" So I ran back and hauled myself onto it, feeling very conscious of my wet hair and bedraggled appearance.

I gave the driver my wet and soggy notes, which had been screwed up in my hand, and one of the female passengers said, in alarm, "Your bag!" and to my horror she added, "They've ripped your bag." Glancing down I saw, with shock, a long slit where my bag had been slashed with a knife. I gasped, thinking about my handbag inside. Had they taken it? Diving my hand into the bag, I felt inside, and to my utter relief, the handbag was there. I sank into my seat near the door and sat quite still. Although outwardly calm, I felt hurt inside. It was a sense of being degraded, which is hard to explain. To be a visitor from another land, left alone stranded in the torrential rain and to have my property threatened, as well, was quite overwhelming. My immediate concern now was that fifteen minute walk that lay ahead of me, in dark unlit places, over uneven, unmade roads and little pathways. I wasn't sure whether the would-be thief was still on the bus with me? One young man, amidst all the sympathisers, was very vociferous in shouting his complaint about the offender. He spoke in the Twi language, of course. But what really alarmed me was that he had a knife in his hand with a very long, curved blade. I felt decidedly suspicious of him and his violent protests. Several bus stops later, to my enormous relief, he jumped off, and I could breathe more easily.

After I left the bus, a very nice young woman spoke to me, expressing her regret and sadness at what had happened. I felt like crying, as I answered her, but we talked for a few moments and I mentioned the Faith, and my reason for being in Ghana. To my delight she said that she would like to know more about it, and she asked my name. I offered her one of my pamphlets, and after thanking me she said, very sweetly, "Nothing else will happen to you that is not nice." Much comforted, I left her, and padded along in the dark, conscious that my dress was getting longer and longer with the weight of water pulling it down. Wading through sandy and muddy patches of water I found that I was not able to see the paths that led across to Bomso Gate, so I went around the road instead. With every step I took, I was drawing nearer to the haven where I could have a wash and dry my clothes. It was after seven-thirty when I reached the house, and with a great sigh of relief and deep weariness, I knocked on the door. The family welcomed me with the utmost love and tenderness, and they were horrified at the sight of my bag with the large rip in it. They felt the shock that I myself was feeling, and their hearts were saddened that such a thing had happened during my beautiful visit to Ghana.

Next morning I should have been meeting Esther again at nine, but my legs felt strangely weak and I was having stomach pains. It was definitely too risky for me to venture out and perhaps find myself in another difficult situation. My courage failed me at the thought of being back at the same place of the previous night's incident. My feelings of desolation, and of being so far from home, were still with me. It was all too vivid, and I decided to remain indoors. During the morning, I rested quite a lot, and in the afternoon walked to David Tanyi's office to leave a message of apology for Esther. My legs were like heavy weights and my back was full of aching pain. I bought a few oranges from a little stall nearby, and a loaf of what is known as tea-bread.

My lesson-plans were finished, ready for Edward to translate, and Eleanor was still in Accra, typing them for me. Thankfulness and joy filled my heart even as I coped with the heaviness and burden of my physical body. A few days later, we had a lovely gathering to welcome the arrival of Mahnaz's father, who had flown over from America. I wore the new dress of palest green that dear Mrs Najaf-Toumrai had kindly made for me. It was a wonderfully happy evening beginning with a discussion flowing joyously into spontaneous singing and dancing with everyone participating. There was a tremendous spirit of love and happiness with Persians, Ghanains, Americans and Lou from the UK. Acceptance of the reality of the oneness of mankind makes every heart feel like one heart, with God's indwelling Spirit flowing through us all. On a night such as that, in the heart of West Africa, it kindled a fire that can never be forgotten.

A few days later, we arranged to go to a village called Adeuwase, where one of the young Bahá'í students had been teaching his people. The whole Najaf-Toumrai family took part in this expedition. We set out together in order to meet two more of the friends at Independence Hall. We were all hot and sweaty by the time we reached the village and made our way to Richard's home. It had been arranged for us to meet the chief at four in the afternoon, and promptly we gathered at the meeting place. A table and some chairs had been set out for us, and then the chief himself appeared. He was quite an old man with the calm dignity that I saw in so many of the African people. After shaking hands and exchanging greetings, he was happy for us to say a prayer, before leading us to the chairs. Many people gathered, including a great number of children, and everyone listened intently asking a lot of questions. Alfred spoke to them in Twi, and it was a wonderful experience to be with those lovely souls in such peaceful surroundings. He spoke of God's love and of Bahá'u'lláh, His Great Manifestation for this Age. How close He seemed, amidst so much harmony, under the high, wide skies of Africa. My heart was deeply stirred, and yet I felt the sweetest peace. Even now, so many years later, I feel again the mysterious wonder and beauty of that time, and those precious days of my life. The light began to fade and the sky grew very grey, just as Barry and Mahnoz arrived with her father, Mr Kazemzadeh. Full of joy, he spoke a few words which Nana translated, and he told the people about 'Abdu'l-Bahá's description of the different flowers in a garden. How dull it would be if all were white, or all were blue, and he explained that it is the same with people of different races and different skin-colour. Everyone seemed to respond to this analogy and enjoyed it very much.

I was asked to speak about education, and especially spiritual education, which starts with the knowledge of God. This led to the importance of the role of the mother, who is the first educator of the child. As I was speaking, I noticed an older woman in the crowd, who was nodding her head in agreement, and smiling broadly. Then the rain began to fall. My chance to speak to this beautiful lady was lost. In spite of the rain the villagers remained, and Mahnoz started singing and leading some of the children in a graceful dance. Very soon, everyone was clapping hands, laughing and singing. Oh, how the Africans love to dance, and are full of rhythm. They would respond immediately. It began to pour even heavier, and we ran for shelter to Barry's large red wagon. It was almost dark and those dear, lovely people reluctantly had to move away and out of sight.

The days soon sped by, and just one more task of love lay ahead of me and that was the One Day Institute for those who had offered to take the children's classes in that region. My heart was uplifted for the blessing of such an opportunity. Being my wedding anniversary it was a day of beautiful memories, filled somehow with an indescribable fragrance, not unlike the delicate and very lovely sweetpeas that formed my bouquet on that day when I was joined with my beloved John. Perhaps he was with me today and sharing in my happiness.

There was a distinct air of eager anticipation as we all gathered together at the Cultural Centre, where our meeting was to be held. It was thrilling to see the Bahá'ís who

Lou with teachers who came for the Training Institute

Bahá'ís on the drums, outside the Cultural Centre in Kumasi

had travelled long distances, having set out from their villages very early that morning. Their faces were alight with happiness. Attentively they listened, as I unfolded the themes of the lesson-plans, and explained the vital part that the teacher must play in loving the children and helping them to love the Faith. I wanted to encourage them to make happiness an essential part of the classes.

It was a beautiful day in its simplicity and harmony. I was sure that the cohorts of His angels and my own dear ones, were mingling with us in that joyful gathering. With a sense of deep gratitude and humility, I felt God had bestowed on me the bounty of sharing with others just a glimpse of my love for Him and for permitting me the opportunity of speaking about the indwelling spirit within the soul of every child. What a wonderful ending to my teaching-trip in Ghana.

The friends were so kind to me, and it was not easy to say goodbye to my loving, generous Persian family, who had in every way taken me into their tender hearts and made me feel so completely at home. My dear Eleanor had taken care of my return flight to Moscow and onward to London. She was with me at the airport in Accra, where we talked and shared a poignant farewell together, before I took my leave. We have always had a close bond of friendship going back to our early days in Cork, when our little family pioneered in 1970.

13

UNEXPECTED DELAY IN MOSCOW

Settling into my seat, as we headed for Moscow, I little thought that another setback lay ahead of me. I sat, quietly dreaming about home and the joy of seeing my dear Zoë and Anisa again. When we arrived it was the early hours of the morning, and the little queue of weary passengers were anxious to reach their beds. It came as a nasty shock when I was abruptly informed that I had no booking to London, and that there would not be room for me for several days on any flight. My ticket had been booked all the way through to London so this was very annoying. My protests, however, fell on deaf ears. I stood, helplessly, as the official in charge consulted the computer. My throat was dry as I gazed into that screen. I silently prayed, "Please God, Please let me go soon." The dates and figures flashed up on the screen. Then they stopped to reveal the date of my release which was three days ahead! It could have been worse, but it still meant that I was captive for those days in Moscow. There was no way of letting Zoë know of my delay, but I realised that I must accept it as calmly as I could. It was a relief to have a room to myself. I slept as a result of utter weariness and, in the morning, started making friends with fellow-passengers from many parts of the world. It was a wonderful experience to talk with people of such varying and interesting backgrounds. They came from China and Africa, Japan and America, all passing through Moscow on their way to and from their various destinations. In the afternoon we had the opportunity of going on a trip around the historic parts of Moscow, and it was certainly good to be allowed out of doors. I went eagerly, just as I had on my outward journey.

It was a pleasant surprise to be given permission to leave the bus, when we reached Red Square. We alighted in a quiet orderly way and stood, much like schoolchildren on a day-trip with their teacher, meekly taking in our guide's instructions. No one was to stray from the group. This was emphasised in alarmingly severe tones, and we walked obediently with the quite masculine-looking lady whose task it was to keep us close to her side. We enjoyed it but were more than a little amused by it all. The buildings were quite beautiful and most impressive, particularly the golden and colourful domes of the Churches.

This little trip had used up some of the monotonous time inside the hotel, while trying to be patient in my longing to fly homeward to my family. I was concerned that they would be wondering what had happened, and at the delay. After the evening meal on my first full day, I took the lift to my bedroom on the eighth floor. I sat by the window, gazing down at the line of trees below, and suddenly an inexplicable surge of happiness welled up inside me. Without knowing why, I felt a great sense of inner peace that is hard to describe. I reflected quietly, and said my prayers before getting into bed.

It was morning, about seven o'clock, when a sudden, urgent knocking on my door awakened me. Scrambling out of bed I staggered to the little hallway and called through the outer door. Opening it, I saw one of the hotel staff, and she was saying with great urgency, "London! London!" Just when my heart was rising up in joyous anticipation, she dashed my hopes by saying that it wasn't me she wanted after all, for my flight was not today. I closed the door and fell back onto my little bed, weak from being so abruptly wakened. The shock and excitement, followed by deep disappointment overwhelmed me, and I cried like a child. Suddenly and unexpectedly I felt very much alone again. I wept for my loved ones who had left this world, and the immensity of effort it takes to go on with one's life, after the trauma of bereavement. I realised how brave we have to be, not to give up, and to be determined to do more rather than just exist. We must strive to live life to the full and as beautifully as we are able. I dried my tears, thankful for so much divine assistance and so much love.

Then, suddenly, another insistent banging on my door brought me quickly to my feet. Again, the lady was saying something about London, and that I must go now. I repeated what I had said before, about the date of my flight, but she insisted that I could go, and that I must hurry. "The bus ... come NOW!" I closed the door and everything was in a whirl in my mind. Yes, it was wonderful! I really could go home today but I was not dressed and neither was I washed. As far as I can recall, I pulled on some clothes, splashed water on my face, and grabbed my toothbrush and other toiletries from the bathroom. Thrusting them into my bag, I collected my books and magazines, and ran out of the room, with my raincoat and jacket trailing over my arm. Gasping, with a mouth as dry as sandpaper, I jumped into the lift and pressed the ground-floor button. Keeping my eyes on the little orange light that indicated the floors we made our downward journey. My heart nearly jumped out of my body when it suddenly started to reverse. We had been going down and down: eight, seven, six, five, four, and now ... five, six, seven, we were going up! I was horrified. My one thought was to get on that bus which would take me to my plane and to England. Now we were back on the eighth floor, and I had to start my downward journey all over again. I always laugh when I relate this story now, as I do when recounting the adventures that befell me on my travels. Often, in the midst of difficult experiences, I told myself, "This will be fun when I tell it in future but it's making me a wee bit anxious NOW!"

That morning in Moscow I eventually caught the plane for London, and it seemed like a dream, once I was settled into my safe, comfortable seat and had time to think about what had happened. From my sleep I had been wakened, and in so short a

Red Square in Moscow

time had been rushed with great speed to the airport, without any breakfast, not even a drink. I was actually travelling westward, and would reach home in the daylight. Joyous and contented feelings of anticipation welled up. Memories of heat and dust and a myriad flies and mosquitos, floated through my mind. Even with all the bumpy rides on the bus and tro-tro, and the hours of struggling to express what I wanted to convey for the children in my lesson plans, I felt that it had been a very good trip. I thanked God for giving me the strength and for granting me the opportunity of going, once more, to my beloved Africa.

14

EAST AFRICA – TOGETHER

In 1982 Zoë and I happily agreed, at the request of the Overseas Goals Committee, to make a six-week visit to East Africa, to explore the possibility of returning there as pioneers. Our plans for going to India when Anisa had reached her fourth birthday were sadly cancelled. We learned from Dr Johnson, principal of New Era, that the government's policy at that time was to reduce the number of ex-patriots being employed at the school. So we were delighted to have been given this new challenge of going to Africa together. Previously Anisa had been in the habit of getting into my suitcase and trying to pull the lid down over her head thinking she was coming with me. This time, as I started packing for the trip, she knew that she was going too, and her joy knew no bounds. I was thrilled for us to be making this trip together, and once in the air we enjoyed the long flight to Kenya immensely. Anisa took everything in her stride, as she was a very adaptable little girl, with wisdom more than her years.

We were greeted at the airport in Nairobi by Hasan Sabri, who had lived in Africa for a number of years. He and his wife, Isobel, made the three of us so welcome and cherished in our new environment. We spent several days in their home, but the Bahá'í centre became our base for most of our stay in Nairobi.

We had a great many adventures during those six weeks. One unforgettable memory was an overnight train journey to Mombasa. We were there to visit a Dr Rawhani and his wife and their young son and daughter, who had been living in East Africa for quite some time. That night-time journey was a most thrilling experience and one that appealed very much to a small girl like Anisa. That rail line between Nairobi and Mombasa is one of the most famous tracks in the world. It was constructed at the beginning of the twentieth

Zoë and Anisa with Isobel Sabri

century and the engine had been built by the British in the 1940's. The whole experience amazed us, as it was luxurious beyond all expectations. Hasan and Isobel had generously financed this trip to Mombasa and unknown to us had booked us into a first-class compartment. There was such a look of happiness on Anisa's face when we entered the dining room for our evening meal.

The crisp snow-white linen tablecloth, the table laid with fine cutlery, and the tall, dignified waiter guiding us to our seats, so impressed the four-year-old that she called out with excitement, "It's like a hotel!" The other passengers turned their heads and smiled.

We slept very comfortably in our bunks, our sheets and blankets wrapped cosily around us as we rolled along through the warm African night. In the early dawn we lifted the window blinds and gazed across the vast, beautiful landscape with zebra and wildebeest roaming peacefully in the morning sunlight. Africa, to me is such a very special place. It fills me with a deep happiness and longing that is impossible to describe. This was my third visit to the continent of my heart's desire.

Mombasa, like all the cities I'd visited in Africa, was hot, very, very hot. The general atmosphere had a different quality, however, rather strange and mysterious. Soon we were being greeted by Dr Rawhani and his wife and daughter. We felt secure. Their home was situated next to the Bahá'í centre in a peaceful, secluded setting, surrounded by many beautiful trees. Anisa was happy there, playing in the brilliant sunshine during the day, and managing to sleep during the humid, sticky nights, protected with a large mosquito net. Our kind friends took us on several trips. On one occasion we went to Nyali beach for a swim in the vast Indian Ocean. Never had I seen water so blue and sand so silvery white. It was just a heavenly spot. Of course, we attracted a great deal of attention from the few bathers who were there. A group of school-age boys were unable to resist touching Anisa's pale arms as she splashed happily in the waves. Their curiosity was not surprising as it was unlikely they had ever seen Europeans bathing there before. It was amusing to see the expressions on their faces.

Later we returned to our base in Nairobi and continued to make teaching trips over quite a large area. Both Zoë and I were amazed that Anisa was able to walk for many miles along hot, dusty roads, in quite intense sunshine. She looked very pretty in her little sun-hat, her cotton dress and sandals. Sometimes we travelled by local transport in small trucks that had no real seating and were open to the sky. The name of this vehicle was a Matatu, and like the Mammy-Wagons, too many passengers were packed into too small a space. We squeezed between sacks, bundles and boxes of all kinds, and huddled together as best we could. Our fellow passengers were always fascinated by the little girl, with her large blue eyes and long brown hair curling onto her shoulders. There were beaming smiles and friendly greetings on every journey, and Anisa would respond as though she had lived there all her life. Children are so adaptable. They accept all the adventures with perfect equanimity. Their innocence seems to protect them from anxiety. The local food, that we quite enjoyed, was Ugali made from maize flour. Anisa liked the idea of rolling it into small balls and eating it with her fingers, as local people did. This was something she continued to do after we returned to the UK, but with her mashed potato! When it was suggested she should use her spoon or fork she would say, "But, Mummy, they do this in Kenya."

One day a group of Bahá'ís took us for a drive to the beautiful Rift Valley, where we gazed with awe at the wonderful panoramic view before us. There was a very strong breeze and the sky was a great expanse of misty blue. It was a breath-taking experience. Although our being in Nairobi gave us many opportunities for travelling and the chance of meeting people in villages and schools, Hasan and Isobel were eager for us to find a niche for ourselves where we would be able to settle. This was no easy task. Being two women on our own, with a small child, we felt somewhat vulnerable. To start a new life in Africa, where Zoë could find a teaching-post and a school for Anisa and all of us a home where we could feel secure, these were vital considerations.

Isabel and Hasan arranged another trip for us, one that would include the adventure and challenge of visiting Uganda and Tanzania. I fell in love with Uganda as soon as we landed in Entebbe Airport. The whole area was beautifully lush and green and one could feel the gentle yet powerful influence of the Bahá'í House of Worship outside Kampala. The beloved Temple, that I had longed to see for many years, was now so close. It brought waves of joy to my heart. So many blessings were flowing that I was overwhelmed with gratitude for all the love that God had poured out upon us.

During our stay in Uganda we found ourselves in the previous home of Enoch Olinga, a very famous African Bahá'í who had been given the honour of being a Hand of the Cause God. A young couple, Fardis and Parvine were living there as pioneers, with their two young children. We felt the immense privilege of being in that house. Mr Olinga, together with his family, had been brutally murdered in that very place some years before. The cruel and horrific regime of the time had brought waves of brutality and terror to the region, disrupting the lives of its people in what had been a tranquil, peaceful spot.

One evening we had been startled and shocked by several bursts of gunfire very close to the house. The children were tucked up for the night, and Zoë and I slid quietly into our bedroom where, thankfully, Anisa lay sleeping quite undisturbed. Without speaking, we lay down, each on our own small bed, keeping well below the level of the windows. We prayed silent, fervent prayers in the darkness, with bated breath and thumping hearts, while we waited till the terrifying sounds of the cracking bullets died away. In the quietness that followed we began to breath freely again with utmost relief.

The following day brought fulfilment of two long-held dreams, when Fardis lovingly offered to drive us not only to the Temple but to Claire Gung's Kindergarten as well. For many years I had wanted so much to meet this wonderful lady whom Shoghi Effendi had affectionately called "The Mother of Africa". Several years earlier I responded eagerly to a call for someone to help 'Auntie Claire' in her work with children. Quite a number had volunteered their services. At the time this did not work out for me. Now I was seeing her very school. After so much time had elapsed,

Anisa's first taste of Ugali fruit   *The calm and beauty of the Temple*

Breezy and beautiful at the Rift Valley; Lou with Anisa and some of the Bahá'ís

Fardis and Parvine on the front steps of
Enoch Olinga's house.

Two little flowers in the Garden of God.

Clare Gung with her staff and her kindergarten children.

Isobel and Hasan were urging me to offer my help again, as Claire had become frail in health. They contacted the Universal House of Justice and in reply, I was given every encouragement to visit the kindergarten personally and offer what assistance I could. The inner joy of being there, fulfilling a yearning, was indescribable.

Auntie Claire, as she is affectionately known, greeted us with warm hugs before we embarked on a tour of her lovely nursery school. We met five ladies, the only remaining teachers on her staff. They moved with a poise and dignity possessed so naturally by African women. Claire Gung had offered to serve the Cause of God on that great continent, in response to an appeal by the Guardian, Shoghi Effendi, in the 1940s. That courageous lady had gone there, alone, and opened a kindergarten that attracted many children. They all had the joy of learning the wonderful teachings and principles of Bahá'u'lláh. For almost forty years her school had flourished, gathering together hundreds of children, like flowers in a beautiful garden of harmony and love.

The numbers of children in the nursery had declined in recent years, and by 1982 only a group of twenty-eight children remained. Life in general had become almost intolerable, with the terror of indiscriminate killings and brutal attacks on innocent people. Added to this was the desperate shortage of food. All this had undermined the great work that had been Claire's whole life, at an age when she was not physically strong enough to withstand so many hardships.

We sat with her, talking quietly, while she described for us the uncertainty of life around her, keeping her almost a prisoner in her own home. Nightly bursts of gunfire, very close to where she was living, shattered all hope of security and normal life. How brave she was. Our hearts melted for her great spirit and unswerving faith. We also learned, beyond the spoken word, that in spite of everything, the nursery was much more than a goal, more than the whole of her life's work, it <u>was</u> her life. We realised, without her having to tell us, that she would remain at her post, alone and steadfast to the very end. I brought away some lovely pictures of her school, and the beautiful teachers and children. Claire has since passed on to those other worlds, where I feel sure she is serving her Beloved, and rejoicing in the work that she undertook so devotedly over so many years.

Fardis drove us to the precincts of the Temple, and we stood for a while, gazing at its beautiful outer structure. There are no words to express the emotions that arise in the heart when entering the sacredness of a Bahá'í House of Worship. Twice before, I had this blessing. In October 1967 my husband, John, and I had been privileged to visit the Temple in Germany, some way out of Frankfurt, during the International Conference held there. Our son had just begun his studies at Cambridge University and was not able to be with us. My second wonderful experience was to the Temple in the United States in Wilmette during my trip to Canada in 1980. Now to be in the African Temple was yet another spiritual gift.

Before we returned to Nairobi, we made a visit to Tanzania where we stayed with a young Bahá'í couple from America. They were teaching at a local school and we were introduced to the Head who invited us both to become members of his teaching staff.

The Bahá'ís of Arusha in Tanzania.

It was a tempting offer and we might have been eager to accept if other conditions in the area had been more secure. There was talk of murders, a lot of theft and other mysterious, unpleasant incidents. Apart from visiting one of the secondary schools to speak about the faith, I didn't feel any great attraction to Tanzania, and we were quite happy to board the plane back to Nairobi.

East Africa had been very different from my trips to Nigeria and Ghana, and our dear friends, Hasan and Isobel, were naturally very disappointed that we felt unable to make our home there. They had been so helpful and kind, and had offered us all assistance possible. For these things we were deeply grateful.

15

VANUATU – A SOUTH PACIFIC ISLAND

After our adventures in Africa, we settled into the quiet, cooler rhythm of life in Colwyn Bay. I have so many lovely memories of those days with my granddaughter, skipping happily down the road towards the sea. She and I spent so many joyful, lazy hours building castles in the sand and splashing about at the water's edge, as we jumped the rolling waves. There is a special kind of happiness that children bring, when we share in their sense of wonder and discovery. Indeed we glimpse the joy of our own childhood when we look at the world and see it all as magical. With Anisa, every little rock-pool became a well of mystery, and every tiny shell or pebble sparkled in the sun with all the fascination of a precious gem.

We sat, one cool and blustery day, on the low sea-wall. As a special treat, we huddled together with a large bag of fish and chips between us, savouring every delicious salty mouthful. And as the seagulls came shrieking and circling above our heads we shared our feast with them. We sometimes went to Rhos-on-Sea, walking hand-in-hand, with many a hop and skip, as we breathed those special seaside smells, so uplifting to the spirit. When we arrived, our first port of call was the ice-cream shop, for one of those very favourite treats I recall from my own childhood. The immense pleasure of grasping a glorious wafer-cone, with its ice cream blob balanced precariously on the top, is never forgotten even in the mists of old-age. To know it would begin to overflow in a creamy trickle down the side, as it melted in the sun, made us lick even more speedily. The summer days flowed along quite happily, and Zoë and I accepted that our path of service was not, after all, taking us to Africa.

One day quite out of the blue, we received a telephone call from the International Goals Committee, and found ourselves facing a new challenge. They were calling to see if we would consider filling an urgent goal in the islands of the Pacific. We were asked to take over the running of a nursery school in Vanuatu, which was previously known as New Hebrides. This would enable the young Canadian Bahá'í teacher there, to take English language classes for the women in the villages. Zoë and I agreed happily to accept this great challenge and, with tremendous excitement, spent the next four months in a flurry of preparation for our big adventure. It would mean spending at least a year overseas. We set about the task of packing four huge tea-chests with suitable clothing and all the basic things we might need in our faraway tropical home.

There were so many things to be done: visas; passports; air tickets; travellers' cheques, and most importantly, to make sure that we had all the necessary inoculations. Our travelling expenses were great, in addition to the cost of more than two hundred pounds for our tea chests to be sent by sea. With faith and earnest prayer we pulled out all the stops in a valiant effort to fill this vital goal of the Six-Year Plan for the world.

We set out on the first stage of our journey on September 13, 1982, by making the thirty-six hour flight to Australia. We had brief stops in Abu Dhabi, Singapore and Bali. Our little four-year-old was marvellous and quite undaunted by such a long journey. Two very dear Bahá'í friends from Chester, Diane and Mehrdad Arjomand, were now living in New South Wales. I had spoken about Bahá'í marriage at their wedding, several years before. They had now invited us to stay with them and their two young daughters for a few nights, before resuming our journey to Vanuatu.

It was an enormous shock to learn that our visas were not being granted. The whole question of visas had proved very difficult and complicated, but we were assured that everything would be all right and we would have no problem being allowed into Vanuatu. Now we were in a terrible dilemma. Having travelled halfway around the world we could not turn back, but neither could we go forward. Our kind and generous friends surrounded us with the utmost love and hospitality, but we were trapped in a situation from which it seemed impossible to escape. The next few weeks were fraught with anxiety as we tried by every means in our power, to obtain the necessary documents. Here we were, thousands of miles from our home in Colwyn Bay. Our heavy tea chests had already been dispatched by sea some weeks before. Totally unplanned and unprepared, we were living in someone else's home for an unknown and what seemed an indefinite period. Diane and Merhdad were truly wonderful. As the days became a week and the week became five weeks we felt a growing desperation. Cables, phone calls, messages to and from Port Vila on Vanuatu and the immigration office flew back and forwards. We made repeated visits to Sydney to see what we could do but to no avail. It was also important to change the dates of our eventual departure from Australia, week by week, to make sure that we would actually have a flight when the time came. It was something of a bounty to see so much of the countryside as well as that of Sydney. It was also fantastic to visit the beautiful Bahá'í House of Worship close to Sydney. That was a gift we did not expect and we spent a calming, wonderful day there.

After consultation and much soul-searching, we decided that the only thing we could do would be to obtain visitors' visas, which would, at least, get us into Vanuatu. Once there, hopefully, we would be given an extended period of time. This plan worked and October 22 was our bright, beautiful day of freedom and flight to our intended goal. The journey by UTA Airways took us to Noumea (previously New Caledonia) on a very comfortable journey to Port Vila. The smiling, happy face of Barbara Pierce, secretary of the National Spiritual Assembly of Vanuatu, greeted us. She was accompanied by her two young sons, Daniel aged eleven and three-year old

Sam. Barbara's husband, Charles from England, was teaching at the local college. We had met briefly in Southport many years before.

The early evening air was delightfully soft and warm, as we walked from the plane to collect our luggage. Anisa, who was clutching her life-sized baby doll, Sarah, was wide-eyed and silent in our new surroundings. We discovered that one of Zoë's suit-cases was missing and the other one was bursting open at the sides. The officials in charge were kind and courteous, and they asked us to call for the missing luggage next morning. Barbara and Charles made us very comfortable in a twin-bedded room, with a little mattress for Anisa. They were eager to show us the house that they had rented on our behalf. So, away we went in a spirit of happy anticipation.

Our new home was a one-storey, timber house, standing in its own grounds, surrounded with coconut palms, paw-paw trees, frangipani and patches of brightly-coloured flowers. It was very attractive and, with a deep sense of relief, we followed Charles indoors to find it surprisingly spacious. It had three bedrooms, a large living room and kitchen. There was also a wide area for drying clothes on a wet day. We found the bathroom, however, to be very basic. The old dilapidated shower had a rusty enamel base and the bath had large patches of black iron showing through. But never mind, it was home. The house was called 'Macmbo' and there was a lot of work to be done. Zoë and I made lists of things to purchase. We felt the most urgent task was locks and bolts for the doors, as we felt quite vulnerable. There were small markets where we were able to get most of these things as well as pillows, electric-light bulbs, buckets and dishes. We managed to buy some very pretty curtain material for the thirteen windows in the house. Oh boy, did that mean a lot of sewing! The mattresses were stained and grubby, but we poured all our energy into cleaning and scrubbing, while we waited eagerly, each day, for news that our tea-chests had reached Port Vila. We were told that they were due to arrive on October 15, but, as they had been off-loaded in Noumea and transhipped to the "Pacific Islander," they should now reach the port by November 4. Our patience had to be tested just a little bit longer.

The heat and extreme humidity left us exhausted, but we were determined to make our little timber house as much like home as possible. The general pattern of our lives was to welcome visitors right throughout the day. Almost as soon as we wakened, Meg Deamer (a pioneer from Australia) with her little granddaughter Zena would arrive. Meg's two sons, Bryn and Tony, were also living in Vanuatu and were full of energy and enthusiasm. Neighbours would call in for a chat and a cool drink. There was also a stream of loving friends who seemed so glad that the three of us were there.

One of our neighbours was an Indian lady, Mrs Ghosh, who became a very firm friend. Quite frequently she invited us for tea and spoiled us with all sorts of cakes and sweetmeats. We became very close. For some considerable time we were without a fridge in our little kitchen, so, in that tropical heat, it was a great problem trying to keep everything cool. Then one day Tony and Bryn arrived with a well-used one from the Bahá'í Centre. Oh, joy of joys! No more sour milk, oily margarine and warm fruit drinks. We were thrilled.

At the end of October we met with the National Spiritual Assembly in the Bahá'í Centre. I found it a moving experience. Their welcome was so warm and their appreciation of our being there quite overwhelmed us. They expressed the view that our endeavours in Port Vila would benefit the country as a whole, as well as the work we would do for the Faith. I was very happy when they spoke about the importance of child education, a subject so dear to my heart.

Sometimes we went swimming with Barbara and Charles, and had wonderfully relaxing days on a beautiful little beach of pure white sand, with the clearest green water and palm trees. On my birthday in November, they invited us for lunch and we all feasted on a delicious meal of roast meat and fish, with a variety of scrumptious vegetables. They also served us laplap, a traditional dish with many ingredients including chicken, coconut cream, and yam, wrapped in a parcel of vine leaves. This was followed by a huge fruit pie and a coconut cake, which Barbara had made. To my surprise and delight, they presented me with a lovely white lace stole and some very pretty stationery, which had a red hibiscus design. Later, Charles drove us to a little spot called Klems Hill, where we lingered to admire the wonderful view before driving to Malee Beach. The sand there was distinctly silver with tiny black stones that sparkled in the sun. On Sunday mornings we held children's classes at the Bahá'í Centre, and Charles played his guitar while we all sang happily. He asked me to tell a story about one of the early believers. I spoke about Lua Getsinger who once walked in the sandy footprints of 'Abdu'l-Bahá and was stung by a scorpion. The children enjoyed it very much and chattered happily about it afterwards.

After many disappointments and difficulties we managed to meet with the Deputy Immigration Officer, as well as the First Secretary for Home Affairs. This encouraged us to feel more optimistic about getting our residence visas. Everything moved so slowly on this far outpost of the world. Nevertheless, we were beginning to feel more at home, as we became familiar with the town. Apart from the smaller shops, there were three large stores, Ballande, Hebrida and Super Marche, and it was a particular joy to visit them as they had wonderful air-conditioning. To step into that crisp coldness, away from the sizzling blaze of the sun was sheer bliss. Macmbo, our house, was quite close to markets, the post office and banks. There were several hotels and restaurants and a small museum. So, thankfully, we hadn't to walk very far to buy the every-day things we needed.

As well as all this, there was an attractive little cafe called Bloody Mary's which was quite close to the water. They sold absolutely wonderful ice cream, apricot drinks and fantastic little sponge cakes. But our favourite treat was to buy three thick shakes that were totally unlike any milk shakes I have ever tasted. Tall, cool glasses filled with smooth chocolate-flavoured ice cream, almost too thick to drink through the straw. In the intense heat of a tropical island, this was heaven indeed.

There were many such delightful moments to help us through the daily frustration of battling against all the obstacles that kept us from moving forward. We were waiting the arrival of our belongings, and waiting for the visas that would give us the

Barbara and Charles Pierce – Pioneers from England.

'Macmbo' our new home

With our next-door neighbours

chance to stay. What frustrated us most was that we couldn't start our work in the kindergarten till they did. We kept reminding ourselves that when we try to serve the Cause of God, we are often tested but never beyond our limit. Sometimes it is difficult to know what that limit is! We should never expect things to be easy. It is a time when we draw on our inner strength. Then our love and faith grows ever stronger.

It was such a great relief when at last we heard that our precious, long-awaited tea-chests had arrived in the port. The first thing was to find someone with a truck who could collect them for us. Our hearts were light as we talked to our neighbours and made all the necessary enquiries. At last, it was arranged for someone to meet us at two o'clock next day in the middle of town. We stood on the main road in the blazing sun, full of eager expectation. The heat was overpowering for us all especially Anisa. We watched and waited, but the minutes dragged by. Half past two came, and then three o'clock. With sinking hearts we realised he wasn't going to come. Disappointment made us a very forlorn little threesome. What could we do? Silently I prayed, "Is there any remover of difficulties save God?" over and over again to dispel the sense of helplessness we were feeling. Something had to be done. It was no use standing any longer in that unbearable heat, so we decided to go, once again, to the office of the

Shipping Agent. We asked to see Mr Naturelle, who had filled in our customs forms for us. He listened to our dilemma and advised us to go to the wharf where he would send someone to transport our goods to "Macmbo". It was a huge relief to have a course of action to follow. Gratefully, we hurried to catch one of the small buses that passed close by.

In the Customs Office there was still more money to be paid. Everything seemed extremely costly. They informed us that our tea-chests had not been brought out of the containers because another ship, 'The Captain Cook,' had docked, and the men were busy unloading it. There was so much delay, and so much patience was needed every step of the way.

The celebration for the Birthday of Bahá'u'lláh, on November 12th filled our room in 'Macmbo' with happy smiling faces. There were twenty-three of us to share the prayers and writings, to inspire our hearts with hidden fragrances of His love. We gathered around the long table for a delightful potluck meal. After our friends left, guess what happened? A truck stopped outside and the precious, elusive tea-chests were delivered, like a reward for being patient! It had been two months since we left our home in Colwyn Bay, and the tea-chests had been sent well before that time. It was very exciting to open them and find everything we had packed with so much thought and care. For Anisa, especially, it was great fun. She brought out various items, one by one, shouting excitedly, "Your typewriter, Grandma! Your books! Here are your sandals! Look, here's my cuddly bear." It was a treasure trove of lovely surprises.

As we found all the things we had packed, I wondered if this is how it will be when we enter our spiritual home in the next world. Will we find there, all those things that we put into our lives, the good and the lovely as well as the mistakes and regrets of a lifetime? Will we find, with great thankfulness, some little treasured kindness, quite forgotten, but clearly present, in that chest of long-forgotten memories? Some things we may regret, while others surely will lift our hearts in gratitude. No wonder that Bahá'u'lláh tells us to bring ourselves to account each day, before we are summoned to a reckoning.

A few days later Barbara called quite early one morning, looking distressed. Charles had received a message at college, from the Minister of Immigration, informing him that our application for visas had been refused. No reason had been given, just a definite and blunt refusal. We felt shocked and dismayed. Having travelled halfway across the world, we would be unable to stay and fulfil the work we so earnestly longed to do. To add to our anxiety, we were suddenly plunged into another situation. At about one or two o'clock in the morning I was wakened by mysterious noises. Some were very close to the house and others more distant. Lying in bed, very scared and hardly daring to breathe, I listened intently, straining every nerve to understand what was happening. There was much rustling of trees, snapping of twigs, and something like the loud flapping of wings. Being on the ground floor, and with windows covered only with mesh, instead of glass, we felt vulnerable indeed. A little way off I could hear dogs barking loudly, and muffled footsteps scuffling. An occasional stone hit the side of the house as I lay there, absolutely still and tense, trying to catch every sound. These disturbances became a nightly occurrence, starting at about two in the morning. After several sleepless nights I felt weary and was very anxious to discover the reason. No one seemed to know what was happening, and even though we questioned our neighbours and all the local Bahá'ís, there seemed no explanation. After almost two weeks of this continuing sleeplessness I was feeling really desperate. Then, one night, as I lay there listening intently, I was startled to see my windows suddenly light up. It was like the beam of a large torch being directed through both my windows. Then, there was a man's cough and a lot of rustling and heavy footsteps in the garden surrounding the house. I jumped out of bed, suddenly very angry, and switched on my light. I had lain in bed, night after night, too tense to move. It was now time to end it. As soon as my light flooded the room I heard voices speaking loudly, and the tramping of feet on the road beyond the garden. They faded quickly into the distance and I breathed the greatest sigh of relief. It remained a mystery until, a few days later, we were told by one of the local Ni-Vanuatu that the flapping wings were those of flying foxes, or fruit bats, that came into the garden to eat the luscious fruit of our sapodilla trees. Apparently, the bats are a favourite delicacy in the hotels and restaurants of Port Vila and at night they were being hunted, all around the house, which explained the different puzzling noises that had frightened us so much.

At the children's class, we talked about Lua Getsinger and her great love for 'Abdu'l-Bahá. They loved the story about the Master, when he asked Lua to visit a man who was very ill and lived in one of the poorest parts of 'Akká. The children listened intently as I told them that this lovely Bahá'í was very distressed when she arrived at the man's home. His room was not very clean and he badly needed a wash. Lua was afraid that she might catch some sort of infection from him. How could 'Abdu'l-Bahá have sent her there? But when she returned He looked very sad. He told her that He had gone many times to visit this poor man, to feed him and make him comfortable. He said, "Can you not go this once?" We talked about Martha Root and May Maxwell who were such great teachers of the Faith. The way they served with complete devotion the whole of their lives. For many, many years they both travelled to different parts of the world to share Bahá'u'lláh's message of peace and unity for mankind. They had no thought for their own well-being and comfort. I told them that although Martha Root was ill and sometimes very frail, she continued faithfully with her travels. We also shared the exciting story of her teaching the Faith to Queen Marie of Rumania, who became a Bahá'í.

At the Nineteen Day Feast, held in the Bahá'í Centre, we were thrilled when Anisa recited one of the Hidden Words of Bahá'u'lláh, in a clear voice.

"O Son of the Supreme. Love Me that I may love thee.
If thou lovest Me not, My love can in no wise reach thee.
Know this, O, servant"!

Anisa at her children's class.

She played happily with all the children and adapted very well, considering the heat and high humidity. Towards the end of November we had a most enjoyable visit from Owen Battrick, who was a Bahá'í Counsellor. I had known him when he was a member of the National Spiritual Assembly of the British Isles. He invited us out for a meal and gave us enormous encouragement about our service in the Pacific Area. He urged us not to give up hope about our visas, but to keep on trying. The National Assembly also assured us that all would be well. This helped us to feel much more confident in our efforts.

Zoë and I asked to meet with the National Spiritual Assembly, to consult about the work that we could do in Vanuatu. I told them of my longing to travel-teach, and as they had received letters from the Universal House of Justice about Tutorial Schools, they decided that I could help with the work of child education, which was so dear to my heart.

Speaking with Barbara, one day, and realising my eagerness to be teaching the Faith, she asked if I would like to go to a small island, known as Tanna, which has an active volcano called Yassur. On wings of joy, I told her how much I would love to do this. I began, straight away, to pack my bag in readiness for this exciting trip.

Next day we received the sad news that Paul Haney a very dear and very famous Bahá'í, had died. His death was the result of a car accident in Haifa. How fondly I recalled him, during our Pilgrimage in 1966, affectionately telling us, while in the

Off to the villages –
Tanna style

Teaching on the island of Tanna

Mansion of Bahá'u'lláh, "Johnny will sleep in the Chamber of Horrors." He meant that our eighteen-year old son would be sleeping in the room that has the names and photographs of the Shah of Persia and those other rulers who had persecuted Bahá'u'lláh so cruelly!

When she saw me packing in readiness for my trip, our little Anisa felt that if I was going then she should go, as well. Zoë was encouraging and enthusiastic about my trip to Tanna but Anisa didn't want me to go. She said, "You shouldn't go where there is a volcano, Grandma." She so much wanted me to stay at home. Barbara had booked my flight for the afternoon of December 15, and it took just one hour. Flying in the small plane we crossed the vast expanse of clear, green water, dotted here and there with tiny islands far below. It was an exhilarating experience. It made me think of Africa and the wonderful times I spent there.

Pioneers, Donna and Eric Lof, from Australia, and Sue and Denis Stitt, from Canada, were eagerly waiting when we landed. They greeted me so lovingly, and immediately I felt at home. This wonderful sense of belonging was a factor in all my travels across the world. The love of God binds the hearts together in an all-pervading unity which will, one day, encircle the world.

Being in Tanna was so much like being on the great African continent with its small, thatched houses, surrounded by tall palms, and the friendly, smiling faces everywhere. Food was scarce and water even more so. Fine, black dust from Yassur, the volcano, covered everything. It seemed even in my mouth and hair. But nothing could spoil my happiness at being there, where teaching was the central theme of each day. Several times I rode pillion with Sue, on her small motorcycle speeding through narrow paths into the bush, to share Bahá'u'lláh's message for the human race with the villagers.

They would spread a large, colourful mat on the grassy floor, where we sat in a circle and talked. It was, as always, the deepest joy to speak about the great Messengers of God throughout the Ages, and the coming of Bahá'u'lláh, in this great Day of fulfilment. They loved to hear about 'Abdu'l-Bahá and His wonderful life. Hospitality was spontaneous and always very generous. Food was piled onto large banana leaves and placed on the ground in the centre of the hand-woven carpet. Fish, with huge amounts of vegetables and fruit were brought as a loving gift, and it was always assigned to me, as their guest, to start eating first.

One day it was suggested that we should go to Fort Resolution, where Captain Cook had landed in 1774. We hired a truck for our journey, and all shared expenses. When we reached there, I discovered to my amazement, that the sandy beach was absolutely black. There were hot springs with little spurts of steam rising up. The heat was oppressive and we decided to have a swim. We had no bathing gear with us, and I happily waded in, wearing a thin, cotton sundress. Suddenly, a huge rolling swell towered over me, and I was thrown down beneath the ocean and totally submerged. It was very frightening. I struggled, feeling utterly powerless, wondering how I was going to reach the surface again. When, at last, I was able to stand up, water was streaming from my hair, eyes, nose and ears. It was scary and I was glad to get out as quickly as possible. In fact, we all stumbled for the shore with great haste.

Later in the day I had my second adventure. My friends were all eager to show me the volcano at close quarters, so we climbed the hilly slopes to the very top of Yassur. This was an amazing and rather frightening experience. It was growling and roaring down below, like a great angry giant, till it suddenly boiled up and flung its red-hot boulders high into the air. Donna and I stood, hand in hand, watching in fascination, and then running back, away from the side of the void. I was not enjoying this. We stumbled rather than walked, as we made our way, in the dark, down to where the truck was waiting for us. It was a great relief to climb inside and start for home.

By this time we were hungry, as we had scarcely eaten that day. Those Bahá'ís living in Tanna were used to going hungry, and I so much admired their wonderful spirit. Along the way, our driver stopped to buy some benzene at a little hut-like store. Eric and Denis bought some small loaves of fresh bread, which they shared between us. How ravenously we munched on this "manna from heaven," breaking chunks of bread with our hands. How delicious it was. The truck rolled along in the warm, dark night and I felt pure happiness within. I was dirty and covered with mosquito bites, especially my arms and back. There was no water for drinking, much less for a bath or shower.

Next day, before leaving for Port Vila, Donna, Sue and I held a short meeting about Bahá'í classes for the local children. They were thrilled that I had written lesson plans for children during my trip to Ghana, the previous year. Sue said that she could translate them from English to Bishlama, ready for me to type. We planned to find people in every village who would like to take these classes, and then we would hold an institute, using my previously prepared notes for the teachers' guidance.

Later in the day, Denis took me to the airport on his motorbike, and the local people smiled and waved to us as we bumped along the dusty roads. It was such a happy feeling. We sat on the grass chatting as we waited for the plane to arrive. Once aloft I settled into my seat, dishevelled and sun-tanned, feeling utterly contented. During the short flight, I saw several rainbows and a complete bow, a whole circle, which I had never seen before. It was very beautiful and I hoped fervently that it would act as a good omen.

At the airport Zoë and Anisa were waiting, also Barbara with her two sons, Daniel and Sam. They were excited to see me, Anisa waving with joy. The first thing she said to me, as she leapt into my arms, was, "Grandma! Your hair looks funny." My hair had been given a thorough soaking in the ocean, and was curly indeed. 'Macmbo' seemed like a palace, and I revelled in the luxury of a shower, and then a gorgeous meal that Zoë had prepared. It was wonderful to be able to wash my clothes of all the dust of Yassur, even though we had an indoor flood because of the torrential rain during that night.

Next morning we went to the Immigration Office to extend our visas for one more month. We were relieved and somewhat amazed that there were no problems. Later in

A group of the Friends at Port Resolution where Captain Cook landed.

Mount Yassur in action! Photograph courtesy of Mike Lyvers.

Mount Yassur and natives. Photograph courtesy of Mike Lyvers.

The Bahá'í House of Worship at sundown

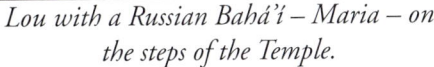

*Lou with a Russian Bahá'í – Maria – on
the steps of the Temple.*

the day, however, we received the drastic news that we would definitely not be granted permission to stay for a full year. Two members of the National Spiritual Assembly informed us, very sadly, that we had been given only one more month to remain in Vanuatu. We were shocked because, usually, the period for a tourist's visa was four months, and we were not even being allowed that. Our hopes and plans were crushed. What a blow! A reversal of all that we had worked for. That night, I wrote in my diary:

> "We have been to U.T.A. and booked our flight to Australia, and on to London, arriving in Gatwick on January 24th. What a shame, especially for Zoë. What efforts! What expense! And it has all come to nothing. It is incredible! I feel for her very much. Such a great disappointment – having travelled right across the world to run a kindergarten and fill one of our pioneer goals for the UK. Despite all our efforts, and emptying our resources, the doors have closed."

For myself, I felt deep down that, somehow, it was right, even though it had cost me the remainder of my modest savings, and the surrendering of my Life Assurance Policy. I continued, in my diary:

> "I have no idea what the future holds. The heat and humidity of Vanuatu are almost too much for me, at times. The dream of a Bahá'í School or orphanage has been with me for a very long time. God knows all that is in my heart and soul, and all things are possible to Him, He doeth whatsoever He willeth."

I lay awake, that night, thinking of the times when I had felt that my dream of working with small children was to be fulfilled. In India, at New Era School, I was invited to take classes for spiritual education for the little ones. Zoë and I had started making plans to go, when suddenly it all fell through. Again, the dream had come very close when we went to see that wonderful Bahá'í, Claire Gung, in her kindergarten. It was something I had longed to do for many years, but the situation in Uganda had then become extremely violent and unstable. We had been advised not to consider working in Auntie Claire's Kindergarten', at that time. The pattern, in Vanuatu, was being repeated again. I had been given the wonderful task of preparing lesson-plans for children in Ghana, just the year before, and that had been a cause of great happiness for me.

It was December, and the weather became hotter with each passing day. It made us feel very weak and limp. Sometimes Bryn and Meg would call and drive us to Erakor Island, for a swim. Anisa loved it. The white sandy beach, shaded by beautiful palms, and the clear green water made it a most delightful spot. We swam and had picnics, and I would feel the sheer wonder of being in such a lovely location. It seemed much like a dream, to be living in the South Pacific.

One morning Zoë and I took Anisa for a treat at the Rossie Hotel. We sat there drinking fruit juice, listening to three musicians who were singing and playing guitars. We relaxed with the tourists who had come into Port Vila for the day on the beautiful liner, The Canberra. It was Christmas, and we were basking in the brilliant sunshine of a tropical island. The ice and snow of England, and mince pies round the fire, seemed very, very far away.

December 28, was Anisa's fifth birthday. Zoë baked a lovely cake and iced her name on it. I started baking at a quarter to seven that morning, and made two dozen little fruit cakes and more than fifty mince-meat slices, in preparation for her party at three o'clock. Ten adults and eight children arrived, happily bearing gifts of delicious food. A wonderful assortment of sweet and savoury dishes, homemade cakes and fruit of every kind were soon arranged in a colourful display on the long table. Everyone joined in the games and competitions, amidst a great deal of fun and laughter. It was a joyful, never-to-be-forgotten birthday.

When Anisa had fallen asleep that night, I typed a letter for the National Spiritual Assembly of Vanuatu on behalf of Zoë and myself. I also included a report about my trip to Tanna. Next day we started to pack our belongings all over again for our departure from the Island. Our kindly neighbour, Mrs Ghosh, invited us to a tea party for New Year. Besides a delicious range of scrumptious foods she had decorated an enormous iced cake with the words "Happy New Year" and we realised how much we were going to miss her when we left.

Gradually, we began to set everything in motion for our return home. We discovered to our dismay that our tea-chests were going to cost a lot more travelling back, than when we had sent them from England. We were quoted £350 Vatu to Hull. It seemed a terrible waste of money, but we realised that we could now contemplate making our pilgrimage to the Holy-Land, which we had booked for March 1983. It was a bright goal ahead of us, to lighten the dark cloud of disappointment. It would have been impossible for us to go from the Pacific, as the cost would have been far beyond our means. We knew that finances were going to be difficult but it was at least within the bounds of possibility.

On January 3, we went shopping and called at the Shipping Agents to see Mr Naturelle. From there, we strolled along to Bloody Mary's, in the sweltering afternoon heat, and drank our thick milk shakes through straws, for the last time. That evening we invited Mrs Ghosh to a slide show of the Green Light Expedition', a recording of Ruhiyyih Khanum's amazing travels in South America. We had a lovely time together, and Mrs Ghosh looked very sad at the thought of our leaving.

As the days until our departure dwindled, we had many visitors calling, including our dear friends from Tanna. Sue and I had become very close and she and Denis seemed unable to stay away. Those last few weeks were very hectic and I was truly thankful when everything was finished. We said our last farewells to Vanuatu and everyone with whom we had shared so much. On board the plane to Australia we had very mixed feelings in our hearts. There was so much to reflect upon. Our wonderful friends, Diane and Merhdad, welcomed us back once again with warmth and love. As they were going to be away on vacation, we were taken to the home of a Persian lady called Nahid. Her husband, Behaj, drove us to the Bahá'í Temple for one last visit. How lovely it was, serene, powerful and so majestic. Little wonder it is that these temples have been referred to as silent teachers. After several days in New South Wales, where we had received overwhelming hospitality and kindness, we were driven by car to the Kingsford Smith Airport for our flight home.

It was January 23, 1983 and our plane was delayed from 9.40am to 2pm, and we had chits to the value of AS$5.60 so we could enjoy breakfast. Young Anisa was, thankfully, an excellent little traveller joyfully taking everything in her stride. An exciting and challenging phase of service had come to an end, and the sense of disappointment it left had now to be overcome. We returned home to Wales, and to wait once more for the arrival of our tea chests. Our friends, in an effort to reassure us, said that we had done everything possible to fulfil our service in Vanuatu and therefore, we had not failed. Eventually, we accepted that there must have been a hidden wisdom behind all the frustrations and disappointment. Our little five-year-old started attending Douglas Road Primary School, which was just a few minutes walk from our home. She adjusted very quickly to our completely different way of life, and the cooler, more changeable climate of the United Kingdom.

16

FROM THE HOLY LAND BACK TO CANADA

The joy and excitement of our pilgrimage did much to heal us of the disappointment we felt after returning from Vanuatu. This was my third journey to the Holy Land, but it was Zoë's first visit to those wonderful holy places. It was a deeply moving experience to be once more in those heavenly gardens of such beauty and peace. It was an added joy to have my five-year-old granddaughter with us, as well. I was very moved to see that little figure kneeling so reverently in the Shrine of the Báb.

Hand of the Cause of God, Mr Furutan called her to sit with him, and with all the happy spontaneity of childhood, she sat on his knee and talked to him. There was a small boy of three from Alaska on pilgrimage with his parents. He and Anisa had a great time together and became inseparable. How much they could understand the significance of those most holy places on earth we cannot know, but I am sure that the spiritual atmosphere and the beautiful gardens must have affected their souls.

Our nine unforgettable days, in the shelter of Mount Carmel, God's holy mountain, serenely glided by as in a dream, far from the world with its agitation and bustle, breathing in the fragrances of a spiritual beauty quite impossible to describe. My inner being felt renewed, and once home, I was eager to travel again for Bahá'u'lláh.

A few months later, I was overjoyed to get a letter from my friends Jessie and Nick in Canada inviting me once more to visit them and make a teaching-trip to Ontario. Although it was always exciting making preparations for a trip overseas, I felt very much the separation there would be from Zoë and Anisa who watched me doing my packing, while asking many questions about how long I was going to be away from home. With many cuddles and reassurances about my return, she and her mum went with me to the little station in Colwyn Bay to say goodbye and wave me off on my long trip. It was going to be wonderful to see my old friends again in their home in Ajax. This time I was being asked to make a trip on behalf of the Canadian National Teaching Committee. This was even more exciting and a big challenge. I was presented with an itinerary, which covered many Bahá'í communities in South Western Ontario. It was decided that Jessie and I would travel in Nick's car and that I would do the driving. Our trip lasted from September 20, to October 21, 1983.

Jessie had booked all the places we were to visit, and the Bahá'ís in every community had eagerly asked us to include them in our itinerary. Never before, or since, have I been given such an extended teaching-trip, with a meeting every day and sometimes two. I really had to pray for assistance, inspiration and particularly the strength to fulfil such an arduous programme. Before every meeting I prayed that my words would be clothed in meaning and spiritual fragrance, and that the hearts of those who listened would be touched by God's love.

Driving Nick's car was not difficult and even driving on the right-hand side of the road presented no problems. It was such a great adventure. Jessie and I had so many humorous moments, and there was lots of laughter.

Our first meeting on September 20, was in Stouffville and was to start at eight in the evening. We set off in high

Jessie and me ready for the Big Trip

Newmarket, Ontario – with Barbara Tree

spirits and had a really happy time in the home of Mrs Alizadeh who gave us such warm hospitality. They asked me to speak about 'Abdu'l-Bahá. Many friends were there, including a young Bahá'í named Robert, who had once visited Ireland for five weeks. We talked about Ireland and Africa and the many people known to us both. We also chatted about the Canadian Bahá'ís who were in Vanuatu. It made the world seem a very small place, like a united global village.

Next day we had a gorgeous lunch at Jim and Bonnie Heiderman's home together with some of their friends. Bonnie had kindly prepared a delicious potato and cheese dish, salad and salmon, eggs, muffins, tea and iced cake! We talked about the Faith and shared experiences and anecdotes. Before leaving we had prayers and then we drove to our next port of call. I began to feel very tired.

We visited houses on the Rama Indian Reservation on September 22, and met some wonderful people. A meeting was held at 2pm. and again in the evening. Jessie's young granddaughter, Julia, performed some lovely Indian dances that she had learned at New Era School in Panchgani. Once again my talk was about 'Abdu'l-Bahá.

On September 23 we went to Newmarket. No, not the horse racing course in England, but in Ontario. Many towns and cities in Canada are named after ones in Britain. This was a full day indeed. There was a morning meeting starting at half-past-nine for women only. Twenty-two ladies and seventeen children were present. A few of the ladies had been attending for some time and were interested to hear more about the Faith. I spoke about the teachings and my travels overseas. Everyone stayed for lunch, and the meeting went on until almost three o' clock. There was a lovely atmosphere making everyone feel close. At another meeting that evening they were mostly men. The responses, and especially the questions, were lively. Someone in the audience asked whether Bahá'ís believe in Jesus as well as Bahá'u'lláh. I explained that Bahá'ís believe in the founders of all the great world religions, because they each brought a revelation from the same divine Source. We don't make any distinction between them. This opened up more discussion and the atmosphere was very warm and friendly.

Next day we were off to Tottenham. This time we drove to the home of Jerry and Brenda Kotras, for another evening meeting. Again I spoke about 'Abdu'l-Bahá. The group of eleven included four Persian friends. Brenda and Jerry have two children, and I slept in the little boy's room. I felt very contented that night.

Then on Sunday September 25, we set off to see the Alliston community. This time I was invited to be the main speaker at a public meeting at two o'clock. The friends there were very kind and afterwards I spoke about our time in Ireland. There was a moment when I felt that tears were not too far away, as I was reminded of those happy days with my husband and son. There was a newspaper reporter present and photographs were taken. The heading in the newspaper the next day was "Turner will speak". Both Jess and I found this very amusing.

There was a Nineteen Day Feast in Barrie the following night, with a pot-luck supper beforehand. There was a most beautiful spirit in that room. Our lovely host and hostess were Mr and Mrs Faramaz Sajed. After the programme of prayers and readings from the scriptures, I was asked to speak. My talk lasted about thirty to forty minutes and I talked about the immortality of the soul and the beautiful spiritual worlds of God where we will be reunited with our loved ones. I also spoke of my search for truth and the difference that finding the Faith has made to my own life. Everyone seemed very happy and full of appreciation for my coming so far to see them.

When we arrived in Orillia on September 27 and made our way to the home of Patricia Katari, we were graciously invited for dinner. They had arranged an open meeting that was hosted by another Bahá'í couple, Georgina and Ian Dowdell. They asked if I would speak about spiritual assemblies and the Bahá'í World Congress, in 1963. I shared my thoughts simply. Because there was no room for us to stay over, Jess and I drove to a motel and this was my first experience of staying in one. We were very comfortable and both enjoyed a good night's sleep.

At the Midlands and Christian Islands Indian Reserve on September 28 we had an open meeting arranged by Bill and Esther Devonshire. Eleven Bahá'ís and two people enquiring about the Faith came along. I spoke about my own spiritual search and of the joy of being a Bahá'í. Everyone seemed to appreciate it very much, and one of the ladies, Sylvia, told me that she had attended meetings for two years but had, only that evening, felt her heart moved. I hoped that her search would bring her ever closer to this new and exciting Revelation. The next day I visited a school and spoke on my travels for the Faith. The children loved hearing about my adventures. A little later that day we had to make a hurried visit to the optometrist because Jessie had broken the frame of her glasses. It was a good thing that she wasn't driving as her sight was very poor without them. It took us some time to find one who would do the repair for her. It meant a lot of driving around the town, and stopping to ask for directions. In spite of our dilemma we could still see the funny side, especially when we tried at first to fix them with some sticking plaster and both of us ended up with our usual bout of the giggles. Eventually we were successful in having the glasses mended and we then continued happily with our trip. Bill drove us in beautiful sunshine and ended up at a lovely restaurant. That night we booked into yet another motel, called The Shamrock, where we talked and relaxed till drifting off to sleep.

We had been given the following day free of any meetings, a rest day to re-charge our batteries. What is a rest day without excellent cuisine? It started with breakfast at MacDonalds, with hash browns, scrambled egg and muffins, tea and orange juice. Then we had a marvellous two-and-a-half hour 'Cruise of 30,000 Islands', the greatest collection of fresh water islands in the world. It is a huge tourist attraction and I was thrilled to go on such a wonderful trip. It was beautiful and peaceful, gliding quietly along on the smooth water, in glorious sunshine. We drifted past many tiny islands, mile after mile on either side of us. It was the most restful few hours one could imagine, and we had needed to relax. Naturally, we took plenty of snaps and then drank hot chocolate on board and later lemon meringue pie, with a pot of tea. Could anything be more delicious except another slice of lemon meringue pie? Then we had a drive around the lovely countryside before starting out for Owen Sound. Unfortunately we were given wrong directions and got lost. It was growing dark so we booked into the Bay Court Hotel. What a gloriously hot, relaxing day it had been.

Saugeen Indian Reserve was our goal on October 3, and a lovely lady named Geraldine made us so welcome in her home. She had two daughters, Cindy who was in her teens, and a very delicate little girl called Nicole. We discussed many aspects of the Faith, and Geraldine was especially interested in the teachings on healing. I think she found it comforting because of Nicole's fragile condition. We had prayers together before leaving.

We moved on to Goderich on October 5 on a hectic schedule. There were so many meetings and moving around that it is now only a blur of warm excitement in my memory. When we arrived the next day on the Forest and Kettlepoint Reserve I was feeling very tired and my head was throbbing. Our bodies were feeling tense, while our spirits were full of the joys of our trip. After a short rest, we were ready to sally forth again and, as always, with the help and sustaining power of Bahá'u'lláh. Looking back at this special time of extended travelling for the Faith, I know full well that it was possible only with the help of those unseen angels, souls who have gone on to the

Bahá'ís in Sarnia – Ontario.

spiritual worlds of God and are closer to the Almighty. It was so interesting to visit the Indian reserves and such a special privilege. The people there have impressive qualities of strength and humility that is difficult to put into words.

In Sarnia on October 7 the Bahá'ís planned and advertised a public meeting. I had been asked to speak about "Living in a New Day". There was a great amount of interest shown and plenty of discussion. They wanted to know more about the Messengers of God Who bring a Divine Springtime whenever They appear on earth. The way Their Revelation affects the hearts of people everywhere, like in nature, when spring comes, it brings fresh beautiful life to the world and everything is made new. Their teachings awaken the inner qualities of the soul, and this helps towards our spiritual transformation. Jess and I felt the evening had been really rewarding.

On October 9, we returned to Ajax for Thanksgiving Day. It teemed with rain all the way home. Driving was not easy as it was very grey and misty on Highway 401 with a great deal of traffic. The windscreen wipers swept rapidly from side to side as the rain lashed down in torrents. I had to concentrate intently, straining my eyes to see what lay ahead. Inwardly, I felt very happy, as though my loved ones in that unseen world were very close. Nick and their daughter, Lynn, were full of excitement, and so delighted to see us when we reached home. In spite of the overpowering tiredness,

With Bahá'ís in London, Ontario. Harper Pettipiece, from England, is in the back row.

sleep evaded me and I remained wide awake all night. This happens sometimes, when we get overtired, and it made me feel really shattered on the following day. We were invited to the home of Pat and Bob Smith for a wonderful Thanksgiving dinner. I was relieved that I had time to catch up on personal things like washing and trimming my hair, and time to iron some of my clothes, and repack my bags.

We went to London on October 11. Funny, all these familiar names but in the wrong place! Again, this was London, Ontario. Jess and I had a very busy morning, getting ready for our trip. We had a sandwich for lunch, and then set off. It was lovely and sunny, and we drove from Ajax on Highway 401 making very good time. That day was young John's birthday, and needless to say he was very much in my thoughts. The memory of that incredibly painful time of parting flooded back to me. I was reassured, however, that he was safe in the spiritual worlds of God and working for Him in whatever capacity required by a loving Father.

We stopped in Cambridge for afternoon tea and cinnamon toast. Yes, I was getting even more confused by names! It brought more memories of John who had gone to university in Cambridge back home in England. At five o'clock we arrived in London and shared a huge pizza in a very nice restaurant.

We had difficulty, at first, in finding Riverside Road, which is where the evening meeting was to take place. Our kind hosts were Rene and Noora Steinburg. While I was speaking, I nearly wept when talking about Dad's death, and Jessie said that she felt an amazingly strong psychic power, which was almost overwhelming! There was a lady from the West Indies present, who was very interested in learning more about the Faith. What a small world. Among the guests was Harper Pettipiece whom I had known in Oakham in England. I was very emotionally moved on this night.

On October 13, a storm blew up on our way to Nanticoke. It was, in fact, a tornado. I have never experienced anything like it in my life. I drove through a cloudburst and couldn't see any car lights in front or from behind. The windscreen wipers were totally useless in such torrential rain, and the wind had uprooted huge trees. I just drove slowly forward into a grey mist. It became so wild that we decided to stop the car as soon as we could. At last, to our great relief, a motel loomed out of the mist and gloom, and, bracing ourselves to face the drenching rain and gale, we scrambled out of the car and dashed for shelter.

We resumed our journey, after an enjoyable lunch in the comfort and warmth of the restaurant. It was difficult to find the address we'd been given, in a place called Peacock Point. Several times, either Jessie or I would venture out of the car, and struggling against the raging force of the tornado, peer at the mailboxes at the front of each garden, looking for the number we wanted. It was really difficult to remain upright. In fact, we were getting more than a little frightened that at any moment, we might be blown into the lake that skirted the small houses. After what seemed an eternity we found the house and, with immense relief, were being welcomed with great warmth into the cosy home of Gail and Mike Emberson. They had a baby girl, just two weeks old. The open meeting that night was held in the home of another young couple, the

Englerts, who lived close by. It was amazing that twelve people came to listen to my talk in spite of the storm.

Jessie and I drove to the shopping mall in Haldimand next day, October 14, and spent some time there, before finding the home of Helen Kelly, a Bahá'í devoted to work with the North American Indians. After a short rest, we went to see a wonderful Indian woman, Emily General. Again it was the Nineteen Day Feast day, so, after prayers and readings, they called on me to speak. Helen asked me if I would repeat what I'd said the previous evening, because she enjoyed it so much. It was mainly a talk on how I searched for truth, and was guided to find the Bahá'í Faith.

Next day I was asked to address a gathering of the Indian Council, on Six Nations Reserve. The talk was to be about our own spiritual development and I had prepared it with much thought. Sadly, it had to be cancelled, much to everyone's disappointment. Instead, it was decided to have a get-together in Helen and Dan Kelly's home. Jess and I bought some groceries as a small contribution. Quite a large number of people came, Bahá'ís as well as their friends. I spoke about my travels for the Faith. Jessie showed a film of the World Congress in 1963. It was midnight when Dan asked her to show slides of Iceland, where she and Nick had pioneered for several years. In the morning we visited again and spent a lovely time with Emily General, a woman of such strong character and with a great spirit.

We drove to Dunneville where a pot-luck meal was arranged for five o'clock. A beautiful devotional programme had been prepared for the evening and a copy was given to each of us as a keepsake. After my talk one of the Dunneville members, Ron Spears, thanked us warmly, and said that a newspaper reporter would call and see us next morning with his wife, Mary-Lou. We were up bright and early, despite being very tired, and were ready when the reporter arrived, together with Mary-Lou and another Bahá'í called Annette. Photos were taken and the reporter seemed keen to hear more about the Faith. Later we drove to Port Colburn and sat by the lake after walking in a small park. I felt desperately tired and, on top of this, was suffering indigestion. Often I was made rudely aware that my physical body can become weary and weak, even though my spirit is eager to keep flying. All tiredness vanished in the beautiful, loving welcome of our hostess, Pidge. She showed us to our separate rooms, very luxurious with large double beds. After an excellent dinner we were taken to the home of a Persian Bahá'í couple. It was a happy gathering made more special when I learned that one of the young men said that he knew Bahman, a pupil in my dorm from New Era High School, in India.

In the morning we talked with Pidge till after 11am and then drove to Niagara Falls. Jessie had a headache and was also feeling the pace of our joyful activities. We went for lunch and then had a walk to the Falls. It was rather cold, so we booked into a motel and had a good meal. Later, we sat in our little beds and did some writing. How much we needed the rest and the sleep so it was lights-out at 9.45pm.

October 19, was the last day of our trip. We met Mr and Mrs Baghdadi and their daughter, Haifa. Mr Baghdadi had met the Master, 'Abdu'l-Bahá, who died in 1921.

Emily General – North American Indian on the Six Nations Reservation.

What a privilege it was just to be with him. They all radiated that indefinable quality of spirituality and humility. In the evening Jess and I had supper with a very gentle lady, who seemed rather sad. Her son had died about two years ago as result of a plane crash. My heart went out to her, as I know only too well what that great loss can mean. She knew that I understood and it comforted her. I have found that our sufferings can be a blessing to others, when we can truly relate to what they are going through.

In bed that night, Jess and I had an attack of the giggles. It seemed to act as a release and relaxed us. Our Trip to Orangeville, which had been planned for the following day, had been cancelled. There had been some sort of mix-up with arrangements for the public meeting, and it was too late for other plans to be made. We were naturally disappointed but this meant that we were free to make our journey home to Ajax, where dear Nick and Lynn were waiting for our return with great eagerness.

Looking back on this teaching-trip, I marvel at the amazing help from the unseen world that made it all possible. The outpouring of energy and inspiration, day after day, was given from a source beyond our own human power. Bahá'u'lláh has promised that if we arise and place our whole trust and confidence in Him, He will assist us with a power from on High. We have to take that first trusting step, and then go forward on our mission to aid his Cause. I look back to that time, with gratitude and thankfulness for such an opportunity. Truly, I thank God!

Joyful home-coming from Anisa – birthday cake and all.

17

RETURN JOURNEYS

I could not have dreamed in 1970, when our little family left Southport to make our home in Ireland that I would return again to Southport sixteen years later. On that summer's day, when we drove with great excitement to catch the ferry for our adventure across the Irish Sea, I basked comfortably in the loving presence of my husband and son. Now in 1986 I was a grandmother with a dear eight-year-old granddaughter and her lovely mum, but without my husband and our dear young John.

I thought of all the changes that had taken place during those sixteen years. Having lived in Ireland until 1975, we had moved back to England for John to work at the Bahá'í Publishing Trust in Oakham, and then we had gone as pioneers to Anglesey, where three of my loved ones passed to the next world. I recalled the seven years that had been spent in Colwyn Bay with Zoë and Anisa. They had been special years when many exciting trips were made across the world. Here I was, about to make my home in Southport for the second time, where we were needed to serve on the Spiritual Assembly (now known as Sefton). A lot of things had changed with the passing of time. The whole experience was now quite different. The greatest change was in myself. I am sure of that. I had now become part of a very different threesome. The years in between held such depths of joy and sorrow. I was happy nonetheless, and there was much to do for the Faith in that area of Southport. We began to hold fireside meetings in our home in North Road, and as a result some people became Bahá'ís. Several Bahá'í Conventions were held in Southport in the Floral Hall on the promenade. We arranged meetings with the R.E. teachers of several schools in the area, and on one occasion I was asked to give a talk to the Business and Professional Women's Association, which was received with great warmth.

Anisa had won a scholarship to Sunnymede Primary School, an excellent private school, where she studied like a student beyond her years. They taught French, music, art and pottery, with open days for the children and their parents on the sports field. Strawberry teas were served to the delighted spectators, much to my personal satisfaction! What with ballet classes and piano lessons, it was a full and happy time for our little girl.

We very often went to meetings in the Liverpool Bahá'í Centre. My sister, Pat, was secretary of that local Spiritual Assembly and, because she lived next door, she always made sure that the fire was switched on in the winter, and the coffee cups were set out in readiness for the meetings. She was absolutely devoted to the Faith and realised deeply, the importance and significance of the Spiritual Assembly. We used to meet every week to have lunch in the Art Centre in Southport. She was a great companion and friend, and we both had received the extra blessing of becoming Bahá'ís. This made an even stronger bond than the one we had enjoyed since childhood. It was lovely to share a strong sense of humour often resulting in bouts of giggling not easy to control.

Our days were very full, and Zoë was eventually offered a teaching post in one of the local primary schools. A year after we had moved into Southport, my longing to make another teaching-trip to Africa opened up the thrilling prospect of a second visit to Ghana.

At the end of June 1987, preparations for my trip were well under way. The International Goals Committee had contacted me with the news that a young Persian Bahá'í, Foujan Kamtarin, from Brighton, was making her first teaching-trip and was going to Ghana. We made plans by telephone to travel together. She was very excited though a little bit nervous, which was understandable. In the weeks before we were due to set off, we had many long discussions about visas, anti-malaria tablets, mosquito repellent and the sort of things that would be needed in a hot African country. My experience helped her a lot. I was beginning to see myself as a seasoned traveller.

Although we had never met one another, it felt as though we were old friends when we finally saw each other at Heathrow Airport. It was June 29, the day after my wedding anniversary, and it was a very happy event for me to be going back to my beloved Africa especially at this time. Once more I had booked with Aeroflot, the Russian Airline, mainly because it was cheaper than most of the others. It meant that we would be spending ten hours in Moscow, and this was a new experience for Foujan.

We had each received letters from the National Spiritual Assembly of Ghana, with a very full itinerary prepared for us. We were being asked to teach and proclaim the Faith right across the Ashanti and Western Regions, and to hold children's classes, and organise deepening sessions for the Bahá'ís on a wide variety of subjects, including the role of the mother in training her children.

Arriving in Accra in the burning African sun, amidst huge throngs of people scrambling and pushing forward, with frantic efforts to get their taxis, was quite overwhelming for us. On my last trip, Eleanor had been there to meet me. Now we were on our own to sink or swim. At last, we managed to get a taxi that would take us to the Bahá'í Centre, but we soon realised the driver wanted to charge us far more than the actual cost of the journey. We were very relieved when we arrived to find that there was a Bahá'í in the office and someone who would confront the taxi driver on our behalf. We were thankful also for the loving welcome and the cooling drink, after our fourteen hour flight from Moscow.

Fujan and I shared a room in the Bahá'í Centre, and after lighting our mosquito-coils, settled down to sleep. Humidity made it difficult to rest peacefully, but our happiness could not be clouded by any small detail such as this. To be in Africa again, and to find myself once more in Ghana, was an irrepressible joy. We were escorted next morning by Tiati, a Bahá'í from Cameroon now living in Ghana. He showed us the large market which Fujan and I found fascinating. The colourful stalls piled high with myriad different fruits and vegetables, and the smiling faces surrounding us. Babies were tied snugly on their mothers' backs, sleeping under the scorching midday sun. We were so engrossed in everything going on around us that time passed really quickly. The three of us had been in the market for more than four hours without seeking any shade. Tiati took us to a small café for lunch. After buying fruit and postcards we returned to base.

Next day we started our itinerary and made our way to the villages of Kwashikuman and Dome. I always loved going to villages, whether it was in Nigeria, East Africa or in Ghana. The inhabitants were always so happy and friendly. In Kwashikuman everyone gathered around beneath the shade of a huge old tree in the middle of a large sandy clearing. We talked about the education and spiritual training of children, and many questions were asked. They were especially interested in Bahá'u'lláh's teachings on marriage and burial. Small children slept on their mother's knee, the older ones sitting quietly, their eyes always shining and eager, as though drinking in every word we said.

We had a lovely afternoon with Tiati, who was thoroughly enjoying his self-imposed duty as our guide and helper. He took us to the beach in Accra, where we comfortably paddled at the water's edge after burning our feet on the hot, silver sand in order to get to the water. It was a delightful spot with many tall, graceful palms dotted along the beach. In the evening, we visited the home of Fredua, a Bahá'í living in Accra who was holding his first ever open-house meeting. I felt it an honour to be asked to speak on that special occasion. The subject chosen was my spiritual search for truth and how I discovered the Faith. This is something that seemed to appeal to so many people wherever I went.

An institute had been arranged in the Bahá'í Centre for the following weekend. Many Bahá'ís had been invited from surrounding villages and in the end, a large number did attend. Various aspects of the teachings were discussed but I was especially requested to speak about pioneering for the Faith. After a very full and happy day, Foujan and I retired to bed, full of excitement as the institute went ahead.

It was Sunday, and everyone gathered in the large room that overlooked a small but very pretty garden. About an hour had passed when we heard someone speaking urgently outside the door. Suddenly the meeting was disturbed with the sad news that Joseph Musa, a member of the Ghanaian National Spiritual Assembly, had passed away in his sleep. Such consternation and shock was experienced by everyone. All our thoughts and prayers were focused on his widow Blanche and their young son, Baba. He was only ten years old and it was he who found his father dead in bed.

The institute came to an abrupt and sorrowful end, and those present left in grief to return to their villages. I was one of a small group who set off for Blanche's home, to pay our respects and convey our condolences. She was distraught, and my heart

In front of the Bahá'í Centre in Accra

yearned for her, as I understand only too well her grief and anguish. On my previous
trip to Ghana, in 1981, I had been very close to Blanche, and she was aware of my past
bereavements. Now, in the midst of her deep sorrow, she turned to me and asked if I
would move into her home and remain with her until after the burial.

My proposed itinerary was cancelled by the National Spiritual Assembly, as they
felt it was important to give whatever help and comfort we could to Blanche, at this
grief-stricken time. I packed a small bag and moved into her home. I had taken one of
my notebooks with me, when I left England, which contained some of my favourite
quotations and passages from the Bahá'í Writings. A number of them were beautiful
teachings about life after death and the immortality of the soul. Blanche and I would
sit quietly together, in the fresh early morning, with the garden before us, and there
we would read from my little book, and say our prayers. This quiet time of peace and
tranquillity refreshed our spirits and granted much needed strength for Blanche to

face the day. We also prepared the devotional programme for her dear Joseph's funeral from readings we thought most suitable.

Every day many people came to the house to pay their respects, and most of them remained all day. At times, the garden seemed to be full of visitors, and I learned that this is a custom in Ghana. In the midst of all this, I began to feel unwell with some sort of stomach bug. I felt extremely weak and sick, and unable to eat food. This continued for several days and I tried desperately to carry on as usual without telling anyone about my condition.

Joseph's funeral did not take place until two weeks after his death. My itinerary was still on hold. Meanwhile, Fujan went off to the villages to continue the work that had been planned for us. I felt a sense of calm acceptance and detachment about what was happening, with a strong feeling that I was where I was supposed to be. The members of the National Assembly expressed the same view, saying that perhaps one of the reasons I had been sent to Ghana was to help Blanche and Baba through this time of grief.

Blanche worked in the Swissair Travel Agents in Accra. Once or twice she took me to see her office but mostly I stayed with her at home, where the visitors kept coming day after day. I found this particularly difficult, as no one spoke, and I felt unsure about what I should be doing. I wrote in my diary:

> The stream of visitors continues.
> Groups under the trees, in the garden, women with their small children.
> I took some 'snapshots' today, of one group.
> I know that Blanche is enduring a great inward strain.

One of Blanche's neighbours, who called fairly frequently, asked me whether I needed anything from the market. I gave her money and asked her to get tomatoes, a couple of corncobs and two tins of sardines. To my dismay, she returned with a huge bag of corn and a massive bag of tangerines, enough to last me for about three months! She explained that they hadn't any sardines, so she had bought the fruit instead.

July 9 was a holy day, when we gathered at noon to commemorate the Martyrdom of the Báb. We met in the Bahá'í Centre and I was asked to take part in the devotional programme. It was lovely for so many of us to be together, though our happiness was tinged by our feelings of sorrow for the loss of dear Joseph.

Blanche's two daughters, Koko and Anne, arrived from the United States, where they lived. Blanche, herself, was a black American, but had been in Ghana for several years after her marriage to Joseph. It was arranged that his body would be buried on the Bahá'í Temple land, which was wonderful because he had devoted so much loving service towards the purchase of that land. It was thrilling to think that, one day, a beautiful Temple would stand on that sacred spot.

It was anticipated that many, many people would be attending the funeral, and there was a lot of work to be done in preparation for such a large gathering. One morning, two workmen arrived to paint the garden wall. Blanche and I sat and talked quietly. She wept heartbrokenly. Then we both prayed. My own tears flowed with her, as I tried to offer the comfort that is in the heart of one who has felt that anguish and knows its pain. She asked me about the death of my own husband, which had also been very sudden. I sincerely hoped that sharing this might bring her some fragment of solace and strength. The strain was almost unbearable for her. The days went by slowly. Blanche was being very brave. One day, I suddenly realised that my clothes were completely unsuitable for attending a funeral. This was emphasised for me when I realised that such an occasion in Ghana would be very formal and that those attending would be dressed accordingly. It was going to be embarrassing if I, as an overseas visitor, appeared in my white casual clothes and sandals. Blanche suggested having a blouse made in black material by a dressmaker friend of hers. I was relieved by this suggestion, while wondering which skirt I should wear with it. The night before the funeral I sat in my bedroom until the early hours, desperately trying to turn a long, dark coloured housecoat into a suitable skirt. With some borrowed shoes, slightly too big for me, I felt far from being adequately dressed for such an occasion. Who, setting out for a teaching-trip, would have foreseen that they might attend a funeral?

At last, the day of the funeral arrived. Chairs, for the large numbers of people who were expected were placed in rows in the garden. They were delivered very early in the morning, along with a large canopy, which was put in place as a shield from the sun. There was a lot of activity going on and there was much tension for dear Blanche, almost every step of the way. The coffin should have been brought to the house before eight-thirty in the morning, but it was more than two hours late and this caused much anxiety for her. Friends and guests started to arrive in great numbers. They looked very impressive in their magnificent robes, and many wore traditional costume. Chiefs and drummers arrived, everyone blending in a marvellous pageant of colour. At least a thousand people poured into the garden. It was an amazing sight. I felt very drab and very white amidst that wonderful throng, which presented such a rich tapestry.

The vast garden filled to overflowing. Many had to stand, while others had to leave because there was no room. The sun grew hotter every moment, while we waited for Joseph's body to be brought into the house. Then, following the custom, we filed slowly around the coffin, so that we could say our last goodbyes. It was a deeply moving experience. Many people wept for he was greatly loved.

The devotional readings were very beautifully read. The prayers of Bahá'u'lláh rose into the vast blue African sky. The air was filled with delightful fragrances. It was a farewell for Joseph and a proclamation of his deep love for Bahá'u'lláh. It was exciting to be standing on the Bahá'í Temple land for his burial later in the day, where crowds had gathered on the hillside. My heart felt honoured to be present at such a historic event, and I thanked God for bringing me back to my beloved Ghana.

After the funeral was over, Blanche agreed to return to America with her daughters,

Anne and Koko. I was uncertain what to do next. Fujan and Tiati had returned from their village teaching trip, and Fujan's time in Ghana would soon be coming to an end. Travelling on my own was a thing I felt rather unsure about. One of my plans had been to go up north to see Bill and Paulina Brown in Tamali. The Bahá'ís in my own community back home had been sending tea-chests full of materials there, such as books, writing paper, pencils, crayons and similar things for their local primary school. We had also sent towels, blankets and clothing for babies who had been abandoned and were staying in a small orphanage in Tamali.

In answer to my earnest prayers for help, Mary Tanyi, wife of Enoch, and daughter-in-law of David Tanyi (Knight of Bahá'u'lláh) came to my rescue. She suggested that I should travel with her and her two small sons as far as Kumasi. My relief was immense. She was my guardian angel and rescued me from my dilemma. How happy and secure I felt to have this little family as travelling companions.

We went to Kumasi by coach. It was a long hot journey of some six hours, travelling along the dusty and uneven roads. We arrived, extremely tired, at Esther and David's home, where I was given a most wonderfully loving reception. I was happy to stay with them for two nights. The little boys were very sweet, and I so much enjoyed watching them being bathed by their grandmother, outside in the sunshine. They were called Nakhjavani and Morsen after two devoted and well-known Bahá'ís. I was glad that they responded happily to my being there, despite the fact that they had very seldom seen anyone with white skin.

I was thrilled when dear Mary suggested travelling north to Tamali with me, to visit Bill and Paulina Brown. We started out very early in the morning. I woke at half-past-three and was ready to leave the house by four o'clock. I managed to get everything I needed into two shoulder bags, one borrowed from Esther. Happily, I set off accompanied by Mary and Enoch. He was taking us to the bus station, but we had to get a taxi first. It was still dark and fine rain was falling. I felt a glow of excitement at the thought of another adventure ahead.

When we reached the State Transport office, Enoch negotiated with the man in charge and eventually bought our tickets with the promise of good seats. Mary and I wandered off to get something to eat as neither of us had had breakfast. The food looked tempting, but, as everything was open to the dusty air and flies, my appetite instantly wore off. To have another stomach bug is extremely difficult to cope with when so far away from home. But as I had to eat something, I found a little stall and bought a roll with fried egg, and some tea. Mary got some Coke for the journey and then we went off to look for a toilet that was not actually in full view of the crowded station yard.

The journey was long and hot, bouncing over potholes in the road, for miles and miles. Evermore passengers were taken on board, until the bus was crammed to overflowing. Inwardly, I smiled at the situation, having someone's head resting on my shoulder and another lady sitting on my feet pressed against my legs. Along the way

Bill and Paulina Brown in Tamali.

The tea-chests for the orphanage had arrived

Heart-breaking visit to the orphanage.

*Paulina and Bill's three lovely children
Hans, Jeffrey and Michael.*

the bus stopped. Everyone took for granted that these short stops were to allow passengers to urinate. This was always expressed openly, without embarrassment, and most of the people just stayed near the side of the road. Mary and I walked quite a long distance to find somewhere more private. This proved almost impossible. Then we heard the bus horn blowing loudly so we had to run, laughing, rather quickly back to the bus.

Hours later we arrived in Tamali, terribly hot and covered with red dust. Thirsty and dishevelled we reached the home of Bill and Paulina and were gathered lovingly inside. We were served with tea and toast, cold meat and cheese. Their electricity went off, which meant that there was no fan, and they were also temporarily out of running water. I managed to bathe with a single bucket of cool water that felt absolutely wonderful. My hair felt stiff with dust and grease, and to be able to wash it was like a gift from heaven.

While Paullina was preparing a delicious cooked meal for us, I spent a welcome relaxing time talking with Bill. Like me he was also from Liverpool. He said that my sister Pat had helped him a great deal in the past to understand the Faith. He called her his spiritual mother. This was a strong spiritual link between us. We made plans to visit the orphanage that very evening, but torrential rain had started so we decided not to venture out. The wind blew fiercely around the house and whipped up to quite a gale. An hour or so later, we received some wonderful news, that the tea chests from England had, at long last, arrived. They had been standing in the port since April. It was now July.

Next morning, after breakfast, we started out for the orphanage with Bill. When we arrived, we were greeted very warmly by Sister Carmelina, who was responsible for overseeing the running of the orphanage. I wanted to see it but also dreaded the thought. There were twelve toddlers and young babies, whose mothers had either died or were unable to keep them. It was a deeply moving experience to see those little souls, completely helpless and unloved, who had been deprived of practically everything. Four women received a small allowance from the government to look after them in relays. The babies were lying on the floor or in one of the few cots, without any covers. Lonely and undernourished, they were not developing.

The surroundings were so drab, with bare walls and floors. As soon as I picked up one of them and held them, the baby's natural instinct was to rest its little head against my shoulder. It was dreadful and my throat ached with a terrible sadness. The babies were so small and thin, and were very much undersized. I bent over a small cot and looked into the eyes of a baby boy. He gazed back at me. There was contact in that long gaze, so I lifted him into my arms and held him close. How can a baby survive without love? What must it feel like to be lying in isolation, with nothing whatsoever to stimulate the thoughts or senses? I picked up a little girl, and she snuggled into my neck with so much trust. I thought of my own young granddaughter back home in England. Why can't every child in this world receive love and care, and warmth? My heart was desolate as we walked away. I wrote in my diary:

These babies have nothing!
They have no one to comfort them, to love and encourage them.
O, Lord, I feel devastated.
It is so sad; it is heart-breaking!

Mary and I discussed the plight of these babies with Paulina, and she assured us that everything possible would be done to ease their situation. The Bahá'ís in Tamali would take them under their wing, as much as they could. We were unable to hold back our tears as we left, and it was with feelings of utmost sorrow that Bill drove us to the bus yard to continue our journey north.

18

RETURN JOURNEYS – PART II

We travelled from early morning until late afternoon on roads that were even worse than those we experienced further south. In the extreme heat and humidity, squashed into our seats and bouncing over the potholes, it was truly exhausting. The relief felt when we reached Jenni and Brian's little home was indescribable. Our happiness, however, was short-lived, when we realised that they were not at home! We were absolutely parched and I could scarcely swallow. We had not had anything to eat or drink since our early morning breakfast. I know that it seems unbelievable but in those years the importance of carrying and drinking water was not emphasised.

We found a small wooden seat where we could sit in the porch to await their return. The sun was at its most brilliant peak and as I glanced at Mary we started to laugh. What a dusty, dishevelled pair we looked. On the journey we had been amused by the slogans written on the side of two trucks. One said, 'Who Knows The End?' On the other were the words, 'How Long?' Now the hours dragged by and still we sat there. Then, to our great relief, a kindly neighbour offered to go back to Navrongo, which we had just passed through. It was five miles away, and he nimbly jumped onto his motorbike and roared off into the distance. It seemed a long time before our knight in shining armour came back, with bread and sardines. Such a feast! Such joy! It was like manna from heaven for Mary and me. We started eating, thankfully, but we had nothing to drink and we were so dry we could hardly swallow. Still, the hours crawled by until suddenly our two lovely friends appeared. It was almost half-past eight in the evening. What a wonderful reunion it was. We hugged each other and chatted as they led us into their home. What bliss it was to savour those long cool drinks. Mary and I shared a double bed and slept under a ceiling fan. It was a great relief to have that lovely cool air wafting over us throughout the whole night. Next morning Jenni left for work, while Brian went out for a supply of water. They urged me to stay with them for the next seven days, so we could do some teaching. I was very happy about this, but Mary had to get back to Kumasi to be with her little sons. I felt very sorry to see her go, and being so close we said goodbye reluctantly. I was deeply grateful for her companionship and help, and I'm sure that I couldn't have coped with everything on my own. During all my teaching-trips I have been helped in just the right way, and at just the right time. Truly, it was what Bahá'u'lláh promised. When we take the first step to serve the Cause, divine assistance will be given to us.

Often there were things that my physical senses shrank from but this never affected my joy of being there. The meat market was one such place, with its flies crawling all over the slabs of meat. It made me think of India, when I lived in the hostel in Ooty. The swarms of flies always astonished me and were a big challenge when it came to sitting down for a meal. Jenni shopped and bargained like one who had lived there for many years. I admired her ease and natural way of doing things. We joined Brian for Coke and Fanta at a club near their home. We sat lazily beside a lovely blue swimming pool, and talked about the trips we could make to the surrounding villages. A few days later I recorded in my diary:

JULY 29, 1987

Had some heavy thunderstorms, especially in the evenings and during the night. Strong, tearing winds, thunder, lightening, and RAIN…. torrents of rain! Heat and humidity are very tiring; makes me limp and I perspire a lot. Mosquitoes attack my legs and arms - despite the Pyrethrum that I use as a repellent.

This morning my stomach has been upset again, so haven't eaten anything today. Went out with Jenni. Drove a long way to inspect fields of rice.

She showed me the nursery beds of young rice, which will be transplanted later. Her work is very interesting and she enjoys it.

One morning we set out in the truck to drive to Bolgatanga. Deciding to have some breakfast we sat outside a small café in scorching sunshine. While we waited for our food, we relaxed and enjoyed two glasses of cold Milo. We had ordered omelette that was served between slices of thick bread. Just as the waitress was bringing our plates over, a young man came and stood beside me. He had intensely sad eyes, and just stayed mutely by my chair. He had leprosy, and to my dismay the fingers of both hands were missing. I had been doing my utmost to balance the plate on my knee while trying to waft the flies off, and now I began groping for my purse as well. It was desperately sad to see someone who had been so disfigured in this way. With the sun beating down relentlessly and swarms of flies determined to squat on my plate all appetite fled. I was

A gift from the Chief of Bolgatanga

now conscious of my unwashed hands. The last thing I wanted was that egg, bread and my glass of Milo. All thoughts of breakfast had disappeared.

One day Jenni and Brian suggested that we visit the Chief of Bolgatanga who had known about the Faith for some time. I also learned that Prince Charles had once been a guest of his. When we arrived, we were shown into a beautiful circular room, with a ceiling fan and attractive furnishings. His title is the Bolganaba, and he greeted us with great warmth. There were many people seated in the centre when we arrived, but they quietly left the room. His costume was of blue and white striped material, and very colourful and distinctive. He showed a great interest in the teachings of the Faith. As we were leaving he presented me with a beautiful Bolgatanga basket, which had a very unusual shape. Brian took photographs of us outside the chief's house. It had been a lovely encounter.

One day, a Bahá'í called Gilbert visited us bringing Musa, a friend. It was quite amazing to learn that he remembered meeting me in 1981. It was in a lorry park, in Kumasi, and apparently I had been talking about the Faith. Years later, when he met Brian and heard the name of the Faith, he remembered our conversation.

Three times a week, Thomas, a houseboy, came to sweep and wash for Jenni and Brian. He was very conscientious, and I always enjoyed a little chat with him. He was interested to see the pictures of my trip to Ghana, in 1981. Sometimes Jenni came home for lunch that was always very simple. Because there was no butter or margarine, we enjoyed spreading avocado on our bread. Sometimes we enjoyed drinks of ginger syrup in cold water with a squeeze of lime, and that was very refreshing.

I spent a very happy afternoon when Jenni took me to visit a lovely Hungarian lady married to a Ghanaian. They had a chubby little boy who was nearly two years old. Jenni went off to her project leaving Ilona and me together for the afternoon, while her little boy went for a rest. She was such a gentle attractive girl, and as we talked she told me about a very sad and awful event in her life. Her first child, who had also been a boy, died in a tragic accident when he was only two. He had been in the driveway of their house and had gone behind his father's car when he was backing out. Their grief had seemed unbearable. We talked at some length about the Bahá'í teachings, and Ilona was very sympathetic towards the Faith.

When we reached home I helped to prepare dinner. Just washing and chopping the vegetables made me feel hot and sticky. Water ran in rivulets down my face. The humidity was completely draining. I dashed into a cold shower before attempting to start the meal. Later at seven thirty we set out for an open-meeting about five miles away.

I noted some details in my diary describing that fireside (open-house), and in memory I can see and feel it all again.

JULY 29, 1987
Met several Bahá'ís on their way to the meeting, and in a spirit of happiness made our way in the warm, dark night, to where the Fireside was being held. Several people were there, including two children who were asleep on

the floor. Apart from a few hard-backed chairs and a low wooden table, the large, barn-like room was absolutely empty.

Mosquitoes, moths galore, and all sorts of beetles and flying insects, touched our necks and faces, our arms and legs. Saw a large black beetle crawling close to Abolga's ear and neck.

In these unusual circumstances our Fireside began. We started with lovely prayers and then I began to speak about 'Abdu'l-Bahá. Realised that I would just have to 'switch off' and become detached, and ignore the fact that a creepy-crawly was going down the back of my blouse or up my legs. So I just tried, unobtrusively, to keep my skirt wrapped tightly around my knees and continue speaking as if nothing untoward was happening.

Other people, also, sat absent-mindedly scratching, or waving away the flying variety. I felt that my mop of hair was a nesting place for untold moths, flies and other swooping insects.

Evening harmonious, unified and loving.

What a marvellous evening, in a far-off place in the very north of Ghana – dim electric light, no refreshments or other attractive things – just being there, and learning more about this Great Day in which we are living!

Reached home about ten-fifteen.

Had mug of sweet Milo, then to bed, <u>under the fan</u>.

One evening Brian drove us in the Icour pick-up truck to Kologo, a small village, where we met quite a large number of Bahá'ís and their friends. We sat outside in the dark warm night, beside some tiny round houses with thatched roofs. It was a truly wonderful evening, reminiscent of my time in Calabar, when meeting with pure-hearted people in remote villages. Theirs is a special quality not easy to define, and far removed from anything we experience in the West.

We sat on benches, with a single storm lantern hanging from one of the walls. Flashes of lightening in the distance lit up the night sky. I spoke about the greatness of this New Day in which we were living, and that we were blessed to have come together to speak about Bahá'u'lláh and His teachings. I referred to His words about the human heart when He said:

"Thy heart is My home; purify it for My descent".

One of the Bahá'ís translated for me as I spoke, and at one point I mentioned that there are many people in England who don't believe in God. There was a murmuring from the group and a ripple of astonishment. They couldn't grasp that there were people who didn't believe in God. Such a thing seemed impossible to them.

It was difficult to explain that people in Europe fill their lives with so many material things such as houses, clothes, pleasures, career and business. There was no way that I could convey our materialistic way of thinking to those who possess nothing. They work very hard to grow their crops of millet, rice or groundnuts. They have no property or possessions, no books or television. They have no theatres, no luxury of any kind, just the sun the wind and rain. Their only source of light at night was a kerosene lamp. Each day they work from early morning in the middle of the bush. Many of them had become Bahá'ís, without any books in their own language, not even prayer books.

It made me deeply aware of the many blessings in my own life, and the many wonderful experiences I had enjoyed as a Bahá'í such as our summer schools and conferences, our vast amount of literature in my own language, and the indescribable bounty of pilgrimage. These simple spiritual people, loving Bahá'ís, had composed some beautiful songs about the Faith, and sang them with great feeling and purity. It had been a marvellous evening of inspiration making me reluctant to leave. Tiredness swamped me once we reached home and my legs felt weak. It was really good to collapse into bed under the ever-whirring fan.

We went one evening to a tiny village and met with a large group of children. We sat on the steps of their school in complete darkness. Brian lit two lanterns and hung them on the wall. The light attracted hundreds of large moths and bats, which circled around our heads. Speaking was difficult even through an interpreter. It was quite laughable to have the distraction of all those flying creatures in my hair brushing against my face. We sang many songs together, including one I had learned in Nigeria during the first trip to Africa. It was called '*The Báb is the Gate of our Faith*', which all the children sang with marvellous joy and enthusiasm.

Jenni and Brian had become good friends of the Chief of Navrongo and his lovely Vietnamese wife. We spent a happy afternoon with them both in their home, sipping deliciously cool drinks and talking about the teachings of Bahá'u'lláh. They asked me to tell them how I had become a Bahá'í. They sat in wrapt attention responding with great warmth and understanding. They had met in Russia where he had been studying for his doctorate. When we were leaving, they extended a very loving invitation to have dinner with them on the following day. That meal was delightful, while seated under a vast night sky, in their open roof-top room. The warm African night, stirred occasionally by gentle little breezes, relieved some of the humidity. We were served a large meal of many different dishes, including rice, fried yam croquettes, liver in sauce, and vegetables. I felt very full, especially as we had eaten very little during the day. We were completely charmed by the loving hospitality of our host and hostess and stayed quite late.

I felt extremely tired once we got back home that night and also sick. I was bathed in perspiration and almost too limp to have my usual long cool shower. Pains in my stomach added to the feeling of faintness. Thankfully, I slept very quickly after rolling into bed and was feeling much more like myself in the morning.

My days with dear Jenni and Brian passed all too quickly, and on Sunday August 2 I started my long return journey to Tamali. It was wonderful that they were taking me in the truck and I was so thankful for their help and kindness. Hour after hour we drove those miles of dusty roads, lurching and bumping, once more, over a myriad potholes, arriving hot and sticky at Paulina and Bill's bungalow. After we had eaten and Jenni and Brian had left, Bill and the family took me to the Catholic Church Mission to see a video film in the open air. It was a well-known Judy Garland film called 'St. Louis'. There were also two short films of the comedian Michael Crawford, which were hilariously funny. How relaxing to be sitting in harmonious company under the stars, and releasing all strains and tiredness in the magic of pure laughter.

Water and electricity were in short supply and had to be used with care. Water was delivered to the Browns' household in large tanks, and electricity had to be switched off in the evenings. They had three delightful sons, who were very good company. Paulina took me visiting the next day to meet some of her friends. One lady was from Bulgaria, another was half-African and half-Indian, and another was from Somalia. They all welcomed me warmly. I went back with Paulina for lunch of fried yams, with herring, onion and tomatoes. It was very tasty.

Later Bill took me to round up some of the Bahá'ís in the area so that we could hold a Fireside. We called at a village called Nyamkpala and several Bahá'ís eagerly joined us. From there we drove on to Kpathi and everyone helped to bring benches for us to sit on. It took us quite a long time to gather everyone together, but at least forty Bahá'ís and lots of children had come, which was wonderful.

It was a double translation situation that I hadn't experienced before. Bill talked with them first about repairing their Bahá'í Centre. They asked for help with their literacy programme and other matters of concern to them. There were so many things that these villagers wanted to know about the Faith, and their eagerness to learn was very touching. I spoke about God's love in creating us, and the suffering of all His Messengers. Bill asked me to say something about 'Abdu'l-Bahá. To speak about His servitude and selflessness, and His beautiful life always brings me joy. We talked about prayer and the role of the mother in the training of her children, and God's teaching that man and woman are like the two wings of one bird. The evening ended, as it so often does in Africa, with singing that truly comes from the heart and the atmosphere being filled with love and pure happiness. We all shook hands, and everyone sang 'Allah'u'Abha' (God the All-Glorious) as we climbed back into Bill's truck, and drove for home.

On August 5, Bill drove me to the airport where I was leaving for Kumasi. The plane was very late but I was so relieved to find that Enoch Tanyi was there to meet me. He and Mary's little boys greeted me so warmly when I walked into their home. They shouted out, "Auntie Lou's back!" When David Tanyi was going to Accra a few days later, I decided to go with him as a travelling companion. I wakened at 4am on the day and by 6.15am was eating a small piece of bread and swallowing a mouthful of coffee, before we set off. My diary well captured the happenings of that day:

> Bus left at 8.40. Felt weak and a bit faint.
> The crowds! The heat! The struggle! The uncertainty!
> My adventurous spirit seems less venturesome than before.

Endured more than five hours of sticky heat wedged together, six passengers squeezed into four seats. Couldn't move to reach my bag to wipe my face. Agony of restriction. Baby's hot little head pressed against my side - the heat was awful. Oh, it has been hard! But David and I teaching the Faith before we reached Accra! Arrived Bahá'í Centre and met by Tiati and Kobbanna. Such a loving welcome. Quite wonderful! Batch of letters from home.... What a joy! Tiati brought some bread and sardines from a little stall, near the Centre. Bahá'ís think that I should go and see Blanche, now back from the States.

Thought about Mary and our journey up north. What next?

On the following day, I went with Fredua to Blanche's home. She was so delighted to see me that there was no question about what I should do. It was good to be with her again and to hear that Isobel Sabri, one of the Counsellors for Africa, was arriving next day. It was exciting to be at the airport in the company of a large group of Bahá'ís, all in high spirits about meeting Isobel. Despite the heat and scorching sun, we were all in a happy mood. Zoë, Anisa and I had previously stayed in Isobel and Hasan Sabri's home in Nairobi, and it was great to see her again.

That evening there was an open meeting in Fredua's home. Even with the torrential rain and thunder more than forty people came. It was a joyful night enveloped in an atmosphere of such harmony impossible to describe. At such times, I ask myself how I came to be so richly blessed, and my heart just overflowed with thankfulness.

Next day started with a meeting in the Bahá'í centre at 10.45am when Isobel inspired us with a talk about the Covenant of Bahá'u'lláh and its huge significance, not just for the Bahá'ís themselves but also for humanity as a whole. Following her talk we attended a women's meeting that sparked a lot of discussion. Blanche invited us to a delicious lunch at her home, before we all drove out to the Temple land to visit Joseph's grave. Blanche preferred not to go, and Mary Tanyi stayed with her. It just seemed too soon and would have evoked too much grief for her. It had been raining heavily and the gravesite looked very bleak with the once lovely flowers now withered and dead. It was fortunate that Blanche had remained at home. It was such a sad reminder of our great loss. Later we were shown plans of the Temple, by the architect. Our spirits were greatly uplifted by the vision of another Bahá'í House of Worship, which would shed its glory over that part of Africa for ages to come. The Temple in Ghana would, in the future, be shedding its glory in West Africa, as the one in Uganda does in the East.

We left the temple-site and drove to meet the Bahá'ís in the village of Jankamma. There was great excitement as everyone gathered round with such a sense of anticipation shining on every glowing face. Isobel spoke first and then asked me to say something. I relished every moment, as I knew that my time in Ghana was soon drawing to a close. Also, I felt in my heart that it would most likely be my last visit to that amazing continent and I wanted to cherish every little thing around me.

A beautiful Bahá'í, Agatha, invited us for lunch with her family. Her tiny son sat happily on my knee and shared my food. Little Nahkjavani stood very close by my side. Mary said, "Children really love you, don't they?" This made me very happy as, ever since I was a little girl, I had adored young children. Isobel and I shared the large bedroom in Blanche's house and this was a good opportunity for us to talk quietly together about the Faith, and about the many openings in different parts of the world for travelling and pioneering. Isobel wondered whether I might like to serve at the World Centre, and then she quickly added that I would probably prefer to continue as a teacher of the Faith as that has been the greatest joy and fulfilment of my life.

Next day we had lunch with Beattie, Pinnock, Leonard and Blanche in a delightful restaurant, where we sat outside under a large sunshade. We enjoyed rice, chicken and plantain, or fufu with sauce and meat, and a variety of other tasty dishes. Later, and in sombre contrast, Beattie took us to his workplace, and in his large, spacious office he showed us a video about the tragedy of people suffering from AIDS. It was so sad to see the pain and anguish which often afflicted totally innocent people. It was terrible and deeply imprinted on my mind.

Isobel and I were then driven for a tour of Accra that included a trip to the beach. Later we went to the village of Kwashie Kumeh, for what was my second visit. To our surprise and joy, about fifty little children gathered in the village, spontaneously clapping their hands and singing with all their might. It was lovely to be able to speak to such an eager group, about those things so deeply cherished in the heart. We drove home in the dark, and got a burst tyre, which made it even later when we arrived back in Accra. As I fell into my bed, utterly exhausted, I realised that I'd been awake since about four o'clock that morning. Oh, the sheer bliss of sleep, when all one's energy has been spent in exhilarating activity.

Isobel was leaving and we were going to miss her a great deal. We travelled in two cars to the airport. She gave me a big hug and we watched her plane soar into the wide blue sky and melt away into the distance. She had paid me a lovely compliment as we were dressing that morning. She said that I always looked fresh and immaculate in whatever I was wearing. In reality I had very few clothes with me. I had been hoping to buy a little dress at the market, but by that time I couldn't afford it. I had felt anything but immaculate, washing and ironing the same few skirts and tops for several weeks. But her kind remarks lifted my spirit.

The economic situation in Ghana was extremely poor. Everything was terribly expensive, especially food. I had asked Solomon, Blanche's house-boy, to get a few things for me, two small tins of Ideal milk, tuna fish and some corncobs and tea bags and was amazed at what it cost. Money was disappearing at an astonishing rate. At least I was able to buy some postage stamps for a batch of letters I was sending home. This helped me to keep in close contact with my loved ones in the UK. After a hasty lunch I was taken to the Bahá'í Centre to meet with some of the National Spiritual Assembly members. Gladys Quartey Papafio, who was then secretary of the National Assembly, explained the work they would like me to do. They had been pleased and delighted with the lesson-plans for children's classes that I had prepared in 1981. Now, there was more to be done for the spiritual education of the children, and it was work that I loved very much. A new pattern of daily routine began, as I slept at Blanche's home each night, and in the morning went to the Bahá'í Centre. The time passed slowly, working in the office on my own. The evenings with Blanche and Baba were sad. Seeing little Baba looking lonely and forlorn, obviously grieving for his father made me also grieve with him in my heart. We tried hard to interest and divert him but I felt great concern for such a young boy trying to deal with such a big grief.

Blanche received an invitation for dinner from a group, who was connected with travel and tourism, and she kindly asked me to accompany her. It was really interesting. There were several speeches, and a special talk by a doctor on the subject of drug abuse. I thought that night when I got back home, that the world was really getting ever more dangerous and terrifying, and the increase in drug abuse was only one of these frightening things. I went back to the Bahá'í Centre to get on with my work, when a young man rushed in. He was in obvious shock and distress. He had witnessed an accident while travelling. Four people had been badly injured and he, himself, had been given two injections. His face was twitching and he looked very pale and extremely agitated. I gave him Rescue Remedy (Bach Flower Remedies) to help with the shock, and then made him some tea. I was very concerned and felt that he should be seen by a doctor. Sitting quietly with him, as he sipped his tea, I was silently saying the healing prayer over and over. It was a great relief when, after what seemed a long time, Fredua arrived and suggested that the shocked young Bahá'í should go with him to a nearby clinic.

That night I lay awake, reflecting on my teaching-trip and hoping that the young man was feeling better. How many unexpected things had happened on my trip? What I could write would only touch the surface, while all the rest will remain within my spirit always. I recorded in my diary, among a multitude of other things, the thoughts that came to me as I lay in bed, reflecting.

> What a teaching-trip! I could never describe it, but I know, deep inside, that all of it is part of Bahá'u'lláh's plan.
> It is what God wills for me and for the other souls I am interacting with. Service comes in many different guises. When we pray for service in His pathway, we may be imagining, and aspiring to, a very different form of service.
> We may picture: Travelling, Teaching, Rewarding Confirmations, bringing a happy, joyful exhilaration to the soul!
> But if we truly and sincerely wish to SERVE, how can we prefer one aspect to any other? To listen to someone's troubles, and to respond with all one's heart, and to 'be there' at the side of one in sorrow - just allowing our silent understanding to flow out and enfold that dear one in their grief! To do the very best we can, in each experience and challenge, and to withhold NOTHING that can possibly be given, whatever the results.

What difference does it make? We shouldn't seek results.
Are the results all seen in this world, at this present moment?
Or are they hidden behind the veil of eternal realities?
Our highest and last aim of all should be to win the good pleasure of our
Creator. If He is our goal and our desire we must long for Him, above ANY
of His gifts, or the praise of any person.

I was still very concerned about young Baba, as he seemed really depressed. One day some of his friends called and we played games in the garden. We had a lot of fun together and devised our own version of the egg and spoon race, using small limes instead of eggs. There was a lot of laughter, and when I tumbled over and hit my head on the trunk of a tree the children came running, full of concern. They were so helpful and kind. It is always wonderful to be with children.

One day Mary called with her young son, Morsen. It was so lovely to see her again, after the adventures of our trip together. We played Scrabble and had lunch of palm-nut soup and plantain. For the next few days Blanche had many visitors and friends. The house was always full.

I now began to count the days till my departure. Though extremely happy to be in Africa I was eager to see my loved ones again. I missed Zoë and Anisa more and more, as time went by. Home was calling me. My work continued, however, at the Centre, as I pressed on to finish the lesson plans.

There was something else I wanted to do before I left Ghana, and that was visit a school in Asseseeso, where Bahá'ís in my community back home had been sending books and all sorts of educational material for the children. Fredua offered to drive me. The journey was fairly long, and, as we travelled, the skies became blacker every moment. Soon the rain was pouring down in torrents. The teachers and other members of staff were overjoyed to see us. Mr Joseph Offei, the head teacher, was especially delighted. It was marvellous to see how the children and teachers were making use of what we had sent. There were writing materials and lots of things for their sewing class. Everything had been put to great use and was so appreciated. They gave me a lovely gift of two African wall-plaques, which I treasure, and a little bracelet they had made from coloured threads. I felt so glad that this visit had been accomplished and that we had met in person at long last.

It was a great relief when Fredua offered to get my air ticket confirmed for my homeward journey. Things that are easy to effect in the UK can seem so difficult and hazardous when in Africa, and I certainly always felt inadequate in dealing with officialdom. I worked hard to get the project on child education finished for the National Assembly. It was a wonderful relief when it was finally completed. I felt a little ill at ease when Fredua brought me the news that my flight had been changed from Tuesday morning to Monday evening. I began to wonder whether this would mean my spending an extra day in Moscow or arriving home a day early. I wakened at half past two in the morning and was unable to get back to sleep. Oh, me of little faith!

I was happy when one of Blanche's friends called, and offered to take me to town, so that I could buy one or two small gifts for Anisa and for other friends at home. It was a lovely feeling to be free to look around and shop, as it hadn't been possible before. Monday was the day of my departure, and what a day of uncertainty and anxiety it was. Because we had no idea what time my flight was scheduled for, Blanche took my air ticket and passport to her place of work, so that she could call at the Aeroflot office on my behalf. When she arrived however, the building was shut. I needed to know what was happening. The suspense was frightening. Later in the day we went back to Aeroflot together and found it still closed. We decided to drive to the airport office where the manager made two phone calls for us. The news was still very vague, and he told us that I should check in at about eight o'clock. I was beginning to feel a sense of panic. Back at Blanche's house, some of her friends had come to say farewell. I then hurriedly packed my bag and left for the airport.

Once at the airport it was complete bedlam. People were pushing and shoving and surging forward. Everyone was desperate to be given a seat on the plane. Two girls from the UK said that they had been off-loaded the week before, in spite of having tickets for the flight. I was gripped with anxiety. Home seemed the dearest sweetest place to be, and I was afraid of not being allowed to go. Blanche fought her way through the throngs, and although she knew several people who worked there, she still had to be forceful and determined. At last, to my utter relief, my ticket was accepted. Oh, how thankful I felt, knowing that I could now make my journey home. We sat and drank mineral water, talking quietly while we waited for departure time.

Hours went slowly by. All passengers had to stand outside on the tarmac, waiting to get on board. It was, by this time, quite dark, and a warm soft breeze was blowing. My only thought was to get inside that aircraft. It was one-thirty in the morning when we actually took off. A deep sigh of relief surged. We were on our way. I was truly going home.

It was a very long flight. One and a half hours to Benin. I mentioned the Faith to a young couple from Newcastle. It transpired they actually knew one of the Bahá'ís living there. We spent one hour in Tripoli and half an hour in Vienna, which was a lovely airport. In Moscow we had the usual overnight stop. I met a delightful and friendly Chinese doctor. Next day, I sat at table with a couple from Somalia, with a three-year old boy named Muhammad. We chatted together and became really good friends.

On each of my flights with Aeroflot, I very much enjoyed the opportunity of meeting people from all over the world. There were two ladies from Uganda who lived not far from the beautiful Bahá'í Temple outside Kampala. They were very warmly speaking about the Faith and those Bahá'ís that they had met. On this occasion I had a bedroom to myself, thank God. I enjoyed wandering round the little gift shop, filled with anticipation at the thought of going home. It was a wonderful feeling, and I could scarcely wait. Next morning, I had an early call at just six-thirty. I suddenly realised that in England it was only half past three. I relaxed on the plane, contented and happy. When we landed, a young man carried my case to Victoria Coach Station.

Such kindness was often shown to me while on my travels. I had a quick cup of tea, and phoned home. A hurried little word with Zoë and Anisa with joyful cries, "I love you, Grandma I love you!"

It was a smooth journey home, in comfortable seats, driving past beautiful tree-lined roads. Once we arrived, Southport looked so lovely with its gardens full of flowers, and everything fresh and green. I relished my sandwiches and tea. My sense of anticipation was mounting. The coach arrived ten minutes early, and I stood for a little while, looking out for my dear ones. Then, suddenly, they were running towards me - breathlessly - and Anisa flung herself into my arms. Hugs, kisses, laughter and pure joy! Two months had seemed a very long time. So much had happened, adventures of all kinds, things planned and unplanned, expected and unexpected. In many ways it had been tough, but strength had been given to me every step of the way and in my heart I was thankful.

My diary states that it had been a hectic, challenging, and quite a different teaching-trip from any I had experienced before. I wrote:

> I feel sure that I was in the right place at the right time, for many reasons, and in my inmost soul I have learned a great deal. Through all of life's adventures we are enriched and blessed. Every moment is important, and all my memories of Africa will stay with me forever.

19

SURPRISE EVENTS IN POLAND

I was surprised and excited during the summer of 1990 to be invited to Poland, to help a family with two daughters to improve their English. Several Bahá'ís from the UK had been taking courses in 'Teaching English as a Foreign Language', (TEFL), and were practising quite a lot in Poland. Edgar Boyett, secretary of the Bahá'í International Travel Teaching Committee, called me to ask if I would be willing to go. It was to be challenging and completely different from my previous trips overseas. There had always been someone waiting at the end of my journey. It also felt very different because it was in Eastern Europe and I knew that my inability to speak the language would be quite difficult. Nevertheless, it was a lovely feeling when getting ready for the trip, and trying to imagine what it would be like.

At last I was all packed. I had included a number of small gifts, which I hoped would be suitable for my Polish family and for other people I might meet during my stay. I travelled to London on the Rapide Coach, which was very comfortable. Tea and sandwiches were served by a friendly hostess, and I now had several hours in which to relax and contemplate what lay ahead. In London, I was met by kind and thoughtful relatives who took me home and, after a restful night, they drove me to Heathrow Airport. We sat there, drinking tea until it was time for me to say goodbye and gave heartfelt thanks for making the start of my journey so pleasant and smooth. I was also saying goodbye to England and the English language. I boarded the Polish 'Lot' plane and, as most of my fellow passengers spoke Polish, I was surrounded by the soft pleasant tones I would be hearing from that moment until my return home.

We flew directly to Krakow where I had been promised that a young student called Iwona would meet me. I prayed ardently that she would be there. The mere thought of having to make a phone call in my non-existent Polish and without any of the local currency filled me with trepidation. Krakow airport was small. As I pulled my luggage off the wagon, a friendly lady, who thank God spoke some English, advised me how to fill in the currency form. Before I had time to feel anxious, two smiling girls came towards me and introduced themselves as Iwona and Kataryn. These two young friends flooded me with kindness and a quiet courtesy. They were wonderful. They carried my bags to the tram-stop, where we waited in the cool of the evening, talking together and speaking slowly and distinctly. Their knowledge of English was a Godsend, even though they kept apologising for it. They made me feel really at home, allowing me to

With Iwona Kacak outside Krakow University.

share their room in the students' quarters where there were three beds. The third one belonged to one of their friends who had gone home for the weekend. They made me a lovely supper. Later I washed in the bathroom, before snuggling down in the nice little bed and popped off to sleep.

Next morning I wakened to bright sunlight and the sounds of whispered conversation, coming from across the room. I enjoyed breakfast of creamy cheese and radishes with delicious bread and butter and a cup of tea. They planned to take me sightseeing around Krakow, and advised me to leave my luggage and raincoat in their room, so as to be unhampered for the day.

It was Saturday, and as we strolled along, I reflected on our Saturday mornings in England. Here there was a sense of relaxation, of being less hurried. The shops were very different with limited choice. At home, the huge variety of everything can sometimes create a sense of stress. In Poland there were no elaborate and beautiful window displays, and there were few goods inside. There was no bewilderment or perplexity for the shopper. The cost of everything was the problem for the Polish people. All those thousands of zlotys were like Monopoly money. The exchange rate was currently ten thousand zlotys to the dollar and I found myself doing sums all the time, trying to work out the cost of everything.

Iwona and Katryn were very proud to show me some of the beautiful and impressive old churches in Krakow, with their intricate ornamentation. There were lots of children everywhere guided by their teachers. Everyone showed a distinct and obvious reverence inside the churches. Adults as well as children knelt quietly or sat

177

with bowed heads in front of the altars. We spent a leisurely morning, stopping at a small café for apple-cake and coffee. Kataryn took me to some shops and the museum, while Iwona returned to their room for my large case and raincoat. We arranged to meet her at the railway station, where I was about to take a train to Wroclaw, about a five-hour journey. We had waited in a very long queue to get my ticket, and I was thankful not to be on my own. The language is really difficult and I would have made a total mess of expressing myself.

When we arrived at the station, Iwona was already waiting for us. She had my case and small hand-baggage with her, but I could see that she had forgotten the raincoat. Realising that we had very little time before the train left, I tried to reassure her. I told her not to worry. But instantly Kataryn said that she would go back for it by taxi. Before I could stop her she rushed away.

I followed Iwona along the platform until we boarded the train, managing to find a compartment with one vacant seat. She lifted my suitcase onto the rack and, because we were speaking in English, became the centre of curiosity for other passengers. There were only a few minutes left and she was still anxious about my raincoat. We were just saying goodbye when a very breathless Kataryn came running along the plat-form with my raincoat over her arm. We beamed our relief as I thanked her profusely and hugged them both. My fellow travellers could now understand our little drama as our actions spoke louder than our words. Language didn't matter, nor was it necessary, as they watched intently our flurry of hasty farewells.

Sinking into my seat I smiled broadly to my five travelling companions who warm-ly smiled back. We began trying to communicate, but only one lady could speak a few phrases in English. In the midst of our efforts, I cannot remember why I said 'nie' which is 'no' in Polish, but their response was amazing and immediate. There was a chorus of bravo, and the clapping of hands, which made us all burst out laughing with pure merriment. Much later in the journey I left my seat to look for the 'Toaleta', and, as I was beginning to feel thirsty, I managed to convey to the young man seated on my right that I would like to buy a drink of orange or mineral water. He kindly offered to get it for me, and before long he returned with a bottle of orange squash. The atmosphere was relaxed and friendly, and I didn't feel I was alone any more in this country far from my home.

I knew that I was going to be met in Wroclaw by Dr Roman Kolacz, and that I would be staying with him and his wife Maria with their three young sons. It seems ridiculous that I had not asked anyone what Dr Kolacz looked like. As the train drew slowly into the huge railway station I realised how difficult this could be. The helpful young man, who brought me the orange squash, was also going to Wroclaw. He lifted my suitcase from the rack and carried it along the platform. I walked beside him still wondering how on earth I was going recognise my host. Even to this day, I don't know what really happened next. My young escort put my case down abruptly and moved towards a tall, distinguished looking man in a white suit. He was coming towards me, smiling a most wonderful, friendly smile. Suddenly Dr Kolacz was shaking my hand warmly in welcome. I just felt completely reassured by his twinkling eyes, so full of kindness. It all happened so quickly. When I turned around my young friend from the train had gone. I hadn't been able to thank him again for his kindness. I will never know how he knew who Dr Kolacz was. I was thankful and relieved to have overcome this hurdle in my journey, and said a prayer of gratitude.

Roman and Maria were kind and loving hosts, and I felt totally at ease with them in their apartment. Their three young sons, Paul, Peter and Simon, were aged thirteen, twelve and seven respectively. They were quite shy in the beginning, but their parents encouraged them to speak a little English each day, when they came home from school. I gave lessons to Simon's little friend, Caroline, as well and they all seemed to enjoy it.

The day after my arrival was a Sunday, and we spent a quiet day together, just talking and getting to know one another. Every time I used a word that Maria and Roman didn't understand they would look it up in their Polish/English dictionary and then write it in an exercise book. They were very keen students and I found it most interesting, speaking slowly and clearly and thinking about the words I used. They had heard that I was a Bahá'í before my arrival, and Roman asked me, in the midst of our conversation, "What is the Bahá'í Faith?"

In my heart I felt poised at the edge of a vast and glorious ocean of divine revelation, wondering which precious drop I could offer first. This lovely family was Roman Catholic and I knew that their beliefs would be strong and devout, so my awareness of this guided me towards the answers I gave them. Carefully and thoughtfully, explanations were given about unity and world peace, and the oneness and brotherhood of mankind. Accepting these teachings, Roman eagerly asked for more. The words of Bahá'u'lláh and 'Abdu'l-Bahá hold a transforming quality which is uplifting. Those moments in our lives when we are teaching are surely the most rewarding and joyful we can ever have. Sharing what we believe, with people who are interested and eager to hear, brings immense happiness to the spirit. On that Sunday afternoon, when Roman and Maria probed deeper and more intently into the teachings, it was a beautiful feeling to have this opportunity of unfolding God's eternal truths. I showed them pictures of the beautiful Houses of Worship around the world. They wanted to know about the soul and life after death as well. The lovely analogies which 'Abdu'l-Bahá has given are so helpful on this subject. The way He explains that the soul is like a bird in a cage during our life in this world, and our purpose is to develop the spiritual qualities that God has given to us, potentially. They were both so eager to know more, that I gave them some small books about the Faith, in Polish.

Their youngest son, Simon, had given his bedroom to me and for this I was most grateful. Meal times in Poland are somewhat differently spaced than at home, but I had no difficulty in adjusting to them. We had breakfast quite early, as the children start school at eight o'clock. Their main meal of the day is served between three and four o'clock in the afternoon. There were several hours between dinner and supper, which was any time between eight-thirty and ten o'clock. At home, I often have snacks

Maria and Roman Kotacz and their sons, Paul, Simon and Peter.

between meals, as you might guess, and yet I didn't miss them here at all. I enjoyed the light uncooked breakfasts, soft cheese with radish or chives, continental sausage and really delicious bread. I even found that cocoa for breakfast was enjoyable and quite an acceptable alternative to tea. At home I would never dream of substituting anything for my pot of golden tea and a plate of hot toast! Perhaps it's good to change our routine from time to time and break free from some of our habits, trying new foods and new ways of doing things.

Maria took me to the centre of town to visit some of the larger shops. They were very different from those at home, and it made me more keenly aware that our western standards of plenty and abundance do not exist in Eastern Europe. Everything was terribly expensive for the Polish people and a struggle for them financially. But, there was a spirit in Poland, which is sadly lacking at home. Free from the constant merry-go-round of our materialistic society, life is less bound by the feverish pursuits of pleasure and self-indulgence. I was very impressed by their love of learning, their culture, and their sense of purpose. These feelings and impressions are not easy to put into words, but those subtle differences permeate the atmosphere and make a lasting impression on the mind and on the heart. I liked what I saw.

Maria and Roman, very slowly and with much difficulty, were in the process of having their own house built. It was going to take them a long time on account of their limited finances, but they were so proud and happy about the project. They asked me if I would like to see it. Of course I did and we drove the short distance from their flat. I took some pictures of them standing at the front of their future home. They pointed out where each room was going to be, and kindly and sincerely assured me that there would be plenty of room for me when it was finished, as they hoped that I would return to Poland again.

On Monday morning Maria and I went shopping locally and I bought a deep-blue blouse, which cost me very little compared with prices at home. I was doubtful about the colour and whether I would really like it in the long run. However, at the end of my trip I was glad I'd bought it as it proved to have a different destiny. At about nine-thirty that same evening Roger Wilkinson arrived, a Bahá'í from Kendal. He had come from Warsaw and was to stay for two nights in Wroclaw with us. He was jovial and charming, and made himself completely at home. Next day, Roman arranged for one of his friends, Leszek, to take us both on a sightseeing tour of the city. He was a very friendly and thoughtful guide and a most pleasant companion. We stopped for coffee in the middle of the morning and then, outside the beautiful town hall, strolled around looking at the lovely and varied art displays. The gentle sunshine was warm to our skin and not blazing hot like Africa. In a great square in the town centre there was an abundance of the most beautiful flowers. They were breathtaking and Leszek, observing my love of flowers, stopped by one of the displays and bought me a gorgeous rose. It was a lovely shade of peach and pink with a gorgeous scent. I was so thrilled that I asked Roger to take a picture so that the rose might not die from my memory even when it had faded.

In the afternoon Roman escorted Roger and myself to a most wonderful spectacle called Panorama. It is noted as being Wroclaw's most important piece of cultural heritage. It is made up of a wonderful painting that was designed to commemorate the 100th anniversary of the famous Koeciuszko insurrection when a Polish rebellion defeated the Russian army. The atmosphere was amazing! It was designed to make us feel that we were actually there, in the midst of the battle. What was unique about that particular war was that peasants, not the soldiers, saved the day for the Poles. Roger and I were supplied with audio-phones so that we could hear the whole drama narrated in English. It was truly unforgettable.

In the evening we were all invited to supper with a lovely young couple, Wlodak and Joanna. They were so hospitable in a modest way, which greatly impressed me. Their manner and speech was courteous. We talked of many things, which touched on the deeper aspects of life. Roger and I were able to contribute with answers from the teachings of Bahá'u'lláh. How sorely is the world in need of His Divine remedy?

May 23 was a Wednesday. It was the anniversary of the Declaration of the Báb and one of the nine holy days in our Faith. It was thrilling and wonderful that we had arranged to visit a Bahá'í family who were living in Olesnica. Farhad and Anna Monadjem and their son Anis owned a farm there. Roger arranged this visit and, to our delight, Maria and Roman asked if they could go with us. It was such a blessing to bring these dear friends to meet our fellow Bahá'ís. We spent the whole afternoon and early evening at the farm, in golden sunshine, mingling in a warm, mellow companionship like old friends. Farhad, his kind, brown eyes glowing, poured out his experiences of life in Iran.

He talked about the dangers and difficulties for the loved ones of Bahá'u'lláh, and how he came to leave the country. As he spoke, I asked his lovely wife Anna (who is Polish) to translate for our two friends, who sat completely spellbound. While we had been strolling leisurely down the country lanes, admiring the three thousand geese that they owned, Anna had been busy in the kitchen, cooking for us. I felt so thankful to be in Eastern Europe, and for the wonderful opportunities of meeting these special people.

Maria and I were close and happy companions. She loved her black coffee and was delighted each time I said that I would like one as well. She took me again to the larger stores in town and I bought a very pretty cotton two-piece dress and top. This was extremely reasonable in price, though in Zlotys it seemed really expensive. It was in pastel shades of blue and pink, with slashes of white and grey. It made me feel sad that everything was terribly expensive for the people, who seemed to have amazingly low salaries. I was more than glad that I had brought a little stock of gifts to show something of my appreciation for all the loving hospitality I received along the way.

Because Maria was at university each Thursday, teaching Russian, she had arranged for a friend called Dorada to come and take me out. After she arrived it felt as though we had known each other forever and we were totally at ease. She was kind and thoughtful, taking me for a leisurely stroll around some beautiful gardens with the most magnificent flowers. It was raining softly, after days of glorious sunshine, but I managed to take a few pictures standing amidst all that loveliness.

The following Saturday was Mothers' Day and the three boys had been out and secretly bought a bunch of magnificent red roses for their mum. It was lovely to watch them. The excitement and joy they saw in their mother's face was a sight to behold. As she hugged them and thanked them, their young faces were beaming in the circle of her love. Throughout the world, humanity seems to be so much the same in the way of showing affection within our families and especially our children. God has given to all mankind the gift and the beauty of the human heart, which He tells us is the dwelling place of eternal mysteries, and, of course, the dwelling place of His love.

Later in the day Maria took me to see her garden once again, which was her pride and joy. Paul went with us to do some watering and weeding. She had cultivated vegetables including lettuce, flowers and fruit trees with such loving care. With little rain the soil was dry as dust so they had to make several trips to the water tap which was a little way away. Maria left Paul, then thirteen, by a lily-pond where he was playing while she worked contentedly at her plants. It was getting late and we began to feel the cool of the evening as the sun sank lower. Maria began calling for Paul to come back. She called several times, louder and longer beginning to feel impatient. She then went to look for him. I waited for them by the car for what seemed a very long time, especially as it was getting colder. Paul had the car-key, which meant that we couldn't get in. I could still hear Maria constantly calling his name over and over again. After a considerable time, I saw their two figures in the distance walking towards me much to my relief. They both looked upset. Maria had felt anxious and worried when he went missing but Paul had been trying to get some water lilies for her from the pond. It reminded me of my own childhood, when some lovely little idea or plan would not be understood by worrying parents, and my good intentions would end in dismal failure. Paul was quiet and sensitive and I could see the inner hurt that almost overwhelmed him. It was his mother that he had been hoping to please and delight, and in his hand he clutched four or five lily stalks with round unopened buds. But, instead, he had upset and worried her by keeping us all waiting. His eyes brimmed with tears as he sat in the back of the car. Now his dearest mum was contrite and full of sadness as he was. My heart flowed out to them both, encompassing this human situation, which many of us have experienced. We made the journey home quietly. Then, walking up those many flights of stairs to the flat, Maria knew that I understood and she also sensed the underlying feelings of my heart. We shared a timeless moment of total understanding. It was Mothers' Day, and so much emotion was being felt by her as well as Paul. Now she glimpsed my own poignant memories of a young son and his mother's tender love, so near and yet so long ago. Our eyes met, and all three of us shed quiet tears of pain and happiness. We reached the flat and dabbed our eyes, as we entered in. The moment slid away into laughter with happy preparations for supper.

Roman went to his mother's home for the weekend. I said goodbye to him because I was leaving on Monday morning for Nowy-Sacz, and would not be seeing him again. I gave him a box of chocolates for his mother, which pleased him immensely. I went with Maria and two of the boys by tram to a park. It was a very important day for the Polish people, as they were holding local elections and were justifiably proud. Elections had been forbidden for so long. Now it was very precious to them. I was happy to be present at such a time and Maria asked me if I would like to go with her

With Leszak and a gift of a rose.

Anna and Farhad Monadjem on their farm.

to the polling station. Everything was beautifully arranged, with cloths and lovely flowers on three long tables. The Polish Eagle looked magnificent, on the wall, and the booths each had dark red velvet curtains, to ensure privacy. Although Roman and Maria and their friends didn't speak very much about political affairs, whenever more recent events were mentioned they expressed deep relief and thankfulness that the oppression had at last been lifted.

My week in Wroclaw had been a last minute suggestion just before I left home. The original request was for me to go to Nowy Sacz, to stay with Maria's sister, Krystina, and her two daughters. It had been a wonderfully happy week and they had made me feel part of their family, loved and close. This was a blessing from Bahá'u'lláh and I am certain that it fulfilled the purpose of my trip to Eastern Europe. Roman had received not only some of the Bahá'í Teachings and the *Hidden Words* in Polish but also *The Promise of World Peace*. I left literature and a little note for Roman to give to Leszek as he also had asked about the Faith. Now Maria and Roman had met and made friends with those precious Bahá'ís, Farhad and Anna Monadjem.

The week fled by, and now I was to travel down to Nowy Sacz, going by train to Krakow and from there by bus. I was to spend the remaining three weeks assisting the little family there with their English. My lovely, kind Maria told me that we would need to get up early so that she could drive me to the station. During our previous shopping excursions she said she'd like to buy a black tee-shirt to match one of her skirts. I was happy to hear this, as one of the gifts I had brought with me was a really unusual but attractive black tee-shirt with a colourful design. I wrapped it for her, along with several items such as hand-cream, lipstick, eye shadow and her favourite chocolate with nuts and raisins. She was thrilled and put the shirt on straight away. I know we both felt the delight of another lovely moment in our friendship.

I felt sad to be leaving her and I could see that she was feeling the same. We sat together at the station sipping our last cup of coffee together. She had given me some coins so that I could phone Krystina's home when I reached the bus station in Nowy Sacz. Meanwhile, she saw me safely into my seat on the train and we said a very tender and affectionate goodbye, as I started the long five-hour journey to Krakow. The time passed not too slowly and again it was a pleasant journey. Two of my fellow-passengers were men of retirement age and were completely different in every way. They were not travelling together but were sitting side by side, opposite to me. One was reading a book in English and was very courteous and polite, while the other seemed more of a country person, very likeable and kind. He spoke to me in Polish, whilst his companion interpreted for me. Time after time he interrupted our more studious friend, but each time he patiently listened and then passed on to me the gist of the 'message'. He would say, "Our neighbour is saying that he has a large house and you can stay with his family." And, "Our neighbour is saying he would like to have your address." There was nothing menacing or unpleasant about it. It all seemed rather unreal and rather sweet. As this continued, I sensed a little twinkle of amusement, though not unkindness, in our interpreter's blue eyes. In fact, all three of us exchanged names and addresses. The gentleman with the book was a Professor at the University of Wroclaw. A little later, I closed my eyes and felt very relaxed and contented. Suddenly, I was roused when the more talkative little man held out a bag of large round doughnuts and generously insisted that we share them. They were quite delicious and I realised that it had been a long time since breakfast. Quietly munching my jam doughnut I felt myself smiling inwardly while looking on at the scene. Far from home, in a country where I could not speak the language, sitting in a train with complete strangers yet contentedly eating doughnuts as though it was an everyday occurrence.

Iwona was meeting me in Krakow and I was looking forward to seeing her again. She had another friend Ysobel with her and they greeted me lovingly as they carried my bags. We went to an old-fashioned restaurant with a quiet, relaxed atmosphere. They ordered coffee and asked if I would like something to eat. I had a tasty cheese omelette with Ysobel, while Iwonna went for my bus ticket. At the coach station I was delighted to find Kataryn waiting for us. She gave me the sweetest smile and handed me a lovely posy of violets, saying "These are for you from us." They led me to my bus and explained that the seats were numbered. In the midst of our good-byes I turned, and in utter amazement, found a beaming Roman with outstretched arms standing beside me. He was on his way back home after visiting his mother, and had come especially to see me. I was very touched by his gesture of kindness. We gave one another a big warm hug and I felt that we were family. Tears of emotion and happiness were mingled with regret at leaving Wroclaw and my dear, kind hosts.

As the bus carried me away from the smiling group I began to feel alone for the very first time. As soon as I arrived in Nowy Sacz, I was to make contact with my new host family and I didn't relish the idea of making that phone call. The numbers on the dial were almost obliterated, and twice I dialled but could not get through. I asked two people for help but, of course, they couldn't understand what I was saying and I was afraid of losing all my coins. My throat went dry and I began to feel apprehensive. I approached a third lady in desperation. She did the dialling for me. What a relief! She retrieved my other coins and then I heard the voice of Krystina's husband Adam speaking on the other end. He advised me to stay where I was until he arrived. Believe you me I was delighted to do just that. I was not about to go anywhere. Almost from the very first moment of my arrival, I knew that something was wrong. It was very hard to understand what had really happened and even harder to explain. My call from the International Goals Committee was a request to go to Nowy Sacz for the express purpose of helping two daughters and their mother with their English. The whole of my preparations including gifts, tapes and lessons had been to this end. All my telephone conversations with the Committee had centred on this project. I had been told repeatedly that they were waiting eagerly for my visit. Meanwhile, a young woman called Jessica, who was not a Bahá'í, had been planning a visit to Poland and she had taken a course in Teaching English as a Foreign Language, (TEFL). She had been asked to go to Wroclaw. We both happened to arrive on the same day. She was redirected to Nowy Sacz immediately. Apparently, she was to stay with Magda who was involved with the English classes that were taking place down there.

For some reason, Jessica was invited to stay in the home of Krystina and her family until my arrival one week later. Jessica called me just as I was about to leave Wroclaw. She asked whether I would mind her staying on at Krystina's, and if I would let her share the bedroom. When I queried the reason for this change of plan and why she was not going to Magda's home as arranged, she intimated that there had been some problem in their relationship which would make this difficult. Naturally, I immediately agreed to share the room at Krystina's. I was reassured that it would be only for a few days. Once in Nowy Sacz I felt a little uneasy. Although Adam and Krystina were really lovely people, and did their best in every way to be hospitable there seemed to be something not quite right. I was shocked to realise that they were not expecting <u>any</u> English lessons from me. Jessica had by this time been fully accepted as part of their little family. I was redundant. Hmm! What to do? It was a long way from home and I was due to remain in Poland for another three weeks. How could I stay with these nice people, accepting their hospitality? The weather was very wet and cool and we were on the seventh floor of an apartment building. I felt a bit out of place, and I really didn't know what on earth I was going to do.

That night Jessica asked if I would help her next day at the club. She gave me directions how to get there, but during the night she took ill. Several times she vomited and, by morning, was really quite sick. All plans had to be changed. Later that day Krystina sent for the doctor. It was quite frightening for Jessica to be in such a plight so far away from her home. I hoped that my being there was of some comfort to her, especially when, towards evening, she suddenly fainted and the family immediately rang for an ambulance to take her to hospital. Together, Jessica and I tried to convince them that she would recover much better by staying with the family. So much was being said in Polish. This was unnerving and confusing for her. At last, everyone agreed to let her remain in bed and stay where she was. Thank goodness, within a few days she was back to her normal self again.

My own situation hadn't changed. It was a bit embarrassing to come to the table for meals and polite conversation, before scurrying back to the bedroom to write a letter or chat with Jessica. I still felt trapped. On the Wednesday we had a visit from Magda, who brought flowers for Jessica and me. She invited me back with her for tea and cake. She then very kindly invited me to go with her to Zakapane in the mountains at the weekend. I was thrilled at the prospect.

Magda advised me that I would need some walking shoes. As I only had sandals and court-shoes we arranged to go and buy some next morning. We walked back to Krystina's in drizzling rain and she promised to call for me at ten o'clock next day. I felt much lighter at heart. Jessica was being coaxed to eat a little and Krystina had prepared some delicious soup with a most beautiful aroma. I had missed lunch and now I sat on my little bed and watched my room mate supping her soup. My stomach rumbled and Jessica kindly offered me some biscuits and peanuts. I felt homesick. What a predicament? I searched for an answer and prayed ardently for guidance. During the night and the early-morning hours my heart turned longingly to Bahá'u'lláh.

When I woke in the morning, I had a sharp pain in my left eye and it was watering. I looked in the mirror, quite expecting it to be inflamed. Thankfully, it looked normal apart from the watering. Krystina was, as usual, at the university where she taught Russian. Adam greeted me pleasantly. Just as we were about to have some breakfast the phone rang. To my dismay it was Magda telling us that she was ill and would have to stay in bed. She apologised for being unable to keep our appointment and sounded quite poorly. It seemed like one problem after another with Jessica's illness, my sore eye and now Magda's flu'! Adam had a very good sense of humour and we both burst out laughing. The lovely plans of shopping and the weekend in the mountains had all collapsed. Magda had invited me to move into her apartment as she was very enthusiastic about learning English. This suggestion, also, would have to be swept aside. It seemed as if everything I tried to do was being frustrated. Again I prayed for help. I needed someone to show me what to do. Jessica was feeling so much brighter and stronger, that she offered to bake a cake for the family. We were alone in the tiny kitchen, discussing what I ought to do, especially as Krystina was very busy preparing to leave for the United States in a few days time. I couldn't stay there with Adam and the girls, and Jessica was planning to go to Wroclaw to conclude her trip. She asked me if I would consider returning to Maria in Wroclaw, and then added, "What do you really want to do? Go to Wroclaw or get a flight home?"

How appealing that felt, but how could I afford such an expense? My return ticket, on Polish Airlines was non-refundable and the date of my return couldn't be altered. I poured all this out to Jessica then realised that in her kindness she had sown a seed of possibility in my mind.

That evening I asked Krystina if I could phone Maria to ask if I could return to Wroclaw. She responded readily and I made my call. Because I knew that Maria's flat was small and that Jessica was eager to stay there, I suggested that perhaps I could live in with one of their friends, who wanted to improve their English. I repeatedly emphasised Jessica's wish to be in Maria's home and my own willingness to go elsewhere. But, as I lay in my little bed, I resolved that somehow I would try to get home. There was no special virtue in prolonging my stay for the whole month. Bahá'u'lláh seemed to be showing me that I should bring it to a conclusion and that everything meant to happen had happened. The purpose of my visit to Eastern Europe had, apparently, been fulfilled.

It's strange, when we feel unhappy in a situation, and then an even more upsetting thing takes place, it is like that old familiar 'straw' that just proves too much. But it acts as a switching-off agent. In some mysterious way it brings a calming effect. Surrounded with yet more prayer, the longing to go home grew into a firm and definite resolve, and I slept 'till early morning. When Jessica and I were seated together at breakfast, I told her of my decision. I needed help to carry out the practical arrangements of getting to Krakow, and then trying to book a flight to England. We told

Maria and Adam that I was leaving, and they kindly made a phone call to Iwonna for me, asking her if she could meet my bus. I held my breath, for if she had been at University I would not have been able to contact her, and everything depended on her loving assistance once again.

She was in her rooms and she said that she would be at the bus station in two and a half hours time. Quickly and eagerly I started to pack my things. It was with an amazing sense of relief that I folded my clothes and took my few belongings off the shelves. Jessica was in the bedroom and she tried to convince me that I should make my way to Wroclaw. It was clear that the right and only thing for me to do was to fly home and, in the best spirit possible, leave the unfortunate muddle behind.

At such times, especially when doing something to serve the Faith, one becomes aware of spiritual help and guidance. The heart is much more attuned to God's Kingdom, and the things of that world appear the most important. During my intense prayers I had somehow been reminded of the Báb and the Master, 'Abdu'l-Bahá. We learn how, at certain times in Their lives, They spoke out fearlessly with regard to any injustice, even a small incident.

From these thoughts I felt I should speak to Jessica, to try and clear up any misconceptions and leave with no disunity between us. I told her that when I make trips overseas, I go on my own, and that I prefer it that way. After our little chat with explanations the burden that had been weighing on my spirit since the previous night was lifted. I said how much I had enjoyed our lovely intimate talks during our few days together, and how much I admired her many qualities. It was a relief to feel that harmony had been restored and we were parting on friendly terms. We had to hurry as we had little time to get to the bus station. I quickly parcelled the little gifts that I had planned with so much loving thought before leaving England, all ready to give them to Iwonne.

We scrambled, as best we could, into their small car, and Krystina kindly gave me some biscuits for my journey. The sun was shining as we drove along, and I glimpsed the town that I had not been able to see or discover. It was very strange. I was leaving so soon after my arrival and it was hard to see why I had gone there in the first place. But I believe that there is a purpose in everything, whether we understand it then or not.

After I bought my ticket, they warmly hugged me and saw me to my seat. At last I settled down, waving and waving to the three smiling faces through the window. We were moving, and I was alone, but on my way with a deep sense of relief. I felt like a bird that had escaped from a cage. I settled down to reflect quietly on all that had happened since my eager arrival only five days before. I pulled the little blue curtain across the window, as it felt more private, and would conceal my face if my tears became too difficult to hold back. I let go of the tension that had been gripping me all week as we sped forward to Krakow.

There was a light rain when the bus drew into the depot and I spied dear kind Iwonna waiting patiently. It had to be a very hurried excursion in order to negotiate all we had to do. First, we made a trip to the Travel Agents to see if I could get a flight to London next day. How I hoped there would be one. Iwonna interpreted for me, while I was speaking to the young lady. I held my breath as I waited to see whether there <u>was</u> a seat available or not. I needed to know how much it was going to cost. Yes! There was a flight next day at two o'clock, and it would cost £116, a lot of money not easy to find, but my plight was somewhat desperate.

Just as I was frantically telling myself that I must do it, the young lady was saying that the flight was not from Krakow but from Warsaw. Another shock! What could I do? Travel on my own to Warsaw? Spend the night there? I had only moments to decide but I couldn't contemplate the alternative. Another two weeks in Poland? Where? Who with? I knew for certain that Maria and Roman would welcome me with the utmost eagerness and warmth but what of Jessica and her dream of being with them on her own?

I had been given some names and addresses of Bahá'ís living in different parts of Poland, and I knew that there was at least one in Warsaw. Where had I put my list? Searching my bag I found it, and although it was a challenging thought to go to Warsaw without previous planning, I decided that I must do it, as I had no choice. It was all too easy to hand over my Access card to pay for my ticket, but we had now to go straight to the railway station and catch the next train to Warsaw. Dear Iwonna picked up my heavy case once again and led the way. First, I needed to change some more zloty into dollars, and Iwonna guided me to a building where, she explained, the foreign exchange counter was on the first floor. When I had my dollars I returned downstairs.

She was standing where I had left her, but obviously there was something wrong, as she looked distressed. She had lost one of her contact lenses, only very recently acquired, and they had been terribly expensive. She was standing at the foot of the stone staircase on a very old black mat. It looked really dirty and almost threadbare. Poor Iwonna was almost in tears as she crouched down staring into the mat. We were desperately short of time already, and now this sudden and unforeseen added catastrophe. Instinctively, I started praying. Over and over, I kept repeating the Greatest Name and calling on Bahá'u'lláh for help. Iwonna was in obvious distress and I felt for her very much, but I couldn't help seeing the funny side. How could we possibly find a tiny clear and virtually invisible object such as a contact lens in the depths of this frayed old mat? Nevertheless, we both crouched there staring with precious little hope, yet expecting a miracle. She whimpered, "Oh, dear, oh, dear." Then she asked me, with her lovely Polish accent, "Have you got one of those 'What I see you with'?" It seems obvious to me <u>now</u> what she really wanted was a mirror. What I thought she was asking for at the time was a magnifying glass and I didn't have one. Two passers-by stopped to watch us. We must have seemed such a curiosity almost like a TV comedy. Suddenly, to my surprise Iwonna turned and went upstairs. I continued to gaze, as intently as I could, onto the ground. We had a ticket to buy, and the station was quite some distance away by tram and there we were, in this seemingly impossible situation. I wondered how it was all going to end. Then, Iwonna re-appeared smiling as she came lightly down the stairs. It was baffling to discover that she now had both lenses. It seemed that she had inadvertently put both lenses into the same eye. This was the source of her request for a mirror, which I didn't understand at the time. The relief was enormous for us both, and we started laughing hysterically.

We were now free to make our way to the station, and both ran like the wind. As we hurried along, I was suddenly aware it was well past lunchtime, and that I had not eaten a morsel since the small piece of bread and soft cheese that I had early in the morning. There would be no time to think about lunch, nor was there time even for a wash, let alone trying to find a toilet. When we reached the station there was a very long queue and Iwonna was beginning to look desperate. It was about three o'clock, and my train was due to leave in a few moments. There wasn't another until after five o'clock and I had a journey of almost five hours ahead of me. We were standing far back in the queue, and Iwonna turned to me and asked whether she should go to the front and ask to be attended to, straight away. As this was our only hope, she would try and see what happened. There was no problem. The people standing at the front were very co-operative and we were both so relieved. Prayers of gratitude flowed from my heart, as Iwonna led the way forward to the waiting train. There was not a moment to spare. We just got there at the very last moment and there wasn't even time to say goodbye, or to thank my lovely friend for all her help. I realised that the two small gifts I had packed in my suitcase were still there and we had no time to open it. Her willingness to help and her continuous kindness was even more amazing when I discovered she had been in the middle of her exams, and had in fact been studying most of the night. I will never forget her and will be forever grateful for her loving presence and support on that day.

Settling into my seat for the long journey to Warsaw, I found myself sharing a compartment with seven other people, as it was not a first-class carriage. A lady sitting opposite to me was sleeping, but now and again she gave quite a loud snore. After some time one of the men in the compartment glanced at her, sideways, and then our eyes met for a brief instant. Amusement and shared understanding were evident in that one glance, and speech and language were not needed. There was an easy, relaxed atmosphere, much more so than in England.

Warsaw! I had not expected to go there. It had not been part of my plan at all. How suddenly and swiftly this decision had been made. How had I found the courage to go there, not having arranged beforehand for anyone to meet me? Iwonna had made a note of the telephone number of a Bahá'í living in Warsaw, Cornelia Meseke, and had promised to phone her and tell her that I was arriving. Reflecting on this, as we sped ever nearer to our destination, I realised what a flimsy arrangement this was. What if she didn't get the message. It had been such a long time since I had eaten anything and I remembered Krystina's little bag of biscuits with gratitude. A girl sitting in one corner had eaten a sandwich with great relish but, apart from this, no one else seemed to be concerned about refreshments. I was hungry and rummaged in my bag for the biscuits and handed them round. My fellow-passengers accepted readily, and we all sat contentedly munching this small snack.

I had expected the journey to be longer than it actually was when suddenly I saw the huge sign 'Warszawo' as we drew into the station. My heart gave a great leap. It was useless to expect that someone would meet me, and the vast station was filled with people going in all directions. As I stood up, one of the young men asked (by gestures) if he could help me with my luggage. I was so grateful. He and his friend both carried it for me, walking slowly ahead so that I would be assured of their good intentions that they were not about to run away with my bags.

By shrugs and signs they realised that I needed a taxi, and we walked quite some distance to the taxi rank. All the while, I followed them like a little child, trusting and full of gratitude. Many times, I said, "Dziekuje bardzo," (Thank you, very much.) How glad I was to know that little phrase. They could speak not a word of English, but I felt their kindness. I never knew their names and probably will never see them again in this world, yet, how could I ever forget them? Always, I will recall my arrival in Poland's capital, with deep thankfulness for the chivalry of those two complete strangers. Seated in the back of the taxi, driven by a pleasant young man, I became aware of dryness in my mouth, partly through lack of drinks through the day, and partly because of anxiety. I had no idea what lay ahead and I was very tired and hungry. It was then about 8.30pm and the whole day had been spent travelling, without a pause for a wash or refreshment.

It was a wide tree-lined road, and the evening sunshine made everything look attractive and bright. I asked the driver whether he spoke any English, and he replied, "Only very little." He was able to answer my questions as to the distance to the airport, and it was a relief to discover how close it was, barely five kilometres down the road from where I was going. Politely, he carried my bags to the kerbside, and with a deep breath I thanked him, glad that one more hurdle had been overcome. Now to find Cornelia's apartment block.

With the help of a kindly neighbour I managed to get inside the building, and I proceeded to climb the long flight of stairs. I stood outside her flat and rang the bell. Hopefully and with longing, I waited for a reply. But none came! I rang again and again, then waited. Inwardly I groaned. There was no-one there. Just managing to keep despair away, I tried to think what I could do. Prayers seem, at times of crisis, to be answered before they are actually uttered, and even as I bent to pick up my case, the neighbour I had met downstairs arrived. She was full of concern for my welfare, and immediately started to ring the bell of the opposite door to where I was standing. Two women appeared, and the tale of my predicament was shared with them (all in Polish, of course.)

Thinking back, I don't remember how Eugenia appeared on the scene. I can only think of her as a Guardian Angel, sent to look after me, in my moment of helplessness. Logically, I know that I could have found a hotel for the night, and could have taken a taxi. It is difficult to imagine a situation without first experiencing it. Not being able to speak to people can be a terrible handicap. This combined to drain away my confidence and, being weary and in need of a wash-and-brush-up, made it seem much worse. Suddenly, like a comforting beam of light in a totally dark tunnel, this friendly and homely neighbour was steering me towards her home. Once we reached her apartment she took charge of everything, like a close and caring friend who knew all my needs. It was wonderful. Speaking sometimes in Polish, but mainly in French, she handed me a clean white towel, and indicated where the bathroom was, with a lovely welcoming smile. "S'il vous plait, madame." Oh, it was heavenly to be able to wash and to be indoors, safe and secure. While dear Eugenia was in her kitchen, I just sat there, gazing with deepest contentment at the beautiful treetops outside her window. They were gently swaying in the breeze. It felt as if my whole being was relaxing in a most peaceful and tranquil manner. Her room was practically lined with bookshelves, and everything was so simple and lovely. This was my haven, after the turmoil of so much uncertainty, and at that moment it was the most perfect place in the world. My heart overflowed with gratitude. Eugenia was preparing a meal for me, and now and then she came back into the living room. Each time, she phoned Cornelia and, each time, she said to me, "Cornelia is absent!" Calling me into the kitchen, she sat me at her table and plied me with delicious ham and bread and butter. She filled a large beaker with hot water that had tea bags on the saucer. She was offering me eggs that I didn't need, and I ate each mouthful of food with immense enjoyment and relish. It seemed that nothing ever tasted so good. Inwardly, I marvelled at my blessings, and again I thanked God for His care and guidance. That lady was truly a most wonderful person. Because we were unable to converse with one another she, several times, phoned a friend who spoke in English, and then handed me the phone, so that I could speak to her. In this way, we had a nice little translation set-up. Eugenia was trying to tell me that her spare bedroom was not good enough and she apologised for this.

Without language we communicated warmly, and I was able to tell her friend, at the other end of the line, how grateful I felt for her loving and caring hospitality. Eugenia made up a very comfortable bed for me, with clean crisp sheets, and then closed the curtains where the evening sunlight was still filtering through the window. I sat on the side of that welcoming little bed, after I had washed and undressed and, with a thousand sighs of relief and pure happiness, I wrote a few lines to Maria and Roman.

In the midst of all this blissfulness, I became aware of a slightly uneasy feeling that warned me to check my air-ticket. I had brushed the thought aside while I got ready for bed, but it persisted. Even as I opened my handbag there was a definite sense of something being wrong with that ticket. Nervously, I pulled it out of my wallet, all the time saying to myself, "Please God, don't let it be wrong." The date was there, June 1, Warsaw to London, Heathrow. I stared at it intently. I was glad at least the date was right, but the time of departure, which I had been given was two o'clock in the afternoon, allowing me plenty of time to reach Victoria bus station for my coach at six. Yet, here it was, clearly, in front of me, three fifty-five. It jumped out at me, and my heart sank. If I left Warsaw so late in the afternoon, there would be no possibility of my catching the Rapide back to Southport. A fresh anxiety, just when everything appeared so calm and secure. I prayed before lying down to sleep, and turned my problem over to God, beseeching His help yet again.

In the morning, Eugenia cooked some eggs for my breakfast, asking me, with gestures and a mixture of Polish and French, how I preferred them. It was like manna from heaven and so snug and warm in her little kitchen. All the while, I was wishing that I could show her my sincere feelings of appreciation and affection. I managed to convey at least in some measure what I felt, and I decided to make her a gift of the deep blue blouse that I had bought in Wroclaw. Now the destiny of the blouse was clear! It had not been my usual colour at all, but on the other hand, Eugenia wore colours that were really strong and bright, and I knew that it would suit her beautifully. Eventually, I was able to convey the problem of my departure time to Eugenia, and she straightaway telephoned the airport and spoke rapidly in Polish. After a few moments she passed the telephone to me. I explained what had happened about the difference in time on my ticket, and the time I had been given on the previous day. The voice on the other end of the line informed me that there was a flight at 1400 hrs and she would arrange for my ticket to be altered.

I breathed a sigh of relief knowing myself to be another step nearer home. It is lovely to travel, and very exciting to do so, but also wonderful to return to one's familiar country and those dear ones waiting there. Eugenia said we would have to be leaving very soon, and there would not be sufficient time for us to walk to the park, as we had planned. We had no need to call a taxi as the bus stop was just outside Eugenia's apartment, so we waited there in the sunshine.

Once at the airport we soon had my flight time changed, and sat together in the restaurant enjoying cold Coke. How much I owed this incredible woman, with whom I could not converse? She knew how I felt, I am certain. I wrote to her many times after returning home and, needless to say, I will never forget her.

Air travel to me is a constant source of enjoyment and wonder. It has never failed to uplift my spirit. It was a pleasant flight and we stopped in Gdansk for forty-five minutes. I was now perfectly relaxed as I reckoned that there would be ample time to get from the airport to Victoria Bus Station. A very nice little boy sat beside me and we talked happily together for a while. When we arrived in London he spontaneously reached up and kissed me as we said goodbye. I felt a glow of happiness as I made my way through the arrival lounge and went to collect my luggage. I tried to be of assistance to a bewildered-looking Polish lady, as she could not speak any English and my heart went out to her, knowing only too well her anxiety. Once I had my luggage on the trolley, I followed the signs for the Airbus. It was warm and sunny and I was taking it easy. Then, I glanced at my watch and immediately my wonderful sense of calm was shattered. It was almost five o'clock, and I could not believe where the hours had gone. The flight from Warsaw had taken much, much longer than my flight to Krakow, at the start of my trip. I saw a notice at the coach-stand, informing passengers to allow between fifty-five minutes to seventy minutes to reach Victoria. My coach was leaving at 1800 hrs. Again I entered the battle for serenity and calm and fought not to give way to panic and stress. We all pressed forward onto the bus and dragged our varying amounts of luggage with us. How slow it all seemed! Would we never get away from the airport? How could we possibly reach Victoria in time for me to catch the Rapide? It was an agony of suspense! To be so near and then have to spend a night in London would be really frustrating. I was praying yet again imploring His assistance.

I tried hard to detach myself from whatever the outcome might be. With gritted teeth I forced myself not to look at my watch again for a long time. An Indian lady came onto the bus and sat beside me. She had a beautiful little girl with her who was gazing at everything with huge, dark eyes. It was her young granddaughter, and we soon began to talk to one another. In a little while, when I mentioned I was a Bahá'í and had been to India, she said that she had always wondered what the Bahá'í Faith was about. She knew that there is a House of Worship outside Delhi and was delighted about this. For the rest of our journey we talked about religion and especially about the Faith. I was able to show her several pictures including some of Bahá'í Temples and the Holy Places in Israel. It was inspiring for me, and the time passed happily, diverting me away from my watch and the inevitable nervous strain. I found I'd ceased altogether from worrying about my bus. Because my large suitcase was right at the front, near the driver, I went to stand up there towards the end of our journey. Everyone was getting off at the last stop, which was not very far from the coach-station. Not far, but very far when time had practically run out and I would have to walk (or run) carrying heavy luggage while already hot and extremely tired. In near panic, I asked the driver, in an outwardly composed manner, which was the nearest way to get to the coach-station. Then, I added, that I hoped I wouldn't miss the Rapide, leaving at six o'clock. The driver gasped in surprise. "Six o'clock?" I nodded. "Hold on," he said, and to my amazement proceeded to drive the bus through the evening traffic saying, "I don't suppose I'll get the sack for just this once." And he drove me all the way. We stopped right beside the arched entrance and he cheerfully told me, "This is as far as I can go." Amazement engulfed me together with gratitude and wonder. Again and again I thanked him, as I pulled my case off the bus. I almost ran along the great line of coaches searching for the Northbound Liverpool/Southport sign. Gasping for breath, my throat almost closed in its dryness, I found myself at the correct stand. Trying to swallow, I spoke to the hostess who indicated that it was the coach I needed. Then I explained why the date on my return ticket was for a Saturday in two weeks time. "Oh, that's alright," she assured me, and when I told her that I had just arrived back from Poland, she said, "Get in the bus and we'll bring you a cup of tea in half an hour." Bliss! The last hurdle had been accomplished and I was really and truly going home!

As I sank into my seat there were more prayers of thankfulness, while weariness of body and mind enfolded me. I just sat there as if I would never move again. I looked in amazement at my watch. It was exactly one minute past six o'clock. Four and a half hours of gliding smoothly along the quiet roads gave me ample time and opportunity to reflect on all that had taken place. My plans for going to Poland had been to stay for one month. Destiny had decided otherwise. Inwardly, my heart was happy and, in spite of everything, I felt that it had been successful from a spiritual point of view and, really, what other point of view is there?

A short taxi-ride took me swiftly from Eastbank Street, Southport, where the Rapide had terminated, right to my front door. During that brief journey I had been telling the female taxi-driver about my adventures while travelling overseas, and she told me earnestly, "You should write a book." A few moments later I was ringing the doorbell to be met by a very surprised family. It was quite late for callers, and Zoë's face showed clear astonishment and delight, when she beheld me standing there. There was much laughter and warm hugs galore shared by Zoë and Anisa, and also my sister Pat who happened to be staying overnight. We all stood in the hall, while my delighted and overjoyed young granddaughter danced up and down, her eyes shining. She imagined she was dreaming. Grandma had come home. Grandma was not in Poland. She was right there.

We talked, Zoë and I, after Pat and Anisa had gone to bed, until three in the morning. Even though I was totally exhausted I somehow needed to talk. Then I slept!

20

A TRAGIC PARTING – AND A PRICELESS GIFT

In April 1991 we had just returned from a trip to Malta where we had hoped to pioneer. Zoë had been looking into the possibility of finding a teaching post there and had also been looking for a suitable school for Anisa. We realised by the end of our visit that we would have to look elsewhere, as the openings we hoped for were not to be found in Malta after all. A lot of mail was waiting for me, on my return, mainly because I was secretary of the Local Spiritual Assembly. The very last letter I opened was from our National Assembly and I read it with total disbelief. I was completely overwhelmed. They were inviting me to attend a historic gathering in the Holy Land, in May 1992. This was to commemorate the centenary of the Ascension of Bahá'u'lláh. It had been decided by the Universal House of Justice that nineteen Bahá'ís from each country should be chosen to represent their community during those five precious days.

There are no words to describe my feelings of shock and joy. How could it be true? How was it possible for me to be one of those nineteen, chosen from the whole of the U.K. Bahá'í community? Never for a single moment had I dreamed that such a thing could happen! I will always remember the reaction of my dear Pat when she heard the news. Her eyes had filled with tears and she could hardly speak. I just felt her love and her overwhelming happiness that such a gift had been given to me. We had no way of knowing, at that moment, that she would not be here to see me go. Only later did we learn that she had only weeks to live. It was the priceless blessing of my trip to the Holy Land that gave me the strength to carry on.

It was a good thing that I had so much to think about as I made all the necessary preparations for this journey of a lifetime, and the months went quickly by, over-flowing with wonder and excitement. The date of our departure was May 25, 1992. Philip Hainsworth, who had been chosen by the National Spiritual Assembly to be our Tour Leader, advised us all to meet at the El-Al check-in at Heathrow Airport at one o'clock. He rendered a wonderful service by making all the practical arrangements for travel and accommodation on our behalf. Now the big moment had come and we were a very happy, excited group, laughing and talking and hugging in sheer joy. There was Pauline Senior, for many years a pioneer in Guernsey, smiling broadly in her wheelchair and, alongside, another valiant pioneer, Alma Gregory, who was also in a wheelchair. Their radiant faces swept all the frailness of their years away as they greeted us. They seemed to me like two queens upon their thrones having spent years in service to our beloved Faith. John Long, who was for so many years Chairman of the National Spiritual Assembly of the United Kingdom and manager of the Bahá'í Publishing Trust, was standing there. With a gentle smile he brought me a very welcome cup of tea. Viv Bartlett, John Wade, and two happy souls who were pioneers to the Falkland Islands and, joy upon joy, my own spiritual-mother Madeline Hellaby were all there. She it was who had given that wonderfully clear and inspiring talk back in 1962 that had awakened the spirit of faith in my soul, and for which I will ever be thankful. Here was a gathering of souls setting out on a very special mission, a never-to-be-forgotten journey of love and devotion.

From outward appearances we were a group of everyday travellers, yet, inwardly, all of us were ablaze with the divine fire of God's love. The Airport seemed like some great 'launching pad' from which we would be transported to another world, a heavenly Spot, so far removed from earthly things where each of us would dwell for a little while in the Paradise of His Presence.

Our flight of about five hours was relaxed and enjoyable. It was midnight when we arrived in Tel-Aviv and several buses were waiting to take us on to Haifa. Ah, Haifa, that magic city and world centre of our Faith! We were drawing nearer to that Holy Place! At three o'clock in the morning we reached our hotel. Madeline and I were sharing a double room in the Shulamit, and being there with her seemed to bring my life full circle, completing my thirty years as a Bahá'í.

Sunlight greeted us next morning and, after a very lavish breakfast, we were free to relax. Penny Sebastion from the World Centre Staff was acting as our helper, and she advised us to rest as much as possible for the first two days because our programme was going to be very full after that. How could we choose to rest when we were on God's holy mountain and our hearts were being drawn, as if by a magnet, to the glorious Shrine of the Bab? That heavenly spot was just a short bus ride away, and then our eager feet carried us swiftly down the pathway to the ever-welcoming Pilgrim House. Always, it is a 'coming home' for the soul and spirit, and here we find true rest. Here is sanctuary and peace where we melt away in humility.

The sun was gloriously hot, and I found myself bathed in the total loveliness of those beautiful gardens. It is breathtaking and beyond description. We were told that it had been raining until just a few days before our arrival and this had enriched the beauty and brightness of the lawns and flowered borders. The gleam of oranges in the branches and the beautiful Cedars and Eucalyptus trees, everything was in perfect tranquillity and order. We feasted our eyes in loving appreciation, while the Golden Dome of the Shrine of the Báb, in its serene beauty, was calling us. What unbelievable joy, to walk with reverent steps and hearts on fire, along those sacred paths that took us to His Threshold. We bowed our heads, and our prayers flowed out to Him from the silent depths of our hearts. No words, just a great longing and nothing that can be told or described, so beautifully expressed in one of the Bahá'í prayers, *'and transcend the murmur of syllables and sounds.'*

I turned, and in a few paces, had entered the Shrine of the Master, our beloved 'Abdu'l-Bahá. A beautiful feeling of love and spiritual power enfolded me, and I felt very strongly that Pat was already there, joyful and eager for my arrival. It seemed as if she was saying, "Come on, Lou, we've been waiting for you." Amidst the devastating grief of losing my lovely sister, it was comforting to know that she had been released from her pain and sickness, only five short days before I left for Haifa. She had been my loving companion through the whole of my life, and the thought of losing her had flooded my whole being with sorrow. When we were told, that fateful day at Clatterbridge hospital, that she had only a few months to live, I felt that my heart would break. We had shared a very special closeness even as children, and it had been the most wonderful blessing when we both joyfully embraced the Faith of Bahá'u'lláh. Now, undoubtedly, she would be there with me in that land of our heart's desire. She had been ecstatic to learn that I had been invited, as one of the nineteen Bahá'ís from the United Kingdom, to be present at this incredibly momentous gathering. I had seen tears of pure love and happiness on her cheeks whenever it had been mentioned. She had been so glad for me and her spirit had rejoiced at the significance of such a soul-stirring event.

It was truly a gift from God to be there with so many Bahá'ís from all corners of the earth. We met and we mingled, faces glowing and hearts attuned to the vibrating melody of the Kingdom. It looked and felt like a garden of human flowers. The beautiful colours of national dresses, and the myriad tints of smiling faces released such radiance. Bahá'ís had come from distant islands and little villages far-flung and remote. Such a glorious diversity! We were experiencing the worldwide family of Bahá'u'lláh. No wonder we were happy and fulfilled as we gathered beside the Pilgrim House, like flowers bathed in spiritual sunshine. Was it real? Were we dreaming?

We had two days of sheer heavenly delight, praying in the Shrines whenever we wished and then back to the welcoming doors of the Pilgrim-House. Inside, it was cooler, even though the rooms were packed. Happiness, laughter and talking, some were sitting while others stood in groups.

It was marvellous the way the World Centre staff had organised and planned it, with so much devoted care to every single detail. In the dining room all day long were trays of delicious cold drinks and constant supplies of tea and coffee with scores of cups and saucers all laid out in readiness. Refreshed in body, as we were in heart and spirit, we came tumbling out again to the heat of the sun and the cameras clicking. Friends were all the while greeting other dear ones who had, perhaps, not been seen for a very long time. What a lot of hugging and so much to share, along with making new friends from across the world. We had each been given an identity card to wear with the name of the country we were representing. Those wonderful people, the Knights of Bahá'u'lláh, had blue borders around their cards and the name of the country that they had opened to the Faith.

(The title Knight was given to those souls who had taken the Faith to a new country. This was an honour bestowed on them by Shoghi Effendi, the Guardian of

Lou and Madeline with other pilgrims

the Bahá'í Faith.) Thursday was the day of their special commemoration when these steadfast and intrepid Bahá'ís were to be honoured. They had very rightly been called 'Knights' for their valour and their steadfastness that had transformed them into spiritual heroes.

We were up early next morning, to meet in the Hotel lobby at 7.45am. It was very exciting and everyone was filled with eager anticipation. We had our sunhats and sun cream, as we had been advised, and when the buses came we scrambled in like children going on a special treat. The greatness of this particular 'treat' would be recorded in Bahá'í history for the next thousand years. I'm sure that the heart of each one of us was humbled in our striving to comprehend our part in it.

Upon our arrival in Bahji there was drinking water, with stacks of paper cups, and, to our pleasant surprise, a row of 'portaloos'. Certainly, we were in the midst of a deeply spiritual experience, but we still had our finite bodies to contend with, and such loving concern had been shown in all these things. We were in Bahji where Bahá'u'lláh lived during his last twelve years of life. The very thought of it brings a loving tumult to the heart. We became hushed and silent as we took our seats on the terraces of the Haram-i-Aqdás, so close to Bahá'u'lláh's Shrine and the beloved Mansion where He ascended from this world (1892). The ceremony started at 10am.

We sat in scorching sunshine, and were enthralled as we listened to Adib Taherzadeh, member of the Universal House of Justice, giving the opening address. Every word could be heard so clearly through the amplifying system that had been set up, and it seemed that each speaker was standing right beside us on the terraces.

The names of 257 Knights of Bahá'u'lláh had been inscribed on a beautiful Scroll, with the name of the country or territory that each had opened to the Faith. It had been placed in a special cylinder that was treated with a gas that will preserve this precious Scroll of honour for thousands of years. It was such an amazing thought. The three remaining Hands of the Cause were present (the last of a total of fifty appointed over the decades) and Rúḥíyyih Khánum led the procession that included the members of the Universal House of Justice. We had been informed that the world's press was interested in the events that were taking place there in the Holy Land. A press conference had been held in Jerusalem during the previous week, and we frequently caught glimpses of cameramen while the ceremony was taking place.

Prayers were recited so beautifully, and then a wonderfully inspiring Tribute of the Universal House of Justice to Bahá'u'lláh. What a poignant moment was this tribute to God's great Manifestation, being rendered in so holy a Place within the very precincts of His Shrine. After the recitation of the Tablet of Visitation the procession of Knights of Bahá'u'lláh followed the Hands of the Cause and members of the Universal House of Justice along the pathway to His Shrine. Slowly and reverently they walked towards that most blessed doorway. Several people were in wheelchairs, now frailer in body than all those years before when they had made their pioneering move with so great a detachment and devotion that no earthly thing could shake. It was so very moving, watching that reverent procession of His followers, coming now to receive some measure of a far greater spiritual reward that must surely be awaiting them in that Kingdom of His Love.

Their names, preserved within that cylinder, were to be deposited at His Threshold in the Shrine of Bahá'u'lláh by dear Rúḥíyyih Khánum. Apparently, the Scroll had been designed according to the Guardian's specifications, and also placed in the spot that had been designated by him. I sat beside Betty Goode who had for many years served as treasurer of the National Spiritual Assembly of the United Kingdom. The sun was very hot on our backs and we were glad of the protection of our large sun-hats. We talked, on our way back to the Pilgrim House, about our loved ones in the spiritual world. Pat had been very fond of Betty and her husband Ken, and the three of them had shared a lot of fun and laughter during National Bahá'í Conferences. Ken had died about two years before and now Pat had recently passed to the Abhá Kingdom. Betty said that they would now be together enjoying life in that other world.

We returned from Bahjí at noon and had our lunch in the Hotel. I tried to rest, as we would be attending the Commemoration of Bahá'u'lláh's Ascension throughout that night. For the most part, sleep had been rather elusive during my stay in Haifa. Excitement, mingling with the unshed grief of my dear Pat's death, prevented my being able to sleep properly. In any case, it wasn't really a time for sleeping. A Holy

Year like this comes once only in a lifetime, and I was trying to realise and appreciate that I was there.

We had been advised to dress warmly for our night-time vigil, as it would quite possibly be very cold during the night. They had also warned us to take precautions against the mosquitoes. Madeline and I lay on our beds until about nine-thirty pm. and then we each took a shower, read some prayers together and then we had something to eat. A small brown roll and some cheese and dates were enough to satisfy us, preparing as we were for such an amazing event. In a sort of hushed excitement we gathered in the hotel lobby for 12.45am.

Settled into our seats on the bus, we were on our way to the gathering where we would commemorate the centenary of the Blessed Beauty's Ascension. It was dark and now approaching that hour of His Soul's departure. The time when He was released from the agonies of a lifetime's suffering in a world that He had come to redeem. Suddenly we were at Bahji again. Our hearts leapt with a mingling of pain and longing.

How beautiful was the sight that met us. All the paths were alight with rows of glowing candles, thousands of them, shining drops of wavering lights in the darkness. Everything was silent as we took our seats, once again in close proximity to His Shrine. The devotional started at 2.20am attuning the hearts of the three thousand Bahá'ís seated around the Haram-i-Aqdás, like multi-coloured flowers drawn to the Sun of Truth from all parts of the world.

A prayer revealed by Bahá'u'lláh was chanted very beautifully in Arabic, and this was followed with a passage from Gleanings in French read by Louis Henuzet. Other prayers and readings were in English and Spanish, and Mark Hellaby (Madeline's son) read from a Tablet of Bahá'u'lláh that was revealed after the Kitáb-i-Aqdas. Excerpts from a Tablet of 'Abdu'l-Bahá were chanted in Persian. Finally, we all arose for the Tablet of Visitation, in Arabic.

> "...Waft, then, unto me, O my God and my Beloved, from the right hand of Thy mercy and Thy loving kindness, the holy breaths of Thy favours, that they may draw me away from myself and from the world unto the courts of Thy nearness and Thy Presence".

How near, how very near we felt as we gazed towards His Holy Shrine.

We arose silently from our seats and the circumambulation of His Shrine began. Slowly, with quietness of mind and body, we trod those sacred paths, wrapt in silent meditation. The brightness of those flames still flickered in their little glass containers, and almost without our being aware the sky was beginning to lighten. The first sweet little chirping of the birds told us that dawn was breaking, and that night of nights was ending. Reverently and lovingly we wended our way around His All-Glorious Resting Place, and now we must leave.

Back in the bus, I almost fell asleep. It was a very tired and overwhelmed group of believers who had breakfast that morning, before taking to our rooms for rest. We were going next afternoon to the foot of Mount Carmel to climb the Avenue of the Kings slowly up those 365 steps to the Shrine of the Báb. The bus was starting out at three fifteen and we had been advised not to attempt that climb if our health was in any way frail. The sun was very hot and it would be quite a feat. They told us that there would be water for drinking all along the way as well as resting places.

Madeline went for lunch in the dining room, but I remained in our bedroom and had some bread and cheese with a few dates and apricots. While resting on my bed, I had been disconcerted by some chest pains. It very seldom happened, although I had been advised that I had angina for the previous two or three years. I began to question whether I should climb those steps, which I longed to do, or take it as a warning not to be foolhardy. I decided on the latter and remained on the bus while others went to do the climb.

We were all later to circumambulate the Shrine, before going to the Seat of the Universal House of Justice to view the portrait of Bahá'u'lláh. That building is so impressive, dignified and beautiful beyond description. We were taken in small groups to the great room where we would see the Face of Bahá'u'lláh. We stood facing a wall with a large screen in front of it. As we did so the lights were very slowly dimmed and, as they faded, a life-size picture of Bahá'u'lláh appeared before us. I had not expected this, and it was very powerful in its impact. I caught my breath and felt that for just one brief instant all of life stood still, a timeless moment containing everything, past, present and future. All seemed one. And in His eyes, so full of suffering, the sorrows of my own poor little heart reflected back. It brought tears to my eyes, and then the picture slowly faded.

Composing ourselves as best we could, we silently turned towards the door. Outside, it was breathtaking in the loveliness of flowers and trees, and the shimmering white marble of that glorious building. I just wanted to stand there forever and marvel. In 1979 - while on my second pilgrimage to that holy mountain - we had been allowed to take away a piece of the marble from that beautiful building. It had been under construction at the time, and each pilgrim had gratefully and lovingly returned home with some precious marble, as a keepsake.

It took a long time for everyone to return to their allocated buses, with all the hugging and chattering and taking of pictures. It was a gathering of inspired souls on that wonderful mountain. His devoted followers had come, with hearts on fire, to commemorate the hundredth anniversary of our Beloved's Ascension. Nothing would hurry that joyful exchange of love and greetings. Again and again, the feeling came that we were like flowers, rejoicing in the brilliant sunshine of Divine Love.

So many times my heart has been humbled, as the silent question rises, in awe and astonishment, "Why me, Lord? Why me?" To be created in God's 'Radiant Century' (the 'Century of Light') and to have been guided so wondrously to the Threshold of Faith, through recognition of God's Manifestation for this great Age of Fulfilment. And now, to have been invited as one of the nineteen souls from the United Kingdom to attend so glorious an event in the holiest place on earth, made me repeat over and

Madeline Hellaby and Lou in front of the Shrine of the Báb.

With two African friends outside the Pilgrim House

over, "Why me, Lord?" No answer comes to the yearning, trembling wonderment. Gifts of love have been showered upon me all my life, yes, through sorrow and great pain as well as through joy.

We were taken back to our hotels. Mark Hellaby came to our room to talk with his mother. I had a leisurely shower and went down to the lounge. That evening we had the pleasure of Elsie and George Bowers' company for dinner. They were my dear friends over so many years, and there we were, together in the Holy Land, together with Madeline, who brought the Glad Tidings into our lives. The guiding hand of destiny is truly amazing.

Saturday morning was our last day before returning to Tel-Aviv, where we would spend one night in readiness for our flight home on Sunday morning. First, though, we had one more lovely experience. We were allowed to spend two hours in the area of the Shrine of Bahá'u'lláh, between 6am and 8am. Madeline and I set our alarm clock to waken us at four o'clock so that we had time to assemble in the lounge ready to leave for Bahji for our last precious visit. I wrote in my little book:

> "The gardens are really perfect in the beauty of their colour and perfume, bathed in the tranquillity and harmony of divine fragrances; like breezes of holiness gently wafting over the soul. My whole being was enraptured and drawn away from the cares and limitations of this wearisome world, into a state of inner awareness and union with that divine world which permeates the soul."

Walking slowly towards the majestic Collins Gate, I found myself face to face with my lovely friend from Ghana, dear Blanche Musa. We gasped in excited surprise and joy. How we hugged one another. I had last seen Blanche during my second visit to Ghana, in 1987. We had shared many moments of anguish, especially on the day of her husband's funeral that was attended by many hundreds of mourners. Now, standing on the pathway close to Bahá'u'lláh's Shrine, there was a deep well of loving, tender memories flowing between us. It was wonderful to meet again in those special circumstances and on such holy ground.

There are no words to express the emotions and spiritual stirrings that are felt when approaching the sacred nearness of Bahá'u'lláh's Resting Place. Although there were many believers present each one is alone with Him, communing with His Spirit. The outside world falls away while we drink it in to our fullest capacity, peace and sublime love surrounding us. We had two hours in which to pray and meditate. I felt humble and overwhelmed, with a sense of wonder and gratitude for so great a bounty. The long drive to Tel-Aviv was made very interesting for me, as I was seated beside a lady from Brazil who had many lively stories to share. Hearts become quickly attuned to one another in our shared love for Bahá'u'lláh and His Teachings. After the evening meal, I went for a stroll with Betty Goode and a Bahá'í from Reunion Islands called Gay Denbow. She and I were sharing a room in the Ami Hotel and we asked for a morning call for seven o'clock. I had understood that we would be leaving for the airport at eight o' clock, but Gay had been told that it was not until nine.

After my shower, I went downstairs for breakfast and was very surprised when I didn't see a single familiar face. Where were the Bahá'ís? I did not have long to wait for an answer. No sooner had I put food on my plate from the buffet table, before even sitting down, when Philip Hainsworth appeared from outside the hotel, beckoning to me urgently. Then, I saw a mini-bus and all the friends were climbing happily aboard. Gay had to be brought from the bedroom, and we hurriedly took our places in the bus. Reminiscences of travel problems of the past! This time we made it!

As soon as we had been allowed through to the departure lounge, after a very strict questioning and scrutiny of our baggage, Betty Goode insisted on buying me something to eat. It was so thoughtful of her and I really appreciated the long, cool drink of fresh orange and the toasted sandwiches set before me. I sat with two Bettys, Betty Reed and Betty Goode on the plane, and we shared our thoughts together with a great sense of peace and relaxation.

When we arrived at Heathrow, it was an ordeal trying to get our luggage. It was worse than anything I had experienced, with cases tumbling over one another in huge piles. It was a relief to see my own bag appear, so that I could grab it and escape the utter chaos. Thankfully, I then walked through to the arrival lounge, where familiar faces of Bahá'ís were smiling in greeting, as they waited eagerly for loved ones. Then, a further lovely surprise! A bunch of long-stemmed red roses from the Guardian's Grave had been sent as a gift to greet us on our return. One of these loving tokens from the Commemoration that had been held in London was presented to me. It was a perfect ending to a perfect journey.

My teaching trips overseas ended in that Holy Year, exactly thirty years after my declaration in 1962. Those days were indescribably happy days and had been one of life's greatest gifts to me. As I look back on those many wonderful adventures, I am filled with overwhelming gratitude. It was the power of God that got me over my anxiety and stress of travelling. I know in my heart that it was the power of faith that lifted me up on wings of joy and carried me to moments of purest happiness.

EPILOGUE

My return from the Holy Land marked the closing of a very special chapter in my life, and the magical quality of those years was not to be repeated.

Two months before making that memorable trip, we had moved to Shropshire, to help the Bahá'ís of Shrewsbury re-form their Spiritual Assembly. It was such a loving, supportive community and we felt privileged to be part of it. Zoë and I were especially delighted to be serving on the Spiritual Assembly with Sohrab and Denise Samari. During our years in Colwyn Bay we had been in the same community as Sohrab, and we have many happy memories of those days.

Much to my joy, opportunities for teaching the Faith opened up in several Primary Schools, in Telford and Oswestry, as well as in Shrewsbury. It was a great thrill to speak to the children during their morning Assembly, on such topics as world peace, travelling overseas, and especially about the life of 'Abdu'l-Bahá and the Bahá'í holy days.

Another exciting challenge was being invited to address groups of trainee nurses, at the Royal Shrewsbury hospital. I was one of four speakers, each from a different Faith. We had been asked to explain the way our religion would guide us in caring for patients in hospital. These meetings, over a period of about three years, took place every two months, and we were given a forty-minute session each. It was a joy to have this wonderful opportunity of sharing the teachings of Bahá'u'lláh, and the response from the students was always warm and enthusiastic.

It was also a happy time for me when I was invited by the Unitarian Church to take a number of their Sunday morning services, and to tell the congregation about the Teachings of Bahá'u'lláh. Various other groups and organizations asked me to speak, and to share some of the adventures I had had during my travels overseas. Zoë was employed at a secondary school in Ellesmere, as Learning Resources Manager. She was really happy there, and enjoyed being with the young students. When the time came for Anisa to go to university she was accepted at the School of Oriental and African Studies (SOAS) in London. The year before starting University she went to Tonga, to work in a Bahá'í Primary school called 'Ocean of Light'. We were thrilled to see her setting off on her great adventure; flying to Los Angeles, on to Honolulu, and into the heart of the Pacific. All the travelling we did when she was a little girl made it seem quite natural for her, and she loved making this long journey on her own.

In 1999, Zoë and I made a short teaching-trip to Cyprus during her Easter break. It was a very happy and uplifting experience, travelling to so many lovely places in glorious sunshine, and being with the local Bahá'ís. Towards the end of our visit we were asked, much to our surprise and joy, if we would like to go by boat to the Holy Land. Such an amazing and thrilling prospect had not occurred to us, and it was with indescribable wonder and delight that plans were made and everything was arranged. Anita Graves was the dear Bahá'í who set everything in motion, and who accompanied us on that exciting journey. We sailed by night and the following morning wakened very early and stood on deck, gazing with great longing, to catch our first glimpse of the Báb's Shrine. Zoë and I had not known that many Bahá'ís from all parts of the world would be gathering in Haifa that weekend, to commemorate the Twin Holy Days which, by the Lunar Calendar, are the Birthdays of the Báb and Bahá'u'lláh. These events were being celebrated, on the first day, in Haifa, and on the following day, at Bahji. It was such an amazing and inspiring experience to be part of that great gathering of Bahá'ís, and meeting dear friends we hadn't seen for many years.

Our hearts were filled with gratitude and wonder that Bahá'u'lláh had blessed us with this unexpected gift. When we were planning our trip to Cyprus, I had been very disappointed that a two-week teaching-trip was all that we could manage. It had seemed so short a time, and here we were, being showered with this great bounty! We kept asking ourselves, what I have asked so many times throughout the years, "Why me, Bahá'u'lláh, why me?"

At the end of those two glorious days, while we were saying our fond farewells, Mr Adib Taherzadeh (member of the Universal House of Justice) came to us with a radiant smile and embraced us so lovingly. We stood together, talking eagerly and happily about the wonderful times we had shared in Ireland. During our days in Cork, Adib had been Chairman of the National Spiritual Assembly of the Republic of Ireland, and we had been very privileged when he had stayed with us in our home, and had uplifted our hearts with his wonderful stories of the Báb and Bahá'u'lláh. For many years he had enthralled the whole community with his inspiring, amazing talks about the early days of the Faith. Now, standing so close to the Shrine of Bahá'u'lláh, he and his dear wife, Lesley, insisted on driving us to the harbour for our boat trip back to Limasol.

The years have flown so quickly, and Zoë and I are now living in Scotland, in the beautiful countryside of the Borders. Anisa was married three years ago, and she and her husband Jonathan are living in Edinburgh with their beautiful little son Joshua. Life continually enriches us, as the wonderful cycle of life opens up new vistas and new challenges.

These days for me are very different days. This is now a time for quiet reflection, to ponder those joyful years of God's bountiful favours, when He completely transformed my life. My heart is filled with gratitude and wonder as my thoughts carry me back to those teaching trips across the world, inspired by the words of 'Abdu'l-Bahá:

> *"Oh! that I could travel, even though on foot and in the utmost poverty, to these regions, and, raising the call of Yá-Bahá'u'l-Abhá in cities, villages, mountains, deserts and oceans, promote the Divine teachings! This, also, I cannot do. How intensely I deplore it! Please God, ye may achieve it."*
> (quoted by Shoghi Effendi, Messages to America, p. 102)